Part 1:

MEDITATION

THE NOTEBOOKS OF PAUL BRUNTON
(VOLUME 4)

Part 1: MEDITATION

PAUL BRUNTON
(1898–1981)

An in-depth study of
category number four
from the notebooks

Published for the
PAUL BRUNTON PHILOSOPHIC FOUNDATION
by Larson Publications

International Standard Book Number (cloth) 0-943914-18-3
International Standard Book Number (Part 1, paper) 0-943914-19-1
International Standard Book Number (Part 2, paper) 0-943914-20-5
International Standard Book Number (series, cloth) 0-943914-17-5
International Standard Book Number (series, paper) 0-943914-23-X
Library of Congress Catalog Card Number (cloth): 86-81949
Library of Congress Catalog Card Number (paper): 86-81950

Manufactured in the United States of America

Published for the
Paul Brunton Philosophic Foundation
by
Larson Publications
4936 Route 414
Burdett, New York 14818

Distributed to the trade by
Kampmann and Company
9 East 40 Street
New York, New York 10016

89   90
2   4   6   8   10   9   7   5   3

CONTENTS

EDITORS' INTRODUCTION

Volume four in *The Notebooks of Paul Brunton* presents, in depth and detail, the fourth and fifth of the major topics in the personal notebooks Dr. Paul Brunton (1898–1981) reserved for posthumous publication. Bound together as a single volume in the hardcover edition, these two topics (*Meditation* and *The Body*) are published separately in softcover. *Meditation* is Volume 4, Part 1, and *The Body* is Volume 4, Part 2.

Part 1, *Meditation*, is an inspiring invitation to the most intimate adventure of human spirituality—the direct experience of one's own soul. Focusing lucidly on a topic for which his extraordinary expertise has been widely acknowledged since he was a young man in the 1930s, P.B. explains the purpose and importance of meditation, provides an unusually rich variety of tested and proven techniques, and explains both what the potential dangers of meditation are and how they can be avoided. This section will prove highly useful to beginners and intermediates alike. It should also be welcomed by advanced meditators and teachers of meditation as well.

The fourth 'category' in P.B.'s overall outline of twenty-eight, this section stands in direct relationship to the twenty-third category, *Advanced Contemplation*. Because of the editorial decisions involved in distinguishing and presenting these two categories, more is required here by way of introductory explanation than has been necessary for any of the previous volumes in this series.

As is the case with previous volumes, the selection and sequencing of material here is the work of students and not of P.B. himself. Because of the general unfamiliarity in many parts of the West with meditation, however, and because some fundamental ideas might appear unnecessarily confusing if paras were printed somewhat randomly, we have taken much more care in the sequencing within some of the chapters than is our custom. In this particular case, the risk of imposing unintended meanings by context is far outweighed by the risk of obscuring the fundamental clarity with which P.B. approaches and explains this important practice.

Progress in meditation, the inward penetration to deeper and more satisfying levels of the inner reality, can be schematized in several different ways. Two of these schemas, however, are more important to understanding the vast majority of P.B.'s writings on meditation.

The first of these two schemas distinguishes "elementary" and "advanced" practices. All the practices involving willed effort, the struggle to overcome the mind's inherent restlessness and focus it one-pointedly on a single image/idea/ideal to the exclusion of all else, are considered elementary in this schema. Only after such one-pointed concentration can be maintained indefinitely does one intelligently change over to the rapt, highly alert, state of inner passivity requisite for the advanced practices.

This division into elementary and advanced practices is the one that distinguishes the fourth and twenty-third categories from one another in P.B.'s general outline. But since the practices considered "elementary" in such a schema are far from "elementary" in the practice of most meditators and would-be meditators, and since these practices include nearly all of what is generally recommended by way of "meditation" to spiritual seekers in the modern West, we felt that P.B.'s title of "Elementary Meditation" could be misleading to the majority of Westerners now practising some form of meditation. Feeling ourselves forced to offer the present form of introductory explanation in either case, we have chosen to use *Meditation* as the title on the cover of this volume rather than the somewhat technical term "Elementary Meditation" from the original outline.

The second general division of stages of practice that it will be helpful for the reader to understand is threefold. Within the generic term "meditation," it distinguishes three stages: concentration, meditation proper, and contemplation. Though there are occasional exceptions and further elaborations, this threefold framework is the one that readers will find most useful in understanding the material in this volume. These three stages are quite clearly explained in the section on "Levels of absorption" in Chapter 1. The reader should also be aware that the word "meditation" is sometimes used as a generic term covering all three of these stages, and that it is sometimes used more technically to mean only the second of these three stages. Informed of both these usages, readers should have little difficulty discovering for themselves which meaning is appropriate to individual paras.

Editorial conventions with regard to the quantity of material chosen, as with regard to spelling, capitalization, hyphenation, and other copy-editing considerations, are the same as stated in introductions to earlier volumes. Likewise, (P) at the end of a para indicates that it is one of the relatively few paras we felt it necessary to repeat here from *Perspectives*, the introductory survey volume to this series.

It is a great pleasure to see yet another volume of this series going to press—one that carries with it still more profound appreciation of the dedicated work and support of our many friends and co-workers at Wisdom's Goldenrod and The Paul Brunton Philosophic Foundation, as well as of the many favourable and helpful responses from readers equally pleased with the progress of *The Notebooks*. Information about forthcoming publications may be obtained by writing the

Paul Brunton Philosophic Foundation
P.O. Box 89
Hector, NY 14841

Part 1:

MEDITATION

Meditation is really the mind thinking of the Soul, just as Activity is the mind thinking of the World.

It is habitual, hence called natural, for present-day humanity to go along with the mental flow to outside things. Meditation reverses this direction and tries to bring the little mind back to its origin—Mind.

1

PREPARATORY

The importance of meditation

Of all the day's activities, this non-activity, this retreat into meditation, must become the principal one. It ought to be the centre, with all the others circling round it.

2

For the religionist, meditation is essential because a nonchalant faith alone is not enough. He who indulges in theological speculation about the soul without having trod the inner way to the actual experience of it for himself is like a man standing outside a restaurant with shuttered windows and purporting to describe the meals being served inside. The religious mode of life is intended to prepare man for and to lead him eventually to the mystical mode, which is a higher rung in his development.

For the moralist, meditation is essential because a code of morals or a creed of ethics is only a preliminary aid to the fulfilment of life's purpose— which is to know ourselves. Our morals will automatically adjust themselves, our credo of ethics will automatically right itself once we have come into spiritual self-enlightenment. The noblest and the highest within us will then be evoked spontaneously. A technique of mind-training is indispensable to true self-knowledge.

Meditation is also essential for the artist. However talented he may be, a man can produce only substitutes for works of genius if he lacks the capacity to achieve self-absorbed states. The cultivation of this habit is a powerful help to the development of inspired moods. This is an age of brilliance. The talent for wit, satire, and sophistication abounds. But the true artist needs to go deeper than that. Art which lacks a spiritual import possesses only a surface value. The sun of inspiration shines upon all alike, but few people are so constituted as to be able to behold it. This is partly because they cannot achieve the requisite psychological condition. The artist who is wrapped up in a semi-trance of creative endeavour hardly notices at the time where he is and hardly remembers his own past life—

such is the intensity of his concentration. Thus mental quiet is not to be confused with mental laziness. It is not only a triumph over the one-sidedness of external activity but also a creative quiet. This truth achieves its fullest exemplification in the sphere of art.

For the overworked man of affairs or the tired man of action, meditation is essential because it affords a wonderful relief by creating a little secret place within himself where the sordid world will be less able to hurt him, the events of life less able to depress him. Moreover, he needs meditation not only because an unrestrained external activity is not enough but also because it brings up out of the subconscious stores unexpected ideas which may be what he was consciously seeking previously or provides him with swift intuitions which throw light on perplexing problems. How much did their early morning practice of prefacing the day's work with a half hour of devotional meditation and guidance-seeking help some famous historical figures!

For the idealist who is struggling in a hard and harsh world, short daily periods of meditation will in time become the blessed sanctuary wherein he can keep alive his repressed aspirations.

Finally meditation is essential for every man because without it he lives at too great a radius from his divine centre to understand the best thing which life can offer him. He must reclaim the divine estate of which he is the ignorant owner. O! it is worthwhile to make this sacred incursion and attain, for a time, a nobler and wiser state of himself. By this daily act of returning into himself, he reaffirms his divine dignity and practises true self-respect.

3

Spirituality is within. If one does not feel it, then one needs to search deeper, beneath the weaknesses, faults, passions, and desires of the ego. It is still there, but the search must be properly made. This is where help can be found, in the words of those who have already found it.

4

It is a fact of mere observation that most Western men live throughout their wakeful existence from morning to night without finding a few minutes—or even caring to find them—for the liberating practice of meditation exercises. They are virtually imprisoned in the five senses and in the thoughts arising from each sense-activity. This fact is a lamentable one. For how can they hope to cultivate a higher life if this essential aid be neglected?

5

The consciousness beyond the usual everyday consciousness can be reached only after a disciplined training of the mind. This suppresses its activity in thinking and banishes its extroverted worldliness of character.

6

It comes to this, that what people try to find in many books is waiting for them within themselves, to be discovered by regularly practising the art of meditation.

7

This idea, or belief, that we must go somewhere, meet someone, read something, to accomplish life's best fulfilment is the first and last mistake. In the end, as in the beginning, we have nothing else to do except obey the ancient command to LOOK WITHIN.

8

The need of meditation is to establish equilibrium in the whole being, for ordinary active life is a "going out" while meditation is a polar opposite, a "coming back" to the source. Whereas ignorant men are compelled by Nature to "come back" in sleep, they do so without awareness. Meditation, being a conscious, deliberate undertaking, restores "awareness."

9

So long as he is looking for the Spirit outside himself—where it is not— so long will he fail to find it. This is the first justification of meditation.

10

He who would find his Soul has to press deep into his mind.

11

To separate the mind from the body is abnormal and ordinarily undesirable. But to free the mind from the tyranny of the body is absolutely essential and this can be assisted by the regular practice of meditation.

12

The uncertainty which reigns among people as to whether there is or is not an Intelligence which presides over the processes of Nature and the fortunes of mankind—that is, a God—as well as the conflicting views of educated persons, shows the lack of inner experience, the failure to practise meditation.

13

Arguments or doubts about the soul can be settled for us once and for all only by *personal experience* of it. This is immeasurably better than logical proof, which is always open to equal disproof. This mystical experience is the challenge of our times.

14

The truth needed for immediate and provisional use may be learned from books and teachers but the truth of the ultimate revelation can be learned only from and within oneself by meditation.(P)

15

The purely intellectual approach to the Overself can never replace the psychological experience of it. This latter is and must be supreme.

16

It is a principle of philosophy that what you can know is limited by what you are. A deep man may know a deep truth but a shallow man, never. This indeed is one of its reasons for taking up the practice of meditation.(P)

17

Reading and travel can contribute much to a cultured way of life, but meditation and reflection can deepen the man himself.

18

It is one of the values of yoga that it can provide a man with the actual experience of feeling that he is only a witness of the whirling of time, whereas metaphysics only talks of this state.

19

Meditation is essential for the abstract thinker because a brooding intelligence is not enough, because it alone operates with the experience-able facts of consciousness, whereas metaphysics operates either with erroneous speculations about those factors or with correct but shadowy images of them. In the latter case, it successfully brings these images into vividly felt actuality.

20

Reflection must needs be long and arduous before it is likely to reach certainty. These truths can be reached and realized only in solitary meditation. Meditation is the first letter in the aspirant's alphabet.

21

Lao Tzu: "The excellence of a mind is its profundity."

22

If something awakens in him, a serious urge to unfold more of his spiritual nature, then the practice of meditation becomes one of the best ways to get into action.

23

What wonderful experiences or realizations, awarenesses or confirmations await the man who successfully contemplates, and becomes absorbed in, himself! But it must be the inward, deeper part.

24

The consequences of putting the contents of his own mind under observation, of becoming fully aware of their nature, origin, and effect, are immeasurably important.

25

With the sole object of calming and clearing the mind and concentrating its power, it is a good practice to sit in meditation for a while each day before beginning to study philosophy. This helps the studies.

26

Prayer is a help, but some method that not only goes still deeper into the human heart but helps to silence the ego is also needed. This can be found through the practice of contemplation.

27

To the work of reshaping character and extending consciousness, the practice of meditation is indispensable.

28

The man who is prone to impatience, irritability, and anger needs meditation even more than other men. He needs its harmonizing effect on the whole personality, its pacifying touch on the darker impulses and passions.

29

If the work and result of meditation seem strange and unearthly, artificial and abnormal, this is only because the average person is not yet a fully human being but is only in the process of becoming one.

30

Those who are incapable of practising meditation are incapable of becoming philosophers.

31

How can you do God's will unless you know what is God's will? How can you know this unless you are able to communicate with God? And how can this happen unless you can go deep into yourself in meditation?

32

Meditation is important in this Quest. It must be learnt. It helps to create a condition wherein the holy presence can be felt, where before there was nothing, and where the holy guidance can be given.

33

A man may live on the surface of life or in the divine depths of being beneath his ego's sub-surface. It is for him to make the effort, dive again and again until there is contact.

34

Withdraw into the inner Stillness: what better thing can a man do? For it will point to the goal, give direction and support to finding it.

35

In most cases, students must be reminded of the importance of practising meditation *daily* and not just occasionally. Lack of time or energy are no longer acceptable excuses: time can be made for other things easily enough, so let it be made for meditation, too; and laziness or inertia can be overcome by simply applying determination and a little self-discipline. The student who deliberately sticks to his task, and persists through the initial irksomeness of this practice, will find that the eventual results justify all inconveniences. Meditation is essential in order to develop sensitivity and intuition, which play important roles on this Quest.

36

Both the necessity and justification of meditation lie in this, that man is so preoccupied with his own thoughts that he is never aware of the mind out of which they arise and in which they vanish. The process of stilling these thoughts, or advanced meditation, makes this awareness possible.

37

Whether we renounce the world or whether we accept it, the need of mental control still remains the same.

38

So long as thoughts remain unmastered, this present and personal experience shuts us out from reality.

39

In the recesses of his own being, a man can find peace, strength, wisdom—but only if he brings his thoughts into obedience.

40

The cerebrum keeps up mental action like a machine. Only when the mind slows by disengaging from this activity, coming to rest by some means, does consciousness show its own treasures.

41

Thought may ennoble a man or debase him. It is not to be dismissed as unimportant. If conquering it is so necessary, stilling it is even more important and more necessary.

42

The prejudiced mind repels true ideas, which can take no hold in it. Hence we give yoga to such people to discipline their minds.

43

The mind must be prepared before it can take in the truth. Its oscillations must be steadied before it can reflect the truth.

44

Psychological methods are not less necessary than religious exercises. The thought-life of man is ordinarily a confused, a wandering, and a restless one. Meditation, practised in solitude and quietude, must be regularly inserted into it, first, to help improve its character, and second, to open a pathway towards conscious knowledge of the higher self.

45

So long as the mind remains untrained and its thoughts move unrestricted, so long will man be a stranger to peace and self-possession.

46

We cannot come to a plain contemplation of life while we allow ourselves to be unduly disturbed by desires and unduly perturbed by disappointments. Hence the need of yoga.

47

We have never learnt to keep our minds still as we sometimes keep our bodies still. It is by far the harder task but also the most rewarding one. Our thoughts continually titillate them and our desires periodically agitate them. What the inner resources of mind are, and what they can offer us, consequently remain unglimpsed and unknown. They are, in their totality, the Soul, and they offer us the kingdom of heaven.

48

To pursue the realization of his dream—an abiding peace which would necessarily lead to the falling-away of haunting fears and negative emotions—he must gain control of thoughts.

49

It is just as valuable for ordinary non-monastic lay people to learn and practise meditation as it is for the monks themselves. And they can do this—at least in the earlier stages—without any reference to religious themes, prayers, or supports should they prefer it.

50

The mere physical act of sitting down to practise meditation is both a symbolic gesture of withdrawal from the world and an actual severance from it. Each time it is done the meditator temporarily renounces his outer personal life, renders himself oblivious of it and of the world in which it is lived. What other withdrawal is needed? Is this not enough? Therefore anyone may continue to remain a householder and need not take monastic vows, may be active in the world provided such daily periods of meditation successfully take him out of it.

51

Meditation can be learned by the orthodox as well as the unorthodox, by the atheist as well as the theist, by the rationalist as well as the mystic.

52

The failure on the part of most people in the West to give a little of their time to personal and private holy communion, bringing no priest or clergyman into the period but seeking in their own solitude to take advantage of the usually well-camouflaged fact that man is essentially alone, brings its inevitable consequences. Their lives may be good or bad, their careers may be successful or failing, but having no consciousness of Consciousness they remain only half-men. They have so little competent guidance from those who are professional spiritual guides that most do not even know the sin through omission they are committing, do not recognize the failure in duty.

53

In the Western world this ability is not a common one. Yet by its absence Western people are less than themselves, are short of true wholeness.

54

It is true that the Occidental peoples have had in the past little aptitude for exercises in contemplation. But that is no reason why they should not make a start at what will inescapably have to be started if they are to put an end to their aimlessness and restlessness.

55

The Westerner must learn to end this endless restlessness, this daily impatience to be doing something, must practise faithfully and regularly "waiting on the Lord," or meditation. Thus he will come less and less to rely on his own little resources, more and more on the Lord's—that is, on his Overself's—infinite wisdom, power, and grace.

56

There can be consciousness without a brain. Hence, there can be consciousness after death. To verify this, it is necessary to isolate the *principle* of consciousness from its products. Such isolation can only be effected through some kind of mystical experience. This experience can be brought about by meditational practice. The materialists who refuse to try such practice or who, trying, fail, cannot be regarded as disposing of the question.

57

We spend so much of the day concentrating on our personal selves. Can we not spend a half hour concentrating on the higher self?

58

The numerous details with which civilized existence has complicated our lives make meditation seem an irksome exercise and the daily meditation period impossible to secure. Yet although we become so engrossed in those details, analysis would reveal how unnecessary many of them really are, or how trivial by comparison with the importance of emerging from spiritual death.

59

Only a small minority of the human race feels the need of giving itself the time for meditation. Consequently, only a small minority ever knows that mystical experience is really factual. The absence of intervals of tranquil meditation from their day-to-day lives is not to be excused but rather explained by the fact that there are many who shrink from these studies and practices under the impression that the former are dark and incomprehensible and the latter mysterious and unholy. So they come to leave philosophical mysticism to the few who are regarded as abnormal or eccentric. But the truth is that they are disinclined in the first case to make the mental efforts and in the second case to practise the emotional disciplines.

60

Those who continue the regular exercises in meditation are outnumbered by those who give them up. The pressure of modern existence is too much for them.

61

It is a great lack in modern life that it allows no time for a short period of meditation, whether in the morning or evening or both, to gain repose of being and elevation of mind.

62

The man who seeks outer peace and quiet to help his efforts to acquire inner peace and mental stillness will soon find the modern world opposing his intentions and obstructing his attempts.

63

Meditation is no longer limited to a few Christian monasteries and Oriental ashrams but has spread among laymen around the world.

64

Too often the Western world sneered at yoga and gave the name a derogatory, even condemnatory, colouring. But this ignorant attitude is rapidly vanishing and more respect is given to the subject, as in earlier times.

65

Field Marshal Montgomery a Meditator! by Alexander Clifford, the war correspondent, who travelled from El Alamein to Germany with Field Marshal Montgomery: "Montgomery's military thinking was as logical and unorthodox as everything else. Once again his simplicity was at the root of it. He believed deeply in long periods of pure thought—of working each problem out from scratch. Way back in the desert he started a routine which he never abandoned. It was built round the same three caravans and the same staff, and probably the essential items in the day's program were the periods devoted to uninterrupted meditation. He could not do without it. Once the King came to visit him at Eindhoven in the autumn of 1944 and, owing to bad weather, was forced to stay longer than he had intended. Monty's program was dislocated as a result, and his staff detected signs of serious psychological frustration because his meditation periods were being curtailed."

66

That the simple act of sitting down for a length of time as unmoving as the heron-bird watching its prey could provide the first condition for self-knowledge may seem strange.

67

There is a deep antipathy in the nature of most Western people toward the effort required to concentrate and introvert attention. It fatigues them excessively. That is clearly due to the lack of familiarity and practice. But this antipathy has also a mysterious element in it, whose origin is hidden in the ego's desire to avoid any deep, long self-scrutiny that penetrates beneath its own surface. For that would certainly lead to its own exposure and its own destruction.

68

Some are frightened by this very proposal to look deep down into the mind, and they turn away in emotional refusal.

69

The fear of losing the known and familiar prevents them from entering the unknown and higher consciousness.

70

Young people are naturally outgoing and are consequently less inclined to take up meditation practice, but this is counterbalanced by their greater openness of mind and readiness to follow ideals. Older people are reluctant to include meditation in their daily program because, they complain, the rush and pressures of modern living fatigue them and make them less inclined to take on a self-imposed duty of such difficulty for beginners.

71

They are trying to find their way to a higher kind of truth but their efforts and understanding are still in the beginning stages. For instance, to them, the idea of meditation still includes thinking, although only in its loftier, more abstract themes.

72

They are willing to look everywhere else than into their own inner being.

73

Not a few have rejected the practice of meditation because it did not seem natural to them; it was too artificial—as if letting muddied water settle down to become clear was an unnatural process! No one who has not successfully brought the active whirling mind to a complete rest through this practice can know how comparable it is to such a process. Hence Japanese mystics call it "collecting the mind."

74

Critics and sceptics are on the outside looking in. Their opinions on meditation are of little value.

75

Those who condemn the hours spent in meditation as wasted ones, have been misled by mere appearances and have fallen into one of the greatest errors of their lives.

76

He needs to remember the difference between a method and a goal: the one is not the same as the other. Both meditation and asceticism are trainings but they are not the final goals set up for human beings.(P)

77

But a man cannot be continuously sitting down in meditation. Nature herself provides him with other tasks, even if he were capable of the feat, which he is not. All his formal practice of such exercises is, after all, only an instrument to help him achieve a given end; it is not the end itself.

78

It is indispensable to attainment but it is not sufficient to ensure attainment.

79

We must not let the forms of meditation become a subtler bondage than the merely obvious ones. We must not let it (or anything else) become a cage. If this has happened then courage must be summoned to shatter the bars and step out into freedom.

80

Yoga is not finished when a yogin can concentrate perfectly and keep his mind utterly quiet. Certainly he who has reached this point has mastered raja yoga—the royal union—but he must go farther and use the wonderful instrument he has now developed for the mastery of the advanced phases of gnana yoga—the union with truth. In the earlier phases he can employ a sharpened intellect, but depth of intuition and an ego-freed will to know are needed for the later ones.

81

The inwardness through which a human being finds his way in meditation exercises to the redirection of attention to his soul, his deeper "I," is needed to restore his lost balance. But it is a process, a means to an end. For him the end must be not a special and limited experience, briefly felt, of his innermost being but a settled awareness of its presence throughout his everyday life, and a consequent sharing in that life.

82

In the life and work of the philosophical aspirant, meditation takes an important place. There are several different ways and traditions in such work, so that the aspirant may find what suits him. Although sometimes it is better for him to discipline himself and practise with a way to which he is not attracted—that is only sometimes. Generally, it is easier to learn the art of meditation if we take the way that appeals to us individually.

Meditation is, however, and should be, only part of the program. The importance given to it can be exaggerated. The work on oneself, on one's character and tendencies, is also important. The study of the teachings is equally important. And so, out of all these approaches, there comes a ripening, a broad maturity which prepares the aspirant for recognition and full reception of the grace—should it come.

83

Meditation is, after all, a phase which is put on and off again as needed. The Quest is much bigger than meditation—although it includes it at times, but not necessarily all the time.

84

He should not make the mistake of taking what is admittedly important—meditation—for what is all-important.

85

It is most unwise to undervalue meditation and overvalue reasoning. By so doing one would fall into the complementary error of another who depreciates reasoning and considers meditation all that is necessary.

86

It is useful to get misguided people to practise meditation, for it calms passion and lulls the ego. Nevertheless it cannot cure them. They are the products of mis-education and so the radical or fundamental cure is right education—that is, right thinking.

87

The whole bodily and mental purificatory regime contributes both to the proper development of meditation and to the proper reception of intuitive knowledge. This is apart from and in addition to, its direct physical and personal benefits.

88

He must cultivate a sense of the value of meditation. It is not to be regarded as a hobby for odd moments. It is to be prized as the way to a peace and contentment worth as much as any material comfort or possession.

89

This is his sacred hour, his time for holy communion. It must be shielded from society's inroads.

90

A period and a place should be set apart for devotional exercises and mystical practices.

91

Père Lacordaire: "To withdraw into oneself and God is the greatest power which exists . . . I perceive with joy the solitude around me; it is my element, my life. A man works from within himself, not from outside."

92

Man meditating successfully is man at his highest moment.

93

"The action of the mind which is best," declared Saint Gregory Pala-mas, Greek Orthodox Archbishop of Thessalonica seven hundred years ago, "is that in which it is sometimes raised above itself and unites with God."

94

It is useless and foolish to try to avoid meditation. One must learn its lessons.

95

We look for loftier experiences than those the common day affords us.

96

"Westward Ho!" was the cry in the old days when a ship left England for America. "Inward Ho!" can be the cry when a quester starts on his spiritual voyage.

97

Before his mind can understand truth, attain the Real, and enjoy happi-ness, it must reach a quiet state. No disturbances, no agitations, and no resistances must get in the way. To make such a state possible, it must first be reached spasmodically during special periods each day, that is, during meditation periods. As it becomes more and more accustomed to the silencing of its negative activities in this way, it will eventually become more and more settled in the state by habit during the rest of the day. Finally the habit becomes a trait of character, permanent and unbroken. Here is the further reason why the practice of meditation exercises is a necessity, indispensable to a complete quest.

98

The following of these exercises is indispensable to train the mind, to create a habit which will make entry into the meditative mood as easy in the end as it is hard in the beginning.

99

In the earlier history of Christianity, the place given to meditation was quite important and prominent.

100

The art of meditation found a favourable climate in which to thrive both in ancient Orient and medieval Europe. Life moved at a much slower pace. Science and industry had not pressed man to give all his attention to the outward activities. The oppressions, hardships, toil, serfdom, and slavery of common people gave them few ways of escape other than the inward one. There, in the solace of religious prayers or the practice of mystical introspection, they might find some of the happiness denied them by worldly society. Moreover, the tropical temperatures of many Oriental

lands drove their inhabitants more easily into lassitude, resignation, defeatism, and pessimism while the wars, invasions, tyrannies, and poverties
of medieval Europe drove a not inconsiderable number of its inhabitants
to wear the friar's garb or enter the monastic house.

101

The practices of meditation were common in the first centuries of
Christian Egypt but largely dropped out of the Church for a considerable
period thereafter. Then came its revival—first in Roman, then in Eastern
sections.

102

The practice of mental quiet was formerly confined to the monasteries
and convents and kept from the knowledge of lay folk. When Miguel de
Molinos tried to alter this state of affairs, he was sternly suppressed.

103

Modern conditions have so vastly changed from those of antique and
medieval times that it is necessary to remind readers that until about the
sixteenth century in Catholic countries, the teaching of meditation to the
laity was prohibited. It was a subject to be studied by ecclesiastics only,
and an art to be practised in monastic circles only. When the Renaissance
brought a relaxing of this reserve, it was at first in favour of the higher
social classes alone. Not till the eighteenth century was it available to all
classes.

104

More medieval Christians practised the techniques of meditation than
modern ones do. But a principal reason for that was the existence of more
monasteries and convents to take care of the meditators. Those who did
not care to be buffeted about in the storms of the world found plenty of
harbours of refuge to which they could turn their boats.

105

The archives of Eastern and Western mysticism teem with instances of
successful meditation practice and a scientific view must explain them from
the inside, not merely criticize them from the outside alone.

The true way of meditation

106

We have tried to build up a form of yoga fit for those who must live and
work in Western cities. The average European, the average American,
cannot imitate the Indian or Tibetan ways of yogic unfoldment, even if he
wants to; they are not always the correct or convenient ways for him.

107

A way suited to our times and our matter-sunk minds is urgently needed. Because the writer was dissatisfied with most paths already formulated, he has shaped out the one which is here offered. This way takes but a fragment of one's daily life, a mere half hour being enough.

108

Let no one believe that these techniques are the same as, or sympathetic to, those which are employed by spiritualist mediums to enter the trance state, or by spiritualist believers to secure automatic writing. The wary student cannot afford, and should not expose himself to, the peril of letting unknown psychic forces take possession of his body.

109

It is certainly possible for the earnest Westerner to live an active life and still practise meditation. However, there are some Indian yoga exercises which could never be practised in active life without leading to insanity or a nervous breakdown. The exercises given in my books are intended for Westerners leading active lives and are absolutely safe.

110

The expanding interest in yoga is in part due to its value as a technique of increasing our understanding of ourselves, achieving more happiness and peace of mind. It can be applied to normal living by normal persons, and its use is not limited only to hermits and monks.

111

The word meditation, and the meaning of the word, are beginning to become known in different Western circles. If this is contrasted to the ignorance of both which prevailed a half-century ago, the change is gratifying. But although no longer so unknown and mysterious, the distance still to be travelled until the word becomes as understood and familiar here as it is in India is quite long.

112

Meditation is not really a safe term to use nowadays. For instance for most people it means thinking about a theme, but for other groups it holds the very opposite meaning—non-thinking.

113

Yoga is a single word covering a multitude of practices. All are based on the principle of yoking the mind to one idea or one object; but since the ideas selected differ with the different schools of teaching, the results are often strikingly at variance. For concentrated thought gives increased power to our present qualities, intensifying the beliefs with which we started. Hence the competing schools of occultism with their clashing doctrines.

114

People who do not know what they are talking about, who lack the sense of responsibility for one's statements which is engendered by the scientific training of the West, have mixed up with yoga much that is totally irrelevant such as childish superstitions, religious fancies, and magical practices.

115

The term "yoga" itself may mean almost anything in India, for it has become a generic name for a number of techniques which are not only vastly different from each other but in some cases even definitely opposed. It need not even have any reference to a non-materialistic end. It is therefore necessary to be somewhat explicit when using such an ambiguous term.

116

The contemporary definition of the word yoga in India is "union with God." To a philosopher this is an unsatisfactory one. For originally the word, when split into its syllables *ya* and *gam*, meant "the way to go." Later it came to mean "the way to perfection." But in both cases the application of this term was not limited to God as a goal, although He was a common one. For there were materialistic, mental, religious, and philosophic yogas: indeed one could be an atheist and still pursue a particular yoga. The correct interpretation of the word indicates therefore that there is a carelessness and looseness in its use, on the one hand, and a radical misunderstanding of its right meaning, on the other.

117

Yoga is not a system for developing personal efficiency in order to succeed better in the worldly life, nor a therapy to get rid of diseases. Those who present it in this way have neither felt the spirit which belongs to it nor understood its most important offering.

118

If he requests advice on how to set about yoga, let it be clearly understood that yoga in the orthodox sense is neither suitable, practicable, nor beneficial to modern Western people. The techniques permitted merely embody yoga elements but are not limited to such elements. Indeed the term "yoga" has been dropped from these teachings to avoid further misunderstandings. Philosophy is the only teaching here offered, using the word in its ancient Greek sense of love of high wisdom.

119

The traditional, orthodox forms of yoga are not quite safe for Westerners living in the environment of Western cities and therefore they cannot be recommended in their old forms.

120

My attempts to clarify the attitude which I had adopted toward yoga, mysticism, and religion has only partially succeeded in its objects, and still there seems to be a considerable amount of confusion and misunderstanding as to what my views really are. Readers still demand a more explicit statement of my present position and this I propose now to give.

Let it be perfectly clear at the outset that I condemn neither religion nor yoga, but staunchly uphold them. So far as religion consists of a sense of reverence for a higher power and an attempt to live a good life in accordance with the ethical injunctions of the great religious founders, it is a definite necessity for the mass of humanity. So far as the practice of yoga consists in the effort to control thoughts and to subdue worldly attachments, it is an invaluable way for distressed hearts to find peace, an excellent means of obtaining that sharpened attention which is required for the adequate consideration of philosophical questions, and, in its advanced stages, a beatific path to rapt ecstasies.

Holding such views as to the importance and personal value of both religion and yoga for the great majority of mankind, it is natural that I should have nothing but respect and regard for those who faithfully follow and practise their yoga, their religion, or their mysticism. On the other hand, what can honest men give but contempt and indignation for those who become pious hypocrites in the name of religion, parasites on society in the name of yoga, or exploiters of superstition in the name of mysticism? Ought he not to make a strong protest against unbalanced abuse and incorrect practice of yoga which leads to the most unfortunate physical and mental results? Ought he not also to protest against the mistakes of mystics when they take advantage of the much-abused word "intuition" to propagate their own personal imaginations as scientific certainties?

It will be seen that I am for a calm and dispassionate appraisal of these important matters and that I wish to avoid either blind, unthinking adherence on the one side or foolish, hasty scepticism on the other. I could not have arrived at such an attitude of candid examination, I believe, if I had not had the opportunity of studying impartially various manifestations of yoga, religion, and mysticism, not only in India but throughout the world, for more than a quarter of a century. And I have had the advantage of knowing these matters from the inside as well as the outside.

121

It is asked why I consider yoga unsuited to Western people. This statement needs clarification and qualification for as it stands it would be untrue. By the term "yoga" is meant the precise forms of practice which are traditional to India and which originated thousands of years ago. They can be followed in their fullness only by renouncing the world entirely, entering the monastic order, retiring to forest mountain or cave retreats, abjuring all family social and national responsibilities, and accepting Hindu deities as objects of devotion. The average Westerner today is not in a position to do this, nor is he intellectually attracted to it. This is all I meant by criticizing the suitability of such methods. The basic principle of yoga, which is the cultivation of power to withdraw attention from the external world to the internal self, stands for all time and all peoples. I therefore believe it better to separate it from the accidents and traditions of history and geography, to free it from local accretions and universalize it. But if this is done it is perhaps wiser not to use the term "yoga" and thus to avoid confusion.

122

In the attempt to scrutinize, analyse, and define the perceptions, the sensations, and the successive changes of consciousness which meditation produced, I questioned many a practitioner, studied many a text, interviewed the few real experts I could find and, finally, looked at my own inner experience.

123

Yoga is both a method to be practised and a result to be attained. It is both going inside the mind and being the undistracted mind itself.

124

Yoga as work to be done is a process but as the unified consciousness it is a result.

125

Yoga is, in the earlier stages, a bodily position to be assumed and a mental practice to be done. But in the advanced stage it seeks to transcend the other two, to move up to relaxed forgetfulness of them and peaceful self-absorption in the Overself.

126

The process of yoga demands the positive introduction of a specific meditation-pattern and the deepest possible withdrawal of attention from sense-experienced external objects.

127

There are various forms of meditative practice and various aspects of meditation itself, but none of these are the heart of the matter.

128

The true state of meditation is reached when there is awareness of awareness, without the intrusion of any thoughts whatever. But this condition is not the ultimate. Beyond it lies the stage where all awareness vanishes *without the total loss of consciousness that this normally brings*.(P)

129

There are different kinds of meditation. The elementary is concerned with holding certain thoughts firmly in the mind. The advanced is concerned with keeping all thoughts completely out of the mind. The highest is concerned with merging the mind blissfully in the Overself.

Part 1:
MEDITATION

406

Example: The sensation of light may be overwhelming. He will feel as if a large electric bulb has been lighted inside his brain.

407

His sensitivity to the thoughts and feelings of other persons will become so developed and so accurate that the mere entrance of another man into the same room will spontaneously register within his consciousness that man's momentary attitude towards or thought about him.

408

It is when the second stage of meditation is fully developed that occult powers may arise. The mind is able so to identify itself with anyone as to reproduce his characteristics within itself quite faithfully. It may even overcome distance and do so even when the other person is not physically present but fifty miles away. Indeed, he who acquires this power of clairvoyance may have to protect himself against mixing up the other man's thoughts with his own, or against mistaking them as his own.

409

One experience which the meditator may get and which many meditators have had is to get a lightness in the body, a feeling as if he is floating in air, in space, or in infinity. It is blissful and to be welcomed, although there have been a few cases where beginners are frightened by it, frightened that it may be the beginning of annihilation, the annihilation of consciousness, and so they stop and withdraw.

410

The sensation of nearly (but not fully) getting out of his body may prove a pleasant or a frightening one, according to his preparedness for it.

411

He need not get either perturbed or puzzled if, after a certain period of the session has elapsed and a certain depth of concentration reached, there is a momentary disappearance of consciousness. This will be a prologue to, as well as a sign of, entrance into the third state, contemplation. The immediate after-effect of the lapse is somewhat like that which follows deep dreamless sleep. There is a delicious awakening into a mind very quiet, emotions gently stilled, and nerves greatly soothed.(P)

412

The feeling of being half-bodiless is of course an illusory one. It arises from becoming aware of, and sufficiently attentive to, the stillness behind mental activity.

413

If in the period of meditation there comes a feeling of expansion in space, of the enlargement of consciousness along with a concentrated tranquillity, the practitioner need not get frightened, but should let the happening take its own natural course.

414

Possible experiences during meditation: (1) drowsy; (2) a feeling of frustration causes abandonment of session; (3) feel presence of a higher power; (4) finished with a sense of ease and lightness; (5) deeper meaning of certain past experiences become clearer; (6) a dynamic energy was felt in spine; (7) feeling benevolent to all; (8) mixed thoughts kept on distracting attention; (9) varied mental pictures of events, persons, or scenes—mostly past—floated through and vanished; (10) sounds from outside bothered and distracted; (11) ended happy in heart and positive in attitude; (12) no special result but generally relaxed; (13) for periods of about a half-minute or so each he gets into complete mental quiet, unbroken by outer sounds even if they were there or by the procession of thoughts; (14) a feeling of failure or anxiety; (15) a sense of general welfare; (16) an arousal of hope and cheerfulness concerning the future; (17) a wish to be helpful to others; (18) general contentment; (19) harmony with Nature.

415

His development becomes mature when the hour for meditation no longer remains outside the day but perfumes its every minute.

416

If the meditative act is used aright by the intellect, will, and imagination, it can become a means to an inspiration and an ecstasy beyond itself. It can be used as a stimulus to creative achievement in any field, including the spiritual and the artistic fields. It should be practised just before beginning to work. The technique is to hold on to the inspired attitude or the joyous feeling after meditation is completed and not to let it fade away. Then approach the work to be done and carry the attitude into it. It will be done with more power, more effectiveness, and especially more creativeness. Anyone who loves his task in this deeper way does it more easily and successfully than he who does not.

417

Among the visions which are possible, there is one of great beauty but which comes more often to Far Eastern disciples than to Euramerican ones. It depicts the sun rising out of the sea and throwing a straight trail of light across the dark waters.

418

Almost any symbolic vision is possible, but certain ones have repeated themselves so often down through the centuries as to become classic. They may appear to the same man only rarely, but each time they will act as bearers of fresh hope, power, or beauty and as incentives to acquire needed humility, purity, or discipline.

419

The aspirant should vigilantly detect and immediately appreciate those rare mystical moments which come of their own accord. They should be ardently cherished and used as they come by putting all other activity aside for a few minutes and concentrating fully on them. Otherwise they display an ephemeral nature and disappear on fleet wings. They can later be used as themes for meditational exercises by striving to recapture them through imaginative remembrance and concentration.

420

There is a twilight, vague, and nebulous frontier between the two states, most often experienced just after waking. It is here that the psychic and occult are most easily felt and, on a higher level, the intuitive and spiritual most easily known.

421

If seen at all, the Light as a lightning-flash is ordinarily seen at the beginning and near the end of the Quest. In the first case, it appears as a slender ray and inclines the man toward spiritual things or wakes him up to their existence. In the second case, it appears as a mass of living brilliance pulsating inside, through, and around him, or throughout the universe, and brings him close to union with God.

422

When a pronounced uplifting feeling comes, identify yourself with it, not with thoughts *about* it.

423

It is important that the practiser should be able to recognize and detect the advent of a higher power: it may present itself in several different ways and forms. One of them is to make itself felt as a mysterious gripping of the head and neck which are quite involuntarily swivelled round to one side and held rigidly there. Or they may slowly, at intervals, be moved in a semi-circle. He should accept the happening, go along with it until it ends by itself.

424

His encounters with other persons may affect him emotionally or interfere with him mentally, so sensitive does he become. This is why it is better to limit his contacts and if possible avoid those who leave undesirable effects until such time as his development brings them under control. He learns by experience how to guard the mental purity and inner peace.

425

Many different kinds of inner experience are possible as meditation progresses, some exceedingly interesting but all merely temporary. Among them are: divorce from the body, seeing bright light, losing inclination to talk with others, losing the sense of personal identity, the feeling that everything has come to a standstill and the suspension of time passing, and a vast spatial emptiness.

426

It is correct to say that many aspirants have undergone strange, weird, inexplicable, unrepeated, or occult experiences in their attempts to practise meditation. But it is necessary to point out that these phenomena belong to the first or middle stages of the practice, not to the real work in contemplation.

427

These are all experiences for a beginner: when they pass away he may know that the beginning phase has passed. He should be satisfied with the verifications which they have produced and know that appearances are turning into realities.

428

Meditation is also a valuable pause from a totally different point of view, that of health and vitality. It allows body, nerves, energy, and functional organs to recoup.

429

Unfamiliarity with these phenomena may cause fright and withdrawal at first, but the confidence that comes with experience usually replaces these negative feelings.

430

Several reported after meditations that they did not feel their body (except head) and did not feel any life in their trunk hands or legs. But one man reported a feeling of sinking *downwards*, not inwards from the head.

431

What is the absent-mindedness which he experiences both in and out of meditation? If this is accompanied by a blissful feeling, it is nothing to get anxious about and would indeed be a sign of the spiritual force working underground. Even so it would completely disappear in time as he will have to get and keep full consciousness. However, if the blissful feeling is absent, then it is a mental difficulty which he must strive to overcome by using his willpower.

432

Their wishful expectations have a formative effect on whatever revelation or vision may happen to them.

433

There is a disadvantage in these practices, too. If they penetrate deep enough, he becomes sensitive to the unseen emanations from other people—to their thought, feeling, character.

434

The mechanical operation of the lungs and heart may be markedly slowed down as the working of the intellect is itself slowed down or, in some cases, it may come very close to suspension.

435

The feeling of dreamy contentedness prevails long after a good meditation.

436

At times he may feel as if apart from his physical body, a strangely detached spectator of it.

437

It is not correct to assume that because the condition of muscular rigidity and bodily coma has so often followed the condition of emotional spiritual ecstasy, it must necessarily and always do so. It is enough in proficient and experienced cases for the ordinary state to be partially obscured.

438

As attention sinks inward, its outward-turned strength gets reduced until physical objects appear blurred.

439

If the penetration goes deep enough, attention may or may not any longer notice the outside surroundings, the external world.

440

As he enters the higher self there is a great intensification of consciousness.

441

A feeling of delicate sweetness may rise in his heart. If so, it is to be surrendered to completely.

442

It is possible that thoughts involuntarily cease, as in swoon, or are deliberately stopped, as in held breathing, yet none of this exquisite peace is felt.

443

Under influence of drugs, the sense of time may slow down or accelerate, the sense of space may become unbounded or squeeze down to a minute point. Yet exactly the same may happen in certain kinds of meditation.

444

Buddha said that consciousness of pain in the body, along with all other sense reports, vanishes in the trance-stage even before Nirvana is entered.

445

One need not fear "letting go" of the body-thought in meditation. If a momentary swoon should ensue, it will be immediately followed by return to full consciousness. In addition, one will feel physically refreshed and spiritually stimulated.

446

It is possible to experience the mind-being as something separate from the body before one has gained control over the body and ego. But the experience will be fleeting until then.

447

If he is unprepared for these occurrences and uncertain of their nature, the encounter may give rise to fears which cause an abrupt abandonment of these meditations.

448

Trance is often a confusing word to use to describe the deepest condition of meditation. It could lead to misunderstanding. Safer words would be "dynamic reverie" or "constructive introversion." The idea of reverie promotes some kind of background awareness continuing through, either from one's surroundings or from oneself, and is therefore truer.

449

It is not necessary that every seeker of the Spiritual Truth should pass through the trance state. A few do, most others do not, on their way to the goal yet both groups arrive at the same goal. It is indeed not advisable for the average wisdom-seeker deliberately to try to get into trance when his environment is not specially suitable for it, and doing so may even be dangerous.

450

By the trance state I mean one where meditation becomes so deep that the senses of bodily sight and hearing are suspended.

451

An outwardly similar condition can be induced by artificial methods— such as suspension of breath, fixation of the *gaze*, or even hypnotizing of the mind—but it is only a counterfeit, only useful on its own physical and mental level, never on the mystical level which it is unable to touch. It has as much spiritual value as the hibernation of animals has. For the true condition does not really come through such effort of the ego, it comes by Grace. This is why the hatha yogi is warned not to get stuck in hatha yoga but to climb higher.

452

He may fall into a daze which, the longer it lasts the longer it will take for him to emerge from. But Nature will have her way and bring him out of the condition.

Dangers, and how to avoid them

453

Right meditation is one of the most fruitful activities anyone can engage in, but wrong meditation is one of the most foolish.

454

It is true that it may now be desirable to spread the knowledge of contemplative practices as an urgent necessity for the masses, but it would be quite undesirable to do so without proper safeguards against the abuses and repeated warnings against the dangers involved. And it is equally true that only a few have achieved the state which is the goal of these practices, so difficult are they to follow.

455

It is because I have affirmed and do still strongly affirm the necessary validity of meditation, that I have also the right to criticize the aberrations, excrescences, mistakes, exaggerations, and deceptions which grow like weeds in the same field.

456

Meditation is still of the highest importance but it has certain difficulties and dangers which must be avoided.

457

The practice of meditation is beneficial, not harmful; but there are persons who are not yet ready for it and who should postpone it until they are. These include: those whose moral values are low; those who suffer from psychoses, mental disturbances, or emotional hysteria; who take drugs, who possess inordinate ambitions, seek occult powers, or practise sorcery and black magic. Such persons need preparatory or purificatory disciplines or treatments, psychological or physical.

458

All aspirants should be warned that self-development in meditation without some co-equal effort and development in morality, intellectuality, and practicality may easily lead to a state of unbalance which would unfit them for the ordinary obligations and duties of life.

459

Meditation is a very delicate technique and incorrectly done may do harm as well as good. Moreover there are times when it is even necessary to abandon it, in order to strengthen weaker parts of the personality which might otherwise affect the meditator adversely as he becomes more sensitive through the practice.

460

It is necessary to understand that meditation performed incorrectly may attract unseen mischievous spirits or else it may unbalance the mind.

461

The practice of meditation is accompanied by certain risks if it is also accompanied by ignorance and indiscipline. The first risk has been dealt with in *The Hidden Teaching Beyond Yoga* and *The Wisdom of the Overself*; it is mystical hallucination, self-deception, or pseudo-intuition. The second risk is mediumship. Whereas spiritualists believe it confers benefits, philosophers know it causes injury. Whereas the former regard it as a process for getting new faculties, powers, and gifts, the latter regard it as a process for losing reason, will, and character.

462

Life is too tragically short at all times and too dismayingly swift-passing at the present time for us to find any pleasure in echoing to the last letter Patanjali's rules prohibiting the practice of meditation before character has been purified, desires dismissed, attachments broken, and asceticism followed. Hence we have not done so in past writings. If meditation is to be wooed only after a monkish virtue has been pursued and found, then the hope and possibility of a mystical inner life for twentieth-century man seem alien and remote. But this did not mean that we could not perceive the value or importance of those rules. On the contrary, by advocating constant reflection upon the lessons of earthly experience, by inserting such a theme into the formal meditation practices themselves, we took some of their essence without taking their appearance. This proved to be not enough, however. We found that the lack of equal or larger emphasis upon moral culture as upon meditation led many readers to neglect or even ignore the first whilst plunging recklessly into the second.

463

Because so many mystics have confused their own personal characteristics—resultant of inborn tendencies, education, and environment—with the particular effects of meditation, many errors of interpretation have been born as a consequence. These personal additions are superfluities and have little to do with the intrinsic process of meditation. When rightly conducted under the guidance of a competent teacher, the practice liberates the seeker from the tyranny, the warpings and distortions of these characteristics; but when wrongly practised, as often happens when it is done alone, it merely strengthens their domination, and leads him into greater error still. Hence meditation is a double-edged sword.

464

After you have been practising for some weeks or months, if heavy headaches or much dullness should appear, they may be taken as signals to stop or diminish your exercises temporarily until you feel better.

465

Some aspirants who fall asleep during meditation welcome this as a good sign. They talk vaguely of yoga-sleep. I would not wish to deprive them of such a pleasurable state, but it is perhaps pardonable to point out that sleep is not samadhi. The state of utter blankness in such a sleep, however blissful, is poles apart from the state of supreme alertness and positive consciousness of Self in samadhi.

466

The ordinary man, with unpurified feelings and unprepared mentality, can not be safely entrusted with the practical exercises involving breath changes and dynamized imagination. Indeed, he is not entitled to them. Their practice may easily harm him and hurt others.

467

Where there is maladjustment between the seeker's moral fitness and his meditational progress, serious dangers exist for him and sometimes for others.

468

Every man has a deep and endless well of truth within himself. Let him cast his pitcher of thought down into it and try to draw up some of its fresh waters. But alas, there is also a pit of mud within him. Most men cast their buckets into this and think that the mud they fetch up is the pure water of truth. The mud is made of his own selfish desires and ignorant prejudices and slavish slothfulnesses.

469

Where a practice like meditation may lead to increased power, especially occult power, it can be safeguarded only when moral growth accompanies it.

470

Some meditation exercises are not without danger, but this is because most exercises share such danger. Hence, they are usually prescribed along with the religious devotions, intellectual training, and moral disciplines intended to eliminate their danger. Where these safeguards have been absent, unfortunate results may be perceived both in the Orient and the Occident, both in the past annals of mysticism and the present ones. The philosophic discipline and the purificatory preparation are also intended to guard against the danger of inflation of the ego. The cultivation of humility, the moral re-education, the rigorous self-examination, and the honest self-criticism form part of these preparations.

471

The danger of sitting passively in meditation whilst in the presence of someone else who is not, and even in a number of cases of someone who is, is the danger of receiving and absorbing from that person his emotional and mental emanations of a negative character. This is one important reason why solitary practice is usually enjoined.

472

It is not advisable to attach so much importance to meditation as to use it indiscriminately. It is necessary at certain times greatly to reduce efforts at meditation for a while, or even discontinue them altogether. Otherwise the sensitivity being brought about may become a hindrance and not a help.

473

If desires arise during his meditation and take him away from its holy subject, it is better to close the session and try again at another time.

474

It is not really safe or wise for anyone to attempt the exercises without some degree of moral development and even of intellectual development. I have explained in my book, *The Wisdom of the Overself*, why the intellectual checks upon meditation are necessary. Unfortunately I have not explained why moral qualifications are also necessary, so this I propose to do whenever opportunity of further publication arises. At one time I was inclined to accept the teaching that the practice of meditation alone would of itself purify the character. Wide observation since then has led me to doubt the wisdom of this teaching. It is better that strenuous effort at self-improvement and self-discipline should go side by side with efforts in meditation.

475

Every good quality of character becomes a safeguard to his travels in this mysterious realm of meditation.

476

The earlier stages of meditation are often associated with psychic phenomena. This has led to the false belief that all the stages of meditation are so associated and to the gross error of taking the absence of these phenomena as indicative of failure to progress. The truth is that they are not inevitable and not essential. When they do appear the seeker is so easily led astray that they often do more harm than good.

477

If he is merely seeking paranormal powers, the meditator runs a grave risk. Nor, when the desire for paranormal powers is mixed up with spiritual aspirations, is this risk eliminated: it is only reduced. The risk results from those beings who dwell on the inner plane, who are either malevolent or mischievous, and who are ready to take advantage of the mediumistic condition into which such a hapless and unprotected meditator may fall.

478

If he carries on these exercises in the right way—with sane objectives, and for not too long a time on each occasion—then there will be no weakening of his worldly capacities and no harm to his personal interests. If he does not, he will become less able to cope with practical life and will find it increasingly necessary to withdraw from social existence.

479

There is no human activity which has not some kind of danger attached to it if it is pursued to excess or pursued wrongly or pursued ignorantly. It is silly to refuse ever to practise meditation because of its own particular dangers. These do not exist for the man who approaches it reasonably, perceptively, and with good character.

480

The aim of meditation is to bring him within his innermost self. If he permits any psychical experience to detain him on the way, he enters within that experience and not within himself. It is a cunning device of the ego to make use of such experiences to trick him into thinking of them as being more important than they really are, more spiritual than they really are. If he does not see through these pretensions, he may waste years uselessly in psychism—sometimes even a whole lifetime.

481

Books tell him what experiences he is likely to have and what he ought to have if he is able to progress smoothly. When, despite effort and toil, he fails to bring about the desired effects, he either despairingly abandons the practice or else artificially imagines that they are happening. In the latter case he is the victim of suggestion, and makes only illusory progress.

482

Where trouble develops as the result of having made some contact with the psychic plane instead of the spiritual, he should take the following course of action without delay: (a) Stop all meditation, breathing, and gazing exercises, until quite cured. After the expiration of this period, he should judge carefully whether or not to resume meditation practice and then only provided further that he feel an inner call to do so. He should conscientiously follow the instructions given on prayer and purification of character. (b) Until the trouble disappears, try to sleep at night with the light on, dim enough however so as not to disturb sleep. It will probably be necessary to wear a mask as eye-shade over the eyes to keep out the light. (c) Endeavour to purify character as much as possible. Especially keep vigilant control over thoughts and feelings, trying to cleanse them and be careful what is allowed to enter your mind. (d) Kneel in prayer at least twice daily, asking for God's help and Grace in this endeavour, confessing weakness and helplessness.

483

By this power of sympathy which is so largely developed in him, he is able to rise to levels higher than his own as well as to plunge to levels beneath it. In the first case, he opens himself to help from sages or saints. In the second, he gives help to the vicious and criminal.

484

If by meditation you mean mere absorption within oneself, withdrawal from the world of the senses and contact with some inner world, this need not necessarily be a holy state, but could be an unholy one and a communion taking place therein could be demonic rather than divine. There are various ways of achieving this deep absorption which to an outward observer may seem to be a kind of trance and these ways include drugs, witchcraft, and black magic, just as they also include religion, spiritual devotion, and aspiration. This difference must be clearly understood. This distinction is both ethical and mystical. Too many half-crazy, mixed-up persons who refuse to acknowledge it have fallen into a spurious mysticism that leads to their downfall and destruction.

485

Any good thing overdone may easily become a bad thing. Any valid mystical practice overdone by the wrong person at the wrong time and under the wrong circumstances may lead to madness. In all cases of doubt, disquiet, or uneasiness, it is better to draw back than to push on to extremes.

486

Although falling asleep is listed as one of the obstacles to yoga by Patanjali, whether it really is so depends both on the kind of sleep and the circumstances in which it develops. If very deep and very refreshing, it has some positive value—either in conferring temporary peace of mind or in healing some bodily ill. And if it occurs while practising conjointly with and in the presence of a master, it is definitely conducive to spiritual progress. But any other kind is certainly a waste of meditational time. To prevent its happening, or to arouse the sleeper from it if it has already happened, the Japanese Zen monks sitting in the meditation hall are supervised by a prefect who either slaps the drowsing man on the shoulder with the broad end of an oar-like pole or else rings a bell every twenty minutes. A different method is used in Siam and Ceylon by monks who meditate in solitude. A few pieces of wood are fastened to a candle about one inch apart. As the candle burns down, the pieces fall at intervals, thus awakening the monk if he is asleep.

487

Meditation, rightly used and sufficiently developed, will silence his personal opinions so that he may hear the Overself's Voice. But wrongly used or superficially developed, it will only confirm those opinions and, if they are erroneous, lead him further astray.

488

The improvement of character is both a necessary prelude to, and essential accompaniment of, any course in these practices of meditation. Without it, self-reproach for transgressions or weaknesses will penetrate the peace of the silent hour and disturb it.

489

A Buddhist ancient text gives the following blocks to meditational work: (a) a settled residence whose maintenance becomes a cause of anxiety, (b) family connections whose troubles require attention, (c) fame drawing admirers who demand attention or drawing gifts which create obligations having the same result, (d) acceptance of disciples or pupils and giving them instruction, (e) getting involved in various public or private works, (f) frequent journeys, (g) friends or relatives requiring services, (h) illness, (i) study without application in practice, (j) yielding to the fascination of occult powers. All these things take up time which has to be taken from that needed for meditation—this is the objection to them, however worthy they may be in themselves. However it must be remembered that the text itself—*Visuddhi Magga*—was compiled by, and for, monks.

490

Because the art of meditation is unfamiliar to most Western people, mistakes in its practice are easily made. To detect them, it is well to describe one's experiences to a more proficient student if a qualified teacher is not available, and have them checked in the light of his knowledge.

491

If the practice is regularly made in a room, it is prudent to lock the door. During the early attempts to attain the first stage this may not be necessary; but during the later periods, when proficiency has been reached, it is necessary for self-protection. If a condition of deep self-absorption is present, and if another person were to burst into the room unexpectedly and abruptly, the nervous shock given would be severe.

492

Some measure of moral culture is indispensable both as a preliminary course and parallel endeavour to meditation. The Path is beset with moral risks and mental dangers for those who have not previously prepared their characters and personalities to engage in its practices, for those who are still largely gripped by selfish instincts and undisciplined passions, for those who are emotionally unstable and intellectually unbalanced. Hence preliminary and accompanying courses of ascetic self-denial, self-control, and self-improvement are usually prescribed. Sensual lusts and low desires have not only to be curbed, but also ignoble thoughts and unworthy attitudes, if meditation exercises are to be done with safety and finished with success.

493

The very way he habitually uses his mind may be so wrong that if it inserts itself into his approach to meditation, the result is self-defeating. His practice of the exercise may be faithful and persistent but yet so wrongly carried out that no other result is possible.

494

Some of the exercises will be of no benefit if practised too soon by unready minds, and may even do some harm.

495

One danger of mystic experience is the possible swelling of the ego. It could make ignored unimportant persons become a centre of attention and give them a feeling of public importance.

496

Men who are drunk, insane, angry, or insensitive cannot practise meditation.

497

Psychotic states and psycho-pathological conditions usually make it undesirable for a person to continue with or take up ordinary meditation practices. He has lost his way and needs treatment from outside himself rather than from within his ego.

498

To mark off a short part of the day or night for such thought, feeling, and aspirational exercise, or better still, two parts, is a way of life which, however uncommon, is highly important. It will prove itself in time and in various results. The self is brought under better control; the character is morally uplifted; an awareness of a link with the Universal Mind will disclose itself. But again, what is here referred to is a *philosophic* practice, and must conform with the ideals, principles, and knowledge of philosophy. It must be properly done by qualified persons if the effects are to be beneficial and not harmful. Otherwise a preparatory study and purificatory course should first be undertaken. Right meditation can bring about changes for the good, the harmonious and constructive in a man, but wrong or premature or ill-intentioned or totally ignorant meditation can develop the opposite.

499

A difficulty arises from the constant practice of meditation in that sensitivity is much increased: sensitivity to the feelings and thoughts of others. And when this sensitivity seems to submerge him in their influences and auras, he is in danger of losing his own individuality or of getting confused and muddled by this mental absorption. Action must be taken to keep the sensitivity without letting it make him the victim of other peoples' emotional emanation and mental projection.

500

The hazards which beset the practice of meditation ought not frighten us away from it altogether. We should of course beware the foolish cults and lunatic fringes and paranoiac leaders. We should also avoid falling into a lazy daydreaming which self-fabricates its own world. But a healthy mental attitude will readily protect us.

501

In a particular case it is sometimes advisable to discontinue practising meditation for a while in order to apply more attention to spiritual needs and requirements. The student should realize that it is of the utmost importance to steadily increase his power of self-control over emotions, moods, and troublesome thoughts and to develop a more balanced emotional state. Meditation, by itself, cannot bring about this state. What is needed here is dogged and persistent application of the higher will.

502

If, while in a highly sensitive state, the individual finds he is arriving at a psychic rather than a truly spiritual level, he or she should substitute simple spontaneous prayer or worship for meditation, at least for a while. It will also be necessary to practise strengthening the will and getting rid of occult fears. The student must increase his faith in his higher Self and call upon it for strength and courage.

503

It is better not to dwell on any visual phenomena other than at the moment of occurrence, or else progress will be impeded. What is more important than seeing is the state of *feeling* produced; this must be pure awareness from which all psychical elements are excluded. Not until this state has been thoroughly established and integrated with active life and intellectual understanding and the moral nature, is it safe to examine or experiment with psychic phenomena.

504

The wise aspirant will throw out all those foolish imaginations and egoistic fancies which beset the way of meditation. They are false leads and hindrances to seeing truth.

505

There is a practice by which a man can put himself into a passive condition by quietening his thoughts. But if this passivity is not directed by aspiration towards the higher consciousness, towards the holier sources, it may be turned into mere mediumship directed not to spirits but to other living persons. In this way he may become sensitive to other people's emotional-mental condition but will not have the higher consciousness.

506

Aspirants who are more intent on getting "experiences" out of their meditation than on getting rid of the ego, risk falling into the quest's sidetracks. For the experiences are mostly wanted because of the pleasure they give the ego's emotions and the flattering they give its mentality.

507

Dr. Carl Gustav Jung, and those disciples who practise his system of psychoanalysis, have shown some interest in certain Chinese and Indian yoga systems. I, myself, once discussed the subject with him in his own home. But, despite his sympathetic interest, he advises Westerners in various publications to avoid any practical attempts to master yoga.

Such attempts, he says, would be false and sometimes dangerous. The proper approach should be by way of strictly scientific and non-religious observation. Moreover, he condemns the personal asceticism and social withdrawals which are usually associated with yoga.

Now, such a view comes quite close at points to the Philosophic one, but it does not coincide with it completely. For the question must be asked how, by following the Western path of turning his eyes outward and his mind towards analysis, can man arrive at the same goal as by following the Eastern path of turning them inward and his mind toward self-quiescence? It is impossible for the result to be the same. Hence, Philosophy says, bring the two paths together; learn how to unite and keep a balance between them. This is modern man's need and duty.

Why does Jung reject yoga, despite the high praise he gives to Eastern wisdom in both his lectures and writings? He decries meditation, which is the heart of yoga, as being unsuitable to Western man, just as Martinus, the Danish mystic, denounces it as dangerous to Western man. Now, both these authorities have a solid basis for their criticism, but not for their conclusions. As regards the unsuitability of meditation, since it is simply the deepening of the intuitive faculty in man, we can reject it only by saying that intuition is unsuitable to man. As regards its dangers, it must be asked why we do not disdain to use automobiles even though their use has proved dangerous to quite a number of people? It is true that there are perils in the practice of meditation, but they exist only for those who are unqualified to enter it and who should therefore leave it alone, or for those who through ignorance or faulty character abuse it. In the category of the unqualified, we may place those who are seeking occult powers, strange phenomena, mysterious visions, sensational and dramatic experiences, or the satisfaction of mere curiosity. Whatever pathological results have emerged from their meditation have done so because the people who practised it had no business to be doing so. Among the unqualified we may further place those who are dominated by undesirable complexes, by negative feelings, by hidden fears; those who are wildly unbalanced and neurotically unstable. For the qualities they bring into meditation become even magnified by the stimulation in which it results. The gravest possible danger of meditation, and the one to which my friend Martinus usually alludes, is that if the meditator passes out of his body temporarily, there is a danger of the body becoming possessed by another entity. Let it be stated at once that such a danger could arise only during the trance state, and that few persons ever penetrate deeply enough to gain that condition.

But, if a person is intelligent, sensible, fairly balanced, and of good character, he need have no fear whatsoever of meditation. And if his motive of coming to the practice is simply to find his True Self, his Best Self, and if he will reject everything else as likely to lead him aside from this path, and if he devotes part of his meditative time to constructive work in self-improvement as an essential accompaniment and preface to the work in mind-stilling, he is quite unlikely to come to any grief.

Since the means used by all religion, mysticism, and philosophy is the denial of self while the end they propose is the realization of the Overself, and since meditation in its most complete stage is such a denial and such a realization, it would be folly to abandon meditation because of its possible dangers and delusions or because Martinus says it is an out-dated primitive technique for backward peoples of the pre-Christian era or because Jung says it is not suited to Western man. For consider that meditation's stillness is corpse-like, that its utter freedom from all emotional agitations virtually begins the ego's death, and that the mental silence which ends thinking completes that death. Is not all this a dying unto self which allows the Overself to replace it in consciousness?

508

Mrs. Aniela Jaffé told me that late in his life Jung himself practised yoga, but those patients who had neuroses had to be cured first before being allowed to do so.

509

There are perils waiting for those who are mentally ill and who try meditation on their own without supervision. It would be better for them to practise simple relaxation, calming their emotions, quietening their thoughts.

510

The mystic, sitting in the silence of his meditation room, may receive great wisdom and feel a beneficent presence or, astray and imprudent, may fall into psychical deception and be possessed by evil presences. If he is to avoid these dangers, he must adopt certain safeguards and find competent guidance. Without them, he had better be content with reading and study and belief.

511

Why reveal knowledge of meditation if it is dangerous to some people? Reply: the facts should be known even if the practice is prohibited. We should learn about the existence of poisons even if their drinking is prohibited. But in the form of simple relaxation there is urgent need for meditation today and no danger is in that.

512

The practice of meditation in any form, including the use of mantrams or mandalas, does not in any way exempt him from the prerequisite or accompanying conditions of cleansing and disciplining his character.

513

He may become so sensitive that a feeling of unease comes with the presence of other men.

514

If a time comes when the stream of meditation dries up, when its practice brings no apparent response and is undertaken with no felt fervour, the aspirant should take these signs as warnings to make a change of approach for some time. He should desist from internal habitual exercises and engage in external, new, and informal activities, or simply take a long rest.

515

Meditation practised by an emotionally unstable and intellectually egotistic personality, may not only be without value for progress but may even increase the instability and the egotism.

516

If men who lack sincerity, purity, and humility take up such a practice as meditation, it will harm them and increase their capacity to harm others. Moral character not only cannot be neglected in this sphere but is quite foundational.

517

Too much meditation could create hypersensitivity and nervousness in certain persons.

518

People with acidulated tempers or gross selfishness, with serious neuroses or wild hysterias, are required to improve themselves until they are sufficiently changed, before attempting to penetrate the deeper arcana of meditation. For the result would be morally or intellectually harmful to them. Yet it is unfortunately the case that so many among those attracted to mysticism are psychoneurotics. It is worse still when they are half-educated persons. They are often incapable of absorbing its moral disciplines, or are unwilling to do so. The well-educated, who might be expected to be more balanced, are also more sceptical of it.

519

This wandering tendency of thoughts can be blocked by undesirable, artificial, unhealthy, or even dangerous means and the seeker should be warned against using them. Drugs are merely one of these forms.

520

To become a mystic is simply to penetrate from within more deeply than is customary into the psychological element of religion. But after all, this is only a single element, although a most important one, in what is really made up of several elements. And this is the defect, or even danger, of mysticism—that it is insufficient because incomplete, that it discards such useful religious characteristics as moral re-education of thought and conduct, personal compassion, social helpfulness, and worshipful humility.

521

The unbalanced seeker will do better to limit the time he gives to meditation and use it to try to adjust himself to the world instead of running away from it.

522

He should clearly discriminate what good is to be had from, and what evil is to be avoided in, these various practices.

523

It is possible to practise badly and thus bring about negative results. Such meditation can degenerate into mediumship, so that new, strange facets of personality appear. Or, a loss of efficiency may become manifest, a kind of apathy, indifference, which will turn the man into a dreamer.

524

Among the Tibetans the prescribed period of meditation will not be used for this purpose if the man is overcome by anger. He is advised to lie down and wait until his temper cools.

525

What is the use of teaching advanced lessons to those who have not yet learnt the primary ones?

526

If his meditation deviates from a correct moral procedure he will have only himself to blame for his fall into black magic and its dire punishment.

527

The mind can explore itself. But to do this properly it must first prepare, train, and purify itself.

528

Emotionally, and especially mentally, disturbed persons should not attempt most meditational exercises, but should get psychologically helped and healed first.

529

Whenever the development of one or more of the four sides of the psyche falls behind the others, nature soon calls attention to it in order to restore the necessary balance. Almost everybody is deficient in this sense but the degree varies. It is not advisable to practise meditation until there is sufficient balance.

530

Jung objected to yoga being done by ordinary Westerners only so far as it was likely to affect their psychic control. He did not object if they had been properly prepared by a trained analyst who could remove their psychoses and neuroses. This was what I understood him to say at our personal discussion in 1937. In his *Collected Works*, Volume 2, "Yoga and the West," he makes a short statement on this subject: "I do not apply yoga methods in principle, because in the West, nothing ought to be forced on the unconscious. . . . On the contrary, everything must be done to help the unconscious to reach the conscious mind and free it from its rigidity."

531

Some of the obstacles to successful practice of meditation have been told by Swatmarama Swami, one of the medieval authorities on yoga in India. He wrote: "Yoga does not succeed when accompanied by excessive eating, by overwork, by overtalking, by carrying out painful vows, by promiscuous society and by fickleness. It becomes successful by energy, initiative, perseverance, reflection and solitude."

2

PLACE AND CONDITIONS

The set period is to be used creatively, for the work to be done in it is no less than self-transformation.

2

Proper conditions help him to realize the first aim, which is to become wholly absorbed in the subject of his thoughts.

3

Where is the expert in meditational theory and practice greater than the Buddha? His recommendation for those who earnestly sought to master the act was to establish two basic conditions—solitude without and perseverance within.

Times for meditation

4

By beginning each day with meditation on the Divine, a man begins well. This act helps to give a spiritual background to the work, duties, and meetings of the day. It comes every twenty-four hours as a reminder that his life has a higher purpose to which his worldly purpose must be subordinate. It refreshes his dedication and renews his self-discipline. Above all, it attracts grace and this may give him moral restraint or support or even a feeling of inner peace at relaxed moments later in the day.

5

Right through his long life, the Buddha always began his day, after washing and dressing, in solitary meditation. Even the Buddha, illumined though he already was, did not disdain to begin his daily program with meditation.

6

A new day can bring a new hopefulness to the most wretched of men, provided he begins it with a meditation at dawn. For then life is really fresh, the mind is quite unfatigued, and contact with the intuitive self is a little easier to get. A meditation at such a crucial yet glorious hour can fix the whole day's pattern.

7

The aspirant who is really determined, who wants to make rapid prog-ress, must make use of the early hour of morning when dawn greets the earth. Such an hour is to be set aside for meditation upon the Supreme, that ultimately a spiritual dawn may throw its welcome light upon the soul. By this simple initial act, his day is smoothed before he starts. Yet of the few who seek the highest Truth, fewer still are ready to make this sacrifice of their time, or are willing to forego the comfort of bed. Most men are willing to sacrifice some hours of their sleep in order to enjoy the presence of a woman and to satisfy their passion for her; but exceedingly few men are willing to sacrifice some hours of their sleep to enjoy the presence of divinity and to satisfy their passion for God-realization.(P)

8

That day which begins with a harmonious meditation cannot be spoiled, disturbed, or wrecked for him.

9

The peace gained in the morning meditation flows over into the whole day, if he takes care to manage his mind circumspectly. The dividing line between that special period and the rest of the day gets fainter and fainter.

10

A man should arise from his morning meditation comforted at heart, calmed in nerve, and clearer in purpose. For one tranquil period, he has bathed in the cosmic stream of benevolence which flows under the ground of everyday existence.

11

This morning practice sweetens the whole day and deprives the work whereby most of us have to live of its power to materialize us.

12

What could be a better way of beginning each day than by seeking the divine blessing upon it? How much more profitable it is to possess the day by first taking possession of oneself!

13

The use of the words "this day" in the Lord's Prayer is an indication that Jesus advises his followers to pray or meditate in the morning. The suggestion is of high importance, though it usually escapes notice. We can set the keynote of the entire day's activities by the attitude adopted during the first hour after waking.

14

If, on awakening in the morning, your sleep has been satisfying, deep, and refreshing, you have the best bodily condition for meditation.

15

The freshness of air, the quiet of environment, and above all the purity of the mind, are all so much more in the early morning that meditation comes more easily and more quickly and more naturally at such a time. But the objection is often made by Western man that he rises under the pressure of preparing for and travelling to his work, so that strain and preoccupation and clock-watching interfere with meditation and make it unsatisfactory. Even the obvious remedy of retiring earlier and rising earlier has some disadvantage because of the colder morning temperature. Against this is the great advantage of sounding a keynote for the whole day by quieting and directing the mind at its beginning.

16

The morning meditation exercise practised on waking up is excellent, only if the sleep has not been marked by dreams. They require mental activity, just the same as the daytime existence. But there still remain three advantages over the latter. The body is rested and relaxed. Nothing has yet happened to create complexes, moods, emotions, or passions that detract from, or obstruct, the course of meditation. And most dreams are broken—there are some intervals of deep, empty sleep during the night.

17

Even if a man claims that he is too busy to practise this "On-Awaking" meditation, he can at least go through the gesture of doing so for one to two minutes: even this will benefit him.

18

Let no one spoil a new day with old complaints. Here, at its beginning, is everyone's chance to discard negative thoughts, to beautify the mind with remembrance of the divine Beauty.

19

A principal reason for setting apart the pre-breakfast hour is that then thoughts are fewer and their movement more sluggish than at any other time of the day. Why wait until they are abundant, stronger, and faster? It will then be harder to overcome them.

20

As the night shrinks and the day grows apace, as dawn makes its colourful appearance, the man who takes time out of his sleep to meditate, profits much.

21

Dawn, which may bring sadness fear or disillusionment to ignorant vicious or erring men, may bring refreshment hope or illumination to practising mystics who use this opportunity to look up reverently toward their divine source.

22

What happens during this early morning period will determine the character of the coming day. It will influence his deeds, reactions, and contacts.

23
To make the set time early in the morning will be to follow a wise tradition which has come down to us since thousands of years ago.

24
The first conscious moment of the morning has a special value to the seeker. If he gives it over to thinking of the Overself he can do no better.

25
Tibetans pick the early morning even though it is colder, because then, they say, the mind is fresh and the rising sun auspicious. They are averse to the afternoon for then the mind is clouded by its warmth and the sun's descent is astrologically a bad omen.

26
It is important to spiritualize the first moments of awakening, for then the entire being of a man is open to the higher impressions.

27
Those who can do so should profit by that short but valuable interval between dawn and the general awakening to activity in their surroundings. It is a fresher, more vital period, yet its strange calmness makes it suitable for meditation.

28
If it is necessary to rise earlier each morning to find the time for this exercise, the sacrifice will turn, by perseverance, into a satisfaction.

29
All hours are fitting for meditation for always the circumference surrounds the center. But some hours make the approach easier, the entry quicker. One is when the evening bids farewell to the day.

30
There are traditionally certain hours of the day which are the most profitable for meditation practices. They are daybreak, sunset, midnight, and the time when one was born.

31
There are certain points of time which are particularly auspicious for meditation. They are the beginning of day, the beginning of night, the beginning of each week, the beginning of each month, and the beginning of each year.

32
Twice a year, the time of the equinox affords the aspirant a chance to benefit by Nature's own movements. The spring and autumn equinoxes bring her forces to a dead-centre, a neutral point, which affects the mental, emotional, and physical being of man as well as the planetary environment outside him. At every point on this earth, the length of the day is semi-annually equal to the length of the night about March 21 and September 21. The aspirant likewise can temporarily gain a balanced stability of the

mind if he will use as much of these dates for the practice of meditation as he can snatch from his timetable.

33

He may set his own times for these sessions, but since the earliest records of Oriental teaching on this matter, dawn, noon, sunset, and midnight have been recommended as particularly auspicious.

34

The meditation period must not only be fixed by regularity but also granted by spontaneity.

35

Since meditation forms an essential part of the Quest's practices, a part of the day must be given up to it. It need not be a large part; it can be quite a small part. The attitude with which we approach it should not be one of irksome necessity but of loving eagerness. We may have to try different periods of the day so as to find the one that will best suit us and our circumstances. This, however, is only for beginners and intermediates, for one day we shall find that any time is good enough for meditation time just as every day is Sunday to the true Christian.

36

There is no better hour of time than that taken in the falling light for the enchanted pause of meditation.

37

That beautiful interlude between day and night which hushes the busy scene and turns the fatigued consciousness toward repose, is good for meditation.

38

There are not only special periods like sunset, awakening from sleep, and going to sleep, but even special moments at no predictable time of the day when he may be more susceptible to the inward pull of meditation.

39

Although it is often better to wait for the right mood before sitting down to meditation, experience shows that this is sometimes not so.

40

It is true that the mind can work at meditation better in the day's freshness and alertness. But it is not less true that when most people are asleep it can work in depth and hence in a different way. Quietude is then reigning in the outside world, obstructions fall off easier in the inner world.

41

Choose a period when all worries can be laid aside, all past and coming activities put outside consciousness, when you will try to "Be still and know that I am God."

42

He may practise a little meditation at odd times through the day whenever his attention is not demanded by other things.

43

He is not likely to wish to meditate nor to do so successfully if he feels too fatigued, bored, or worried. It is better therefore at such times to miss the exercise altogether; but compensate by putting in an extra period as soon as possible.

44

Some people feel too sleepy to practise meditation when retiring at night and would merely waste their time if they engaged in it. Yet others find that this is the best time for their efforts, that the coming to an end of the day's outward activities enables them to give themselves up unreservedly to this inward one. When a meditation period seems to be a failure, it is sometimes worthwhile to experiment with a change in bodily posture—for instance from squatting to kneeling or reclining—and note if improvement results.

45

Housewives who can find no other free time for meditation than that which comes after their husbands have left for work and children for school, may ignore the advice about the most favourable hours of the day, and should train the mind to make the best of, and live with, this situation.

46

It is not necessary to get up at dawn for this practice if the hour is inconvenient. What is necessary is that any hour will be the right hour if approached in the proper frame of mind.

47

Let him choose a time when there is least street noise in the case of the city dweller, or when there is least likelihood of interruption, in the case of the rural dweller.

48

When he feels the first signs of a mood favourable to meditation, he ought not to let the chance go. It ought to be sufficient excuse for putting aside either his laziness or his other activity.

49

The brain tends to rest from sunset to midnight, if not artificially stimulated or deliberately provoked. This is Nature's hint to us that its own quietening down provides the best time for the practice of meditation.

50

Although the inner conditions needed for meditation are best had on an empty stomach, the outer conditions may not always make this possible. One may be unable to be alone except when allowed to lie down and rest after a meal. In that case, the rest period may be turned into the meditation period. The mind will have to be trained to the practice while the body is recumbent, and the rule concerning an erect spine will have to be ignored. Good results can still be secured, although not so good as they otherwise could have been.

51

The quiet of dawn and the hush of eventide are the two best times of day for all yoga practice. When Nature becomes still, it is easier for man—who is only a part of Nature after all—to become still.

52

Not only acts of religious devotion or mystical contemplation, but acts of ordinary work cannot be done so well immediately after a meal. This is one reason why meditation exercises are to be performed before eating.

53

If he should wake up during the night suddenly, with thoughts reverting to spiritual things, it is a good time to meditate upon them. It is not necessary to get up and dress, nor even to assume a sitting posture. He may even feel a kind of internal shock which precipitates him out of sleep into wakefulness in the middle of the night, after which he will find it difficult to fall asleep again. This, too, is a signal to start meditation immediately.

54

To keep a time and place for this secret retreat into meditation practice is to keep available a secure refuge.

55

Even if the exercise is missed under pressures, the remembrance is enough. And some uplifting contacts are equivalent to meditation.

56

If they come to this practice with a certain amount of fatigue after a day's work, its soothing restfulness may act as a counterweight to that fatigue and remove it. But if they come worn out completely, then it is better to postpone the exercise.

57

At night when the busy world quietens, thought can come to a central point more easily and pierce its way through riddles.

58

If he cannot fit this period into the early morning or late night, let him fit it into any time of the day that is convenient to him. But if, in the pressure and busy-ness of modern city living, he cannot even do that, then he can adopt the two practices of, first, beginning and closing the day with short prayers and, second, repeating a declaration semi-mechanically during the day's activities.

59

It takes so little part of our time to meditate daily that we ought to be ashamed of searching for excuses or surrendering to pressures.

60

The act with which you start the day and that with which you finish it are particularly important. They can become, if you wish, the means of promoting spiritual progress.

61

The soft beauty of twilight is companion to its beneficence. What a fitting time it provides for the irradiating practice and transforming ritual of meditation.

62

This was the amazing paradox of those meditational evenings, that as the outward light grew less and less, the inward light grew more and more.

Places for meditation

63

If finding the time is the first need, finding the place is the second one. It should be where nobody will disturb him and, if he is exceptionally sensitive, where nobody will even observe him. It should be where the least noise and the most silence reigns. If he can use the same time and place regularly, so much the better.

64

We need new thinking about old mysticism. It must begin to look around at the world in which it is living and meditating and particularly to become aware of the problems which so greatly retard its own practice of intense introspection. The physical conditions of everyone's life enter today into the background of all his thinking as never before and affect even more his attempts at mystical non-thinking.

65

It is good to practise meditation in a place where the sun's play of light and colour joins Nature's grant of friendly trees and protective shade.

66

If some students find that artistic surroundings or a religious atmosphere help them to get started with meditation practice, others find that these things are distractions and that a completely neutral background is indispensable.

67

While practising meditation, he should take every safeguard against possible interruptions whether they be the hearing of noisy sounds or the intrusion of human beings. It is possible to continue with this practice despite them, of course, and he will have to train himself to learn how to do this when necessary; but it is foolish to let himself be exposed to them when the conditions are under his control. Every break in his attention caused by outside factors which could have been shut out is an unnecessary one.

68

It is better to choose a place for meditation where there will be the least changes of temperature, the least disturbances by loud noises, the most shelter from high winds, and the most freedom from interruptions by other persons. The desired result will be achieved here when he can completely forget his surroundings, as he should forget his body during the meditation.

69

A house which has no little room set aside as a shrine, or an apartment which has no alcove or niche fitted up as one, is not serving the higher needs of those who live in it. For here they should see daily a simple reminder of the Overself: a figure, picture, photo, or lamp suggesting life's goal and recollecting them to prayer or meditation upon it.

70

The worst obstructions to this exercise are noise and discomfort.

71

A household atmosphere of neurotic scenes and mutual recriminations is not suitable for meditation practice. A church is better.

72

For meditation or worship it is a fitting posture to face the east where the sun rises, the west where it sets, or the south where it is strongest. But the north is less desirable, not only because it is sunless but because it is the direction whence come the powers active in the body during sleep.(P)

73

They ask me, "Will it require a special journey to India and a stay there of several months or some years to find the Overself, or at least to get a glimpse of it?" I can only answer that the journey required is into a quiet room and a period of solitude each day, that these are to be put to use in meditation, and that this with the practice of constant remembrance and the unremitting discipline of character, will suffice.

74

Those who practise at dusk or at night usually need a little light. The candle or the kerosene lantern which, until recently, was used in the Orient for this purpose is not favoured in our electrified world of the Occident. Shaded electric lamps are used by most practitioners working alone, or a door communicating with an illumined corridor or room is left slightly ajar. The others—members of groups, societies, and so on—are generally taught to employ small-sized electric globes of blue or red glass. I find them slightly disturbing—these colours are more suited to psychic development—and prefer darkness. But invention has provided a perfect answer to the problem. It is a night-light for a child's bedroom. Small, almost unbreakable, made of plastic, it fits into electrical wall sockets or skirting-board outlets. It gives an extraordinarily mild, pleasant, mysterious, and phosphorescent pastel-green light which is too low in intensity to disturb anyone. This handy appliance is made by a number of large international firms, so it may be presumed that meditators around the world who want one will find their way to it.

75

Meditation sessions find a better environment if violet or heliotrope coloured lamps are used, or if oil is perfumed with cloves or cinnamon and warmed, or if a pure grade of incense is burnt. But this is more a suggestion for beginners.

76

It is good for anyone to keep one little corner of his house or his room for recollection. It may be furnished and decorated appropriately to this purpose. It becomes a reminder of what he really is and what he ought to do.

77

When we find a place where mechanical noises and natural sounds are impertinences, where human intrusions are insults and loud human voices are indecencies, we find a place which may—if other factors concur—be suitable for meditation.

78

The original idea of a mosque was a simple bare place where there were no things to distract attention and no sounds to disturb it, where the decorations were plain enough to suggest no idea at all. This is the kind of place which helps some temperaments to get on without hindrance with the work of meditation. But there are others—with imaginative artistic or poetic temperaments—who need quite the opposite kind of place to stimulate or inspire them.

79

If he is to become a good yogi, he must learn to do his daily meditation as easily in a flat in Chelsea as in a hut in the Himalayas.

80

It is hard yet not impossible to practise meditation in the large cities of today. They are filled with the disturbing uproar of mechanized traffic and the agitated haste of semi-mechanized crowds with pressures and tensions. The nervous fatigue and restlessness which such conditions create tend to limit effective meditation to determined, persevering characters.

81

The mystical aspirant has always been enjoined since earliest times to seek an environment for the practice of his exercises amidst the solitudes and beauties of Nature, where nothing disturbs and everything inspires.

82

The aura which permeates such a place is something one can feel and something friendly to the soul's growth through meditation.

83

For the practice of meditation a cave has several advantages over a dwelling-house, but a man cannot meditate all day. For the rest of the day, a dwelling-house has several advantages over a cave.

84

His little shrine should be kept private and sometimes it may have to be kept secret.

85

Sensitive persons, ascetic persons, refined persons, and monastically secluded persons may find it helpful to put on special garments for the period of meditation. Those garments, being reserved for such a practice only, become permeated in time with a mental deposit or aura, an influence suggestive of meditation and conducive to its practice. These garments should be kept apart from others and put in a separate drawer, or a separate box, or a silk bag.

86

The lively waters of a mountain stream dash down over its stony bed through the ancient village nearby my modern apartment and soon reach Lake Leman. So I dwell between the city and the village, on the border which divides them by several centuries. There is plenty of suggestive material in the contrast for my thoughts. And when I walk to the little bakery for a fresh loaf, a bridge carries the street over a deep narrow gorge where the stream emerges with the musical sound of a waterfall. This reminds me of the inclusion of such a place in the traditional list of suitable surroundings for yoga practice.

87

To sit in semi-darkness with the only light coming from a well-shaded coloured lamp, surrounded by silence, and the room perhaps perfumed with incense, helps to create a condition suited to meditation.

88

Certain parts of a country are more favourable to contemplation than others. The rules laid down in the old yoga textbooks are that the place for meditation should be secluded, quiet, at a distance from city or village, and preferably in the forest, on a mountain, in a cave, or possibly by a running stream. The chief points to look for are the grandeur of landscape and the freedom from noise, disturbance, and intrusion.

89

The meditator not only needs to protect himself against other people's influences, but he needs to protect his environment also; he should choose a place undisturbed by noise, by machines, and by past mental deposits of a low nature.

90

The monks of Mount Athos were advised to seat themselves *in a corner* of their cell, when about to practise meditation privately, why? Clearly there is a protective value in this position, for two walls will partially enclose the meditator. He will then be in a partial cave. The advantages of such a place for retreat purposes have been described in my other books. A further curious counsel to the Mount Athos monks was to recline the chin on the breast so as to gaze at the navel.

91

To sit in the same spot, on the same chair, in the same room, and at the same hour every day is to gain the powerful help of regular habit.

92

Most devotees of the Mid and Far Eastern faiths turn eastwards when they worship. My instinct and practice is the contrary one, for I turn westwards to the sunken lingering sun.

93

Although only the proficient and protected can safely exercise in a completely dark room, and may even welcome it, the beginner, the novice, and the unprotected will be helped by drawing the shades down just enough to leave a dim light.

94

A place where agitations, quarrels, and passions have often marred the mental atmosphere is unsuited for meditation because they make it more difficult.

95

You do not need to enter a special building for this purpose, be it a church or an ashram, but you may do so if it helps you.

96

Fit up a private shrine corner in the home where meditation is practised or study is done, decorated with leafy plants or colourful flowers. Keep up this contact with Nature, if immured in a city apartment. But cut flowers should not be used as they are dead, bereft of a soul, and are mere empty forms. Use only living ones or potted plants or climbing, trailing ferns in pots.

97

Heavy curtains help to protect the meditation-chamber from disturbing sounds.

98

The expert may be luckier, but for most persons it is most likely that meditation can be practised with less difficulty in one place than in another. This is to say that they can go farther into its deep parts because the interferences are less.

99

If he can make his room sound-proof by cork-lining it, or by using some other material, so much the better.

100

Altitude and seclusion are favourable conditions for meditation.

101

It is advisable to lock the door against any possible interruption.

102

Incense not only helps to calm the atmosphere but also to purify the mind.

103

He does not have to go sit in a cave; any peaceful place is just as good as the Himalayas, probably better because many yogis contract chronic rheumatism among those snow-clad mountains. He can sit in his office instead. The truth is in his head, not on the mountains, nor in monasteries. Wherever he goes it will go with him.

104

The idea of having a sanctuary room is an excellent one and should be helpful. There is great power in having a regular place, time, habit, and manner of approach to God. Nevertheless at times excessive strain and work may render this difficult and even impossible. He then should simply do the best he can and should not worry about the matter. He will probably find that when he can take up his meditation or study again, after a period of enforced neglect, he will be able to do so with renewed zest and with greater inspiration.

105

If the air of a room is heavy with incense smoke, the meditator gets a little sleepy: this is useful for those who have difficulty drawing the mind inwards. But carried too far it may carry him into sleep!

106

The ancient manuals of yoga say that meditation is not to be attempted where the people around are wicked, when the body is tired or sick, or when the mind is unhappy and depressed. The reason for these prohibitions is simply that these undesirable conditions will render the practice of meditation much more difficult and hence much more likely to end in failure.

107

The yogi in the *Bhagavad Gita* is instructed to spread on the earth where he is to meditate some grass covered with a deerskin. Gautama spread only grass under the tree where he found final enlightenment. He had opposed the slaughter of animals and did not want to encourage or benefit by the widespread practice.

108

The metronomic rolling of railway carriage wheels along the tracks helps one person into the meditative state but hinders another.

109

When I enter the solitude of my room, whether it be in a resplendent city hotel or in a peasant's dirty hut, and close the door and sink into a chair or squat on the ground, letting off thoughts of the world without in order to penetrate the world within, I know that I am entering a holy state.

110

The semi-darkness, the shut door and shuttered windows help to cut off disturbances from without; the fixed topic and the positive attitude help to cut off distractions from within.

111

Do not expect to practise easily in a place where doors are frequently banged and voices raised to shout. Do not expect to move smoothly toward the inner stillness if you are startled again and again by other violent noises. Do not even expect that flight to an Indian ashram may solve your problem for if it removes some distractions it may replace them by new ones—such as mosquitoes zooming down to attack and steamy heat oppressing flesh or nerve relentlessly.

112

Dr. Surahman, an Indonesian herbalist guru-yogi, found privacy at home hard to get; so he meditated in a lidded coffin. This was a sign to his young wife and children that he was not to be disturbed.

113

The most advanced mystics in the Pope's circle used the subterranean crypt of the Vatican for prayer and meditation. It is the equivalent to the Indian yogi's use of a cave.

114

Since these sessions are to be constantly recurring, the place chosen for them should be quiet or, if that is not possible, anti-noise precautions— such as the use of ear-stoppers—should be taken.

115

Burn, if you wish, an agreeable incense to help remove stale or undesired auric magnetisms.

116

It is the desert's spaciousness and timelessness which make it so different from all other places and so attractive to those seeking a suitable environment to practise meditation. There is no hurry and no worry among its dwellers. Here is the place where people can most quickly shed superficial baggage and find the essentials of being. Among the Oriental mystics especially, it is regarded as expansive to the mind and therefore helpful to meditate gazing before an expanse of water or of desert. Alone in the immensity of a desert, the sensitive mind easily yet indescribably feels itself taken out of time, brought into the eternal Now. The stillness of desert life and the openness of the landscape contribute towards a gradual and natural stilling of the thoughts. Or perhaps it is because the procession of events is stilled here that the procession of thoughts about them is also stilled. Here the human intruder begins to comprehend, intuitively rather than intellectually, what eternal life means, what inner peace means. Here amid sunshine and silence, petty feelings, negative thoughts, animal desires begin to lose their hold and their vitality. The mystic and the ascetic have since the earliest times been associated with the desert. Its own austere face, its harsh, rocky, sparse, cactus-grown wastes, its rough, arid, comfortless, jumbled surface fit it well with the rigid ideals of these human types. Moses at Sinai, Jesus in Syria, Muhammed in Arabia, Saint Simeon in Egypt—all felt, knew, and tapped the desert's silent power for their own and for humanity's profit.

117

The philosophical student in semitropical or tropical climates who is unable to attend properly to his meditation because of interference by mosquitoes, may, without compunction, kill the disturbers or have them killed for him. He will not be doing wrong. If he had to kill human beings, the Nazis, during the war in defense of mankind's spiritual future, how much more may he kill mere mosquitoes in defense of his own spiritual endeavours? Those who follow a useless asceticism and those who pursue a merely emotional mysticism, may rebut this with their belief in non-violence but such counsel is not tendered to them. It is tendered to students of philosophy, that is, to lovers of *wisdom*.

Solitary vs. group meditation

118

The next point is whether he should practise alone or in a congregation. The answer depends on the stage of progress. Absolute beginners often find group meditation is helpful to them, but those who are somewhat proficient often find it a hindrance to them.

119

The student should try to be alone when he practises. The presence of other people may disturb him by the noise of their movements or their speech, even by the impact of their gaze upon him. For this gaze carries their magnetic aura and their thought-currents and, if preoccupied with him in a personal, emotional, or inquisitive way, will cause him to make more effort in overcoming the distractions to concentration than would otherwise have been necessary.

120

The notion that meditating in an assembly is easier or better or stronger than meditating alone, can only have been fostered by someone who has never experienced the deep penetration which Hindu yogis call "*nirvikalpa samadhi.*"

121

Self-interested organizations may assert otherwise, but it is neither proper nor helpful to meditate with a group. There are risks of being disturbed by fidgety or noisy members of the group. Meditation is in the end a solitary process, an attempt to realize the relationship between a man and his Overself, not with other men. Group work is only allowable when there is no other opportunity to practise with a guru.

122

It is so essentially private a practice that it is better done alone than in a group, better followed in one's own room than in a crowded church.

123

Meditation is best done alone. Group work and team work—so helpful in other occupations—is a hindrance here. For its very purpose is to probe the "I." If a man seeks to get to know his own first person singular, being surrounded by an assembly of other men can only distract him from his purpose.

124

It is much easier to practise meditation in solitude than in a crowd. But the aspirant who would rise from the grade of neophyte to that of proficient must learn to find the inner silence amid the crowd.

125

Those who have to go to a group meeting for meditation or for inner support are in the very early stage of the quest. This is well so long as it helps them. But if they stay too long it will hinder them. A man may then find it better to stay at home and meditate there.

126

To sit with so many varied people is simply to disturb mentally or even disrupt the meditation of more sensitive or more advanced members. Why expose them to this risk?

127

It is better for some persons to meditate in individual isolation, but for others in like-minded groups. The advisability of one or the other method must depend upon the person's temperament, his spiritual status, and the presence or absence of an expert during the meditation.

128

In the privacy of his own room, he need not look around to observe the other sitters, *that is, to fix his mind upon them,* which is what often happens at group meetings. He can go straight to the business of centering himself.

129

Is there any value in community meditation? Is it better to sit in the silence with a group rather than by oneself? The value of each kind of meditation largely depends on the degree of evolution of the individuals concerned. For most beginners, a communal meditation is often encouraging and inspiring; but to advanced meditators it is often a hindrance and an obstacle. They can practise better in solitude than in society; group meditation only hinders them. If they join an assembly or society, it will not be to better their own meditations but to better the meditations of others, that is, to render service.

130

In the end, and after he has long tried group or community work, he will find that meditation is easier, more quickly arrived at, with no other companion than Nature or Art—that is, alone. There is of course the obvious exception to this truth: if the companion is himself a competent meditator, or better still but rarer, an enlightened person. But personal weakness, circumstances, usually make solitary work seem undesirable.

131

It is better for the beginner perhaps to work with others in a group if he wants to learn meditation, provided the group has members or leaders more advanced than himself. But for the person who has made sufficient progress, this presence of a community around him only brings distractions. He ought not to divide his attention between his theme and these presences; his mind should be free, as his surroundings should be, from every possible sort of distraction.

132

Whether in a monastery, a church, or an ashram, I never cared for group prayer or group meditation. It seemed that the people were too conscious of one another when they ought to have been conscious of what was going on in themselves.

133

If he is to remember the Overself with all his undivided attention, he must forget everything and everyone else without exception.

134

Here he is to enter into real as well as apparent solitude. So he must cast out all thoughts which connect him with or recall the presence of other people.

135

I cannot recommend group meditations. The presence of so many other persons interferes with his own concentration. This is not only because they introduce unnecessary noises of movement and coughing and fidgeting but also because they introduce psychic distractions through the impact of their auras.

136

Too much of a group's time is taken up with making itself absorbed, for the thoughts of individual members are too much taken up with the presence and appearance of the others.

137

It is an affair between the Overself and himself, which is to be conducted unperceived by others around him, unknown to them, and unadvertised to the larger world.

138

In these sacred minutes, one must have solitude. Human presences, voices, and glances—unless they are of a quality far superior to one's own—become disturbing and discomforting.

139

The reasons why solitude is to be sought for the time of this practice are several. Here are two. First, he can give greater attention to it than when the presence of others draws thoughts to them. Second, there is a psychic aura which pervades the body and spreads outside it. If he is near enough to come in contact with it, he may be afflicted as by a contagion. Alien thoughts will then intrude upon his mind and hinder the meditation.

140

Meditation may be done individually at home or in groups at their meetings. A beginner may benefit by their joint work only if a competent leader is there, and to a lesser extent, if some among the other members present are more advanced than he. Against this, he may be disturbed by the restlessness, the fidgetiness of others. A developed meditator will prefer to sit alone and avoid a group. The impingement of auras is a nuisance.

141

Another factor which may disturb the serenity or interfere with the success of his meditations is the sceptical, inimical, or over-personal thought originating in someone else's mind. It may be a friend or it may be an enemy who is thinking about the seeker; but if his thoughts are of such a character and are strong enough to do so, they will penetrate his aura and affect his meditations. The result will be either inability to concentrate at all or much difficulty in elevating a concentrated mind to a higher theme. For this reason, there is a traditional custom among adepts of warning the pupil to keep his inner progress quite secret and to maintain silence about his mystical experiences.

142

It is better that what passes in those meditative periods remains a secret between him and his higher self. They are sacred, anyhow. What is coming to birth in them is so delicate, so subtle, so tender, and so sensitive that other people's intruding thoughts may deal roughly with it and hurt it.

143

The Tibetan monk is generally told not to talk privately about any occult power he develops or display it publicly: that would cater to his vanity and bring on the punishment of a shortening of his life span.

144

This is a part of his life which must be kept inviolate, closed-off to all others, to friends, enemies, neighbours, and especially to the world's curiosity. For here he enters mystery, the mystery of his own being.

145

This is one place which he must shut and bolt against the world, one activity which is entirely his own affair, his own secret, from which human inquisitiveness and human intrusiveness must be kept out for it does not concern them.

146

He is here on sacred soil: to tell anyone of these intimate experiences is to vulgarize them and, worse, to impede his further reception of them.

147

He should forbid himself the satisfaction of communicating his occult experiences to others, especially when their effect is self-glorification.

148

Whatever inner experiences you have, it is generally best to keep them to yourself. Otherwise they become new sources of vanity, and strengthen the egotistic wish to be looked up to with admiration.

149

It is true that yoga and meditation are best learned from a personal teacher rather than from written descriptions. This is partly because a process of osmosis and telepathy develops at a certain stage. But since a competent and genuine teacher is hard to come by for most people, the written description must suffice and can be a great help.

150

The rarity of competent living guides in this strange territory of contemplation was noted and deplored by the Russian writer on asceticism,

Ignatii Brianchaninov, more than a century ago. He advised seekers to turn to the books left behind by such guides as the only resort, despite the risks of self-delusion, which he acknowledged. He stated that books for beginners, giving detailed instructions and definite exercises, were even specially written by a few of the remaining mystics to counterbalance the scarcity.

151

It would be advantageous for him to sit in meditation for a few times with anyone who has succeeded in disciplining the mind in concentration and meditation. There is a telepathic interaction at such periods which does help one to progress in thought-control.

152

On Meditation by Bhikshu Wai-Tao: "The advancements will be more varied to each individual, and should be permitted to develop and manifest themselves spontaneously, but it is wise, if possible, to talk the developments over with some qualified Dhyana Master, to see if they are in the true path and to gain his confirmation and encouragement."

153

Students do not understand the role played by the teacher in group meditation. In order to reproduce in them the condition of yoga-with-drawnness, he has first to produce the deeper condition of trance within himself. If therefore he does this and appears to fall asleep—whether it be faint, moderate, or deep—they must understand that he has done it for their benefit. Although he may show all the outward signs of sleep, they will be much mistaken if they take it for ordinary sleep.

154

Just as one who is being taught cycling must not be supported too long by another person but must eventually be left to himself more and more or he will never succeed, so the aspirant who is learning meditation must not depend too long on any guru or he too will never succeed in the practice.

155

He is an expert in meditation who is able to practise it at any time and for any period.

156

You may rightly consider that you have mastered meditation when it becomes easy and natural.

Postures for meditation

157

What is the best bodily position to assume for the practice of meditation? The answer depends on the particular kind of exercise to be done, on its objective, on the previous experience, or lack of it, of the meditator himself; but most of all it depends on what he finds easiest and comfortable. But once started, he should try to sit perfectly still and not to move his seat or fidget his hands. It is better to sit upright than to slouch or to recline.

158

The middle-aged especially need to use this precaution for they have a tendency to be stooped or roundshouldered in a slight or large measure. Let them straighten up the neck, drawing in the throat and chin, and feel the head pulled-up.

159

The variety of meditation postures is more numerous than one would think possible. I have seen holy men who covered their faces (including eyes) with their hands while meditating, others who bent over forward, still others who leaned backwards. There is also some variety in facial expression, although examples are less often found. Some smile, others look grave. Some sit on gilded lotus thrones, but others on cemetery stones.

160

It is of the highest importance to anyone who wants to learn meditation to first learn how to sit still, to keep the body in one place and, if possible, in one attitude for lengthening periods of time with each day's—or perhaps each week's—practice. This is the beginning as it is also the end. For as he learns to keep the body quiet, Nature begins to ease his thought into the quietness too until at length one day there is a perfect harmony of mental and physical quiet. Then Nature can speak to him and tell him the great truth about herself and about himself.

161

The posture to be taken in meditation is partly a matter of individual preference, partly dependent on the kind of exercise he intends to do. Power, peace, truth, and so on—each of these goals is different and requires a different posture.

162

Although the lying-down posture cannot be ruled out for some people, the sitting posture is usually best for meditation and is found most convenient by most people. It may be adopted in either its Occidental or Oriental forms. The first entails the use of a chair or couch seat. The second does not, but requires squatting with folded legs. In the first case, take care to have the small hollow of the lower back supported and made comfortable, and to let the forearms rest quite lightly upon the thighs or knees.

163

It is not necessary to squat with crossed legs on the ground in any formal yoga posture in order to practise these meditation exercises. It will be enough to sit upright in an ordinary chair. If, in this position, meditation is still found difficult, the student may try experimentally to recline in a deep or long chair. What is essential is that he shall be comfortable enough to forget his body and remember meditation alone. If he seeks to meditate for long periods at a time, attention to this rule becomes very important.

164

It is not at all necessary to assume unbearable physical positions and torment oneself trying to maintain them. The less attention one need give to the presence of one's own body the better will be the conditions for successful practice. What is really necessary is to obey one simple rule: keep the body still, refuse to move it about or to fidget any limb. This physical quiet is both the prelude to and preparation for mental quiet. Any position in which one feels able to settle down comfortably and sit immobile is a good position.

165

The question of what meditative posture to adopt is important only in the case of those exercises whose objective is the awakening of Spirit-Energy, and unimportant in the case of most others.

166

The higher objective of meditation is to transcend the personal self, which must include of necessity the power to forget it. This cannot be accomplished so long as the physical house of that self—the body—keeps on forcing itself into the area of attention by reason of its own acute discomfort.

167

A favoured posture used by Sufi mystics for meditation practice imitates one of the positions of the human embryo when curled up in its mother's womb. The meditator sits on the floor, with knees drawn up and chin held just above the knees, and hands covering the eyes.

168

Let the chin fall upon the breast if it is inclined to do so.

169

The Indian yogi sits with his legs gathered inwards, the Japanese Zen monk sits with his legs gathered under him, but the philosopher sits as comfortably as he can.

170

The position in which he can continue to remain most comfortable for the longest time is the one most suitable for practising meditation.

171

Posture: Assume the half-Buddha posture only: that is the safest. The full Buddha posture should only be practised by those who have renounced the world; it is particularly bad for married men as it may block the nervous system communicating with the sexual organs and sometimes cause impotence.

172

Whether with taut erect spine the meditation brings out his inner strength and determination, or with forward bent torso and chin to chest it shows the element of humility in him, it renders equal service in his development at different times.

173

Before anyone can make anything out of meditation practice, he must prepare himself for it. The first thing to prepare is his body. He must discipline his movements and especially discard fidgeting his fingers, hands, legs, and feet. Such unnecessary motions betray the existence of nervous tensions and the inability to relax. They imprison him in his ego. They effectually prevent him from sitting still, and the mind from becoming still.

174

Physical stillness is a necessary part of the technique. The first period may have to be kept for this purpose alone—the time passes so slowly and seems so dull and troublesome that a strong desire to rise and resume ordinary activities overwhelms him. Constant practice, relentlessly and regularly kept up daily, is the cure for this condition.

175

Those who have difficulty in squatting for meditation may find the Japanese style easier. They then put a bolster (long and round, such as is used to support pillows) beneath the crotch and under the buttocks. Legs are bent *inward* at the knees.

176

If bliss is to come into the mind, discomfort ought to go out of the body.

177

If the body is uncomfortable at any point, it will draw attention to that point.

178

The object of adopting a completely immobile posture in yoga is to prevent any attention and energy from being lost by muscular movements, so that the concentration is as full as possible.

179

Not only the Indian Jains practise their meditation while standing up. The mystical Hebrew sect called Hassidim contained various groups who followed different ways of physical posture during their meditation or prayer. One group would stand quite still. Among them was a group headed by Dov Baer, the most famous of all the disciples of the founder of this eighteenth-century movement. He was quite used to standing un-moved for a period of two hours or even more during his deep contempla-tions.

180

Religiously disposed persons who have been accustomed to assume particular postures during their prayers or at some points during their prayers need not abandon them when they take to philosophy if they do not wish to do so. A special series of physical positions is available for their use either for prayer or for meditation according to their inclination. The illustrations in my essay "The Seven Sacred Physical Postures and Mental Attitudes of Philosophical Worship" show what these are [see Chapter 9, paragraph 2 in Part 2 of this volume, Category 5—"The Body"—*Ed.*]. In addition, the postures normally used in Near and Far Eastern religions may be added, such as bowing the head and the body or covering the face with the hands, prostrating on the floor at full length, bending the knees or putting the face and head between the knees. The purpose of some of these, like prostration, is to express, through the channel of the physical body, humility in the presence of the Higher Power and turning aside from the ego in the remembrance of that which transcends it.

181

The posture for orthodox yoga, squatting, is to hold both head and spine upright, to keep the gaze lowered, and to place the left hand on the right hand. For my own practice, I modify the above slightly by drawing the chin well in so that head and neck, although still held straight, incline forward a little, dervish-style. I do not trouble to double-cross the legs in lotus-seat, nor even single-cross in half lotus, but put right foot on gap below left knee joint.

182

The reason why a lying-down position is to be avoided is that it tends to sleep.

183

In the Lotus Posture, the hands are placed in the lap, one on top of the other. There is both a symbolical and practical meaning in this posture. The hands folded in the lap stand for complete rest from all earthly labors and worldly activities. By stilling the mind and body, the man withdraws from the Not-Self into his meditational quest of the True Self.

184

It may seem curious that the physical preparation for a mental process like meditation should involve the feet, as is evidenced, for example, in statues of the Buddha sitting with loosed ankles. This is because there are nerve centres and endings in the soles which when pressed or when the blood flow is inhibited, have a reflex action on their opposite number—the head.

185

The shoulders come in first for attention, because any tenseness of feeling is reflected in them. Loosen the shoulder muscles and then shake the nape of the neck a few times to free it from strains.

186

Nor should the physical preparation neglect the hands. Free them too from tensions, the fingers from being taut. Let them rest lightly on the knees or, one palm inside the other, on the lap. Relax the hands—and it will be easier to relax the thoughts.

187

Perhaps the only part of the body which is not to be allowed to fall into this relaxed state is its back.

188

The simplest position for a Western-born student is to sit in a straight-backed chair, to place the hands on the knees with palms down resting on them, to hold the chin in and head up. The place where he practises should be one where he can be alone, see no people, and hear no voices.

189

In all relaxation and meditation exercises which involve sitting in a chair, both feet should rest flat on the floor.

190

These physical details are important so that he may make himself sufficiently comfortable to forget his body.

191

Although the practice of sitting still is the commonest physical position, it is not the only one. There are other ways of reaching the higher level of consciousness. A swaying of the body, to-and-fro or round and round, is another. A sacred, silent, rhythmic dance is still another.

192

Any posture which is painful to the body, or which soon tires it, should be tried for a limited period only before being abandoned. If it continues to be uncomfortable, then it ought to be discarded.

193

Consciousness continues to receive impulses from the muscles even when a sleeper lies on a bed in a dark quiet room. This may help to explain why successful accomplishment in meditation requires the body's muscles to be well relaxed or even motionless.

194

He should not engage in muscular contractions of the forehead and muscular stiffening of the eyebrows. This frowning is the wrong way to concentrate attention. It is also an exhausting way.

195

There is an interaction between the body and the mind. The practice of physical immobility, done deliberately and regularly with high intent, sitting like a sculptured figure for a while, helps to bring mental immobility.

196

Whatever posture he adopts and whether he sits in the ordinary way or squats in some special way, once adopted it should be held with rigid stillness. It will then serve a threefold purpose. First, by refraining from any kind of movement he will refrain from expressing impatience—a quality which simply defeats meditation. Second, the body's quietness helps to induce the same condition in the mind. Third, such outer physical rigidity is a perfect symbol of the inner ego's death, the cessation of the ego's will.

197

The head, the neck line, and the shoulders should first be pushed up and then kept straight and still.

198

The squatting position can be made easier, for those unaccustomed to it, by keeping the legs one in front of the other, instead of pressing one down on top of the other.

199

That is a suitable posture wherein one can sit perfectly still and wherein the body can send no messages to the mind, be they of pleasure or of irritation.

200

It is quite possible to sit for meditation without adopting any conspicuous posture, without chanting peculiar exotic words or otherwise making public announcement of the fact.

201

Saint John of the Cross varied his customary sitting posture by lying on the ground under an olive tree in a garden, stretched out in the shape of a cross.

202

Few have noticed that part of the spiritual effects felt just after waking from sleep is due to the fixed and sustained bodily posture it involves. For the physical rule for meditation—being still—is faithfully followed through the night.

203

There were sound reasons why the Buddha included fidgeting of the body along with agitation of the mind in the list of hindrances to the would-be meditator which he formulated as a warning. There is a direct line of connection between the two. Those who would heed this warning need to remember that this bad and ugly habit must be avoided in everyday life if it is not to intrude into meditation practice.

204

A seat too hard, too high, or too low may produce enough discomfort to interfere with, or obstruct altogether, the effort to meditate. Elderly persons may get a tormenting ache in the small of the back from a hard seat; long-legged ones may feel awkward in a low one.

205

He should find a posture of the body which is not only comfortable and convenient but which he can maintain steadily for several minutes, or even, when well enough advanced and expert, for a half-hour or hour.

206

Sit like an Egyptian statue, hands reposing on knees, the whole body kept in concentrated power.

207

Keep head, torso, and hips faithful to the central line of straight upright spine.

208

Various postures have been prescribed for meditative work but the commonest is the sitting one. The others are usually related to some special temperament or need, and may call for stretching of arms or legs combined with breath controls.

209

For those who cannot enter into the cross-legged posture of meditation, it is enough if they put only one leg in the squatting position with its foot against the belly and let the other leg remain stretched forward.

210

One suitable posture for meditation is to let the arms rest upon the knees with palms open and upward, the back straight and neck and head in line with it.

211

Whatever the body's posture, I can and must learn to surrender to the Overself in that posture. Surrender must not be confined to sitting straight up alone like the yogis.

212

If you prefer sitting in a chair, I recommend using one whose seat is lower than the average.

213

Philosophical prayer and philosophical meditation are assisted by adopting certain bodily postures which have been tested since antiquity by the religious experience of humanity. This arises from the fact that there is an interaction between body and mind since both arise from the same source.

214

Those who find the squatting posture too difficult and too painful should not abandon it too soon. Let them try long enough to overcome its unfamiliarity at least before deciding against it.

215

A little attention to physical details will be repaid by a lot of reward. If there are persistent, strident street noises or loud-speaking neighbours or radios to disturb him, the windows should be shut. If there is more than a grey soft dim light, the blinds or shutters should be half-drawn or half-closed. He is free to choose the position of the body as he likes, whether in a chair, on a couch, or on the floor; whether ordinary sitting or cross-legged squatting. Once his body is comfortably settled down he is free for the next step: to take his mind off his personal activities and put it on his spiritual aspirations.

216

"Keep your chin *in* and head *up!*"

217

The proper physical pose for one who wishes to learn from a master or his Overself is with hands folded, legs crossed, say the ancient Orientals. The proper mental pose is to hold the consciousness like an empty glass and wait for an inpouring of the spirit.

218

To sit with less discomfort Japanese-fashion on the back of the heels, put a cushion over them and another under the toes.

219

The physical condition is important because of its effect on the mind; the mental condition is important because of its effect on the body.

220

Out in the Egyptian desert near Luxor where I went with an Egyptian friend of mine who was a Sufi, we sat down one evening to meditate. I saw him assume a form, a posture, which I had not seen among the Indians and which he later told me was used by his particular Sufi order. He sat with his knees high up, his chin and face resting between his knees, and his forehead down so low that his face was quite covered.

221

There are some persons whose past lives predispose them to sit cross-legged. This is the posture indicated for their practice. But others are hindered by it and should use a chair.

222

A Jain yoga meditation standing posture is shown by Colossus at Shravana Belgola, Mysore. The figure stands erect, toes slightly turned out, feet three inches apart, arms hanging down at sides, and the palms of hands touching the side of thighs.

223

In the crouched-together, knees-up position of the original Sufi mystics and the chin-locked, leg-tucked figure of the original yogi meditators, there is obedience to and harmony with Nature's instinctive dictate. For Nature so arranges the body of an unborn child inside the mother's own body.

224

A fidgeting body is one of the first obstructions to many who want to practise meditation. They cannot make progress until they learn to sit still. A stable body is necessary to sustain the stability of a meditation.

225

There must be outward quiet not only in his physical surroundings but also in his physical body. Hands, fingers, and feet must share this stillness.

226

You may seek to commune with the Overself in any posture that suits you—squatting like a Hindu, kneeling like a Christian, sitting, or standing.

227

The Eastern Orthodox Christian mystics of Russia recommend sitting on a low stool for practice of their mantra, "Lord Jesus Christ, Son of God, have mercy on me, a sinner."

228

The yogi who squats with crossed limbs, and the Zennist who sits with legs tucked under him, use physical forms to suit the particular doctrine they are following.

229

A good meditation hand-pose (*mudra*) is to place right palm in front of left hand, both resting in the lap. Do not interlace the fingers.

230

The shoulders ought to be kept in a straight line with one another, so that they will neither be pushed forward or pulled backward.

231

He must not budge from the body's settled posture and the mind's fixed focus. His attention must not deviate from its predetermined course.

232

His body follows his mind, his mind follows its body, both being rigid, the one on its seat, the other in its concentration. But all this is only a preparation for the further and higher work.

Other physical considerations

233
Failure to advance in meditation may also be due to physical causes. Where the meditator sits down with his body filled with toxic products, his intestines clogged with an ill-digested mess of fermenting foods, and his energies sapped by the toils consequent on over-eating, the dulling of the mind, its inability to concentrate, is not a surprise. A change of diet and limitation of quantity are indicated.

234
You have not entered the stillness if the muscles, nerves, and sinews are taut or tense. Stress the importance of *relaxing* the body first, then thoughts and feelings. Examine the limbs, arms, legs, and hands to find out if they are tensed, taut, clutching, or gripping. Let it all flop down loosely. Do all this before meditation.

235
To prepare himself for meditation, he should allow a couple of minutes to become collected, poised, and settled.

236
Because of inferior auric magnetism of other persons picked up during the day, the washing of hands and feet and face is prescribed in Islamic religion before prayer and recommended in philosophic mysticism before meditation.(P)

237
He should not start immediately when exhausted or tense after a day's activities. Instead he ought to wait a few minutes to rest and relax first, preferably lying flat on his back or in a very comfortable easy chair.

238
There are four chief points in the body which may be used to hold the attention of the eyes if the latter are to be kept open or partly open during meditation. They are: first, the navel; second, the tip or the end of the nose; third, the space between the eyebrows, or the root of the nose; and fourth—which is rather a Chinese exercise—on the ground a little in front of the feet, which sights the eyes somewhere between the second and third exercise.(P)

239
I have not given in the previous paragraph about the sighting points for the eyes during meditation a fifth exercise although it is also used among some of the raja yogis and hatha yogis. This is to squint the eyes, producing the well-known cross-eyed effect. I did not give it because it has risks attending it just as the holding of the breath and the alternation of the

breath had risks attending them. The risk is to become permanently squint-eyed or cross-eyed if the exercise is overdone either for too long a time at each session or for too many sessions. All these sighting exercises are intended to help, first, the practice of concentration, and second, the further advance into self-absorption or withdrawal from the senses. "And the third purpose is to stop the flowing currents of thoughts." The safest exercise of the five is undoubtedly the Chinese one which I gave as number four. There are no risks attending to that one.

240

The method of breathing used to help quieten the thoughts and thus induce the meditative state is different from that used in the physical yoga practices, whose goal is also different. It should be gentle, although it can remain deep and long, but it should not be forcible, strong, or violent as the physical exercises are. As they say in China, a feather held before the nose should not be moved or swayed, so gentle is the in-and-out breathing.

241

What should he do with his eyes while he is meditating? The answer is that there is no fixed universal rule which will cover all stages from the most elementary to the most advanced in the practice. But there are two ways in which he can deal with this problem, both of which are effective for that purpose at the particular time or stage when they are to be used. The first is to let the eyes be open only a bit, about one-quarter open, so that he is looking closely downward and shutting out most, but not all, of his surroundings. The second way, is to let them be widely open, staring into the distance but not seeing it clearly.

242

For practising meditation with open eyes, the best place is one which gives a long view of landscapes or seascapes.

243

A full long deep breath practised until it becomes the normal way of breathing is not only beneficial for the vitality of the physical body, but also for the command of the inner being—the emotional and the mental being. Lao Tzu recommends us simply to sit quietly and to do nothing if we wish to come into harmony with the Tao. Sitting quietly in his view is to be not only physical, but emotional and mental also. It is not that this exercise creates anything new, but rather that it lets the tensions in us die down and prepares one of the necessary prerequisite conditions for a glimpse to happen. Another condition is coming to the exercise with the longing, the strong aspiration, to find the Overself. Otherwise any cat sitting by the fireside for hours would soon attain enlightenment. But the cat has no interest beyond its own physical welfare.

244

Youth, with its tremendous physical exuberance, is less attracted to, and less fitted for, the practice of meditation than age, with its slowed-down body.

245

It is better for many aspirants to begin their exercise with long, deep breaths. This helps them to (a) banish negative thoughts and (b) arouse the spirit-fire. Only after this initial phase should they try the shallow breathing recommended in *The Secret Path*.

246

During the period of practice, breathe as slowly as possible without feeling discomfort. This is done in order to come nearer to the possibility of holding the breath altogether, for in the arrest of its movement an arrest of the movement of thoughts automatically follows. The slowness is achieved by prolonging the time given to inhaling as well as the time given to exhaling. This must be done by degrees, gently not forcibly. It is really an attempt to imitate the slower breath rhythm observable in a sleeping man, for the layers of consciousness through which the meditator must pass are comparable to those which accompany the dreaming and dreamless states. Holding the breath means holding the inhaled breath—a physiological condition in which there are certain dangers to the lungs, the blood-vessels, and the brain. Consequently, a grave warning must always go out to those who risk health and sanity by carrying breathing exercises to this extreme extent.

247

The deepening of inhalation is a prelude, and then an accompaniment, to the deepening of meditation. It comes of itself, or can be deliberately done to help the inner work.

248

The breath-watching exercise is done with closed eyes. It begins with attentively noting the upward and downward movements of the abdomen as breath passes in and out of the body. The rate of this passing must not be quickened nor itself deepened specially for this exercise but should be the usual one. Otherwise fatigue will be induced and the meditation obstructed. Aim at making a perfectly clear mental picture of the regular rise and fall in abdomen and breathing. Continue with this patiently and unwaveringly throughout the time of exercising. It is important to become fully aware of what has happened each time the mind wanders from the objective set before it, and after that to pull the mind forcibly back to this objective. Once he is familiar with and practised in this method of achieving concentration, the aspirant will find it very easy and very simple to do.

249

The breathing exercises end up in holding the breath for short or long periods which in turn holds up brain activity. The stillness which follows is very pleasant, very unusual, and very satisfying. But it is not the same as the mystical stillness in which there is a definite experience of knowing the Overself.

250

It is a simple exercise to combine the work of watching the in-and-out breathing with quietening the mental activities or concentrating them. Yet it is also an effective exercise. And when it has been sufficiently practised, he may go farther and combine the watching with moral discipline or reflections.

251

Although closing the eyes is best for most beginners, it has the disadvantage of inducing sleepiness in some cases.

252

Quietness of breathing is also important during most of the meditation period.

253

Just as some persons get rid of the distraction coming from noisy sounds by using wax or cotton ear plugs, so others get rid of the distraction coming from visual sensations by using silk, cotton, or plastic eyeshades.

254

It is hardly necessary to point out that stronger drinks, like whisky and cocktails, are obstructive to meditation, and should not be taken during two or three hours preceding the practice: better if renounced altogether in favour of the milder wines or beers.

255

Whether looking straight to the front or drooping the head toward the knees, whether the eyelids remain wide apart and unflickering, in the end the purpose is to pass through the stage of concentration to that of withdrawal, absorption.

256

If he has before practised meditation only with open eyes, then he needs to learn how to do it with closed ones to complete the picture of his practice. When the two ways are united, he becomes a complete and finished meditator.

257

Visuddhi Magga Sutra (a Pali text): "By extreme cold the mind is prevented from exercising continued thought."

258

It is a help to the beginner if all attention is gathered together and put upon the incoming and outgoing breaths. There are other devices used in other meditation methods. This is one of the simplest and safest.

259

It is better to practise meditation neither with eyes fully closed nor fully opened but to direct their gaze towards the floor or towards a spot on the floor which is neither too near nor too distant, but which seems most suitable to you.

260

Professor Radhakumud Mukerjee introduced me to a useful procedure which he had learnt from his teacher, who had also been the teacher of the celebrated Swami Yogananda. This was at the beginning of meditation practice to move the body a little from one side to the other until it gets into an easy comfortable posture.

261

A simple but effective meditation-form with which to start is going along with the breathing process: go in with it; then go out with it. But when doing this breath-watching and identifying exercise, the eyes should be fixed on the end of the nose.

262

Meditation must be faithfully done daily—with closed eyes at the beginning of each period but they may open of their own will later. If so, let them.

263

A Twofold Exercise: The inhaled breath is long and deep but not strained, while the exhaled breath is shorter. This allows some of the carbon dioxide to remain so that eventually a sleepy feeling is induced. The mind begins to retire into itself, the will slackens, the body relaxes. The other part of the exercise depends on whether you choose a chanted or whispered mantram or a pictured form, figure, scene, or diagram. The sound must be repeated constantly but slowly, the imagery must be held intensely.

264

When shutting eyes do so lightly, not tightly. Meditation with open eyes will bring *onset* when shut eyes will not, but vice versa also.

265

He is unlikely to be able to get settled in the first stage if his body is disturbed by stinging mosquitoes or uncomfortable seating, by freezing cold or sweltering heat. It is prudent to take the requisite preventive measures before sitting down to practice rather than to have to abandon the attempt after pursuing it in vain.

266
The eyes being the most active of the sense organs, the act of seeing tends to reproduce itself even when the physical world is being shut out in meditation. This is recognized by science in its noting of the "after-images" as a visual phenomenon. But even after the image vanishes, the tendency remains, and a half-conscious activity in the optic nerves continues. This is one of the causes which, combined, make for a feeling of tightness or tension in the head and which impede the relaxation so essential to the successful attainment of proper meditation.

267
Mystical customs in this matter are not the same in every land. The Persian Sufi closes his eyes during the time that he is sitting, but the Indian hatha yogi opens them.

268
In the early stages of meditation the body dominates his experience and it is ostrich-like to ignore this fact. No matter how he tries to do so, it will keep on stepping into his field of consciousness, and even taking control of it. Let him try to meditate, without proper precautions, while a thousand mosquitoes torment him or a low temperature freezes him!

269
Just as the Japanese and Burmese monks used tea to keep alert for their pre-dawn meditations, so the dervishes of Mecca used coffee to keep awake for their all-night prayers.

270
The Russian Staretz Silouan, who lived in Mount Athos, shut out sights and sounds by pulling his woolen cap over his ears and eyes.

271
Generally, in the early and middle stages of development, it is best to meditate with nearly-closed eyes but beginners do better with fully-closed ones.

272
As the mind closes upon the outer world, the eyes in sympathy may close on it too—or they may remain open and glaze over little by little. Or they may stare, far-seeing.

273
If the thoughts are not to wander then the eyes must also not do so.

274
It is not advisable to keep the eyes too widely open, for this will tire them.

Proper mental attitude

275

Meditation needs a loving commitment to it and a warm devotion to its object if success is to be achieved. Merely to practise it mechanically like a physical exercise is not enough.

276

In this period, when meditation will take the place of action, the remembrance of God should become paramount.

277

The Overself is drawing him ever inward to Itself, but the ego's earthly nature is drawing him back to all those things or activities which keep him outwardly busy. On the issue of this tension depends the result of his meditation. If he can bring such devotion to the Overself that out of it he can find enough strength to put aside everything else that he may be doing or thinking and give himself up for a while to dwelling solely in it, this is the same as denying himself and his activities. Once his little self gets out of the way, success in reaching the Overself is near.

278

Bring a real hunger of the heart to this work, come to it with a great love, feel that it can be productive of many benefits; then any difficulties in keeping to the program of regular meditation, or in sustaining the period itself once started on the day's exercise, will sooner or later go.

279

When the time for practice comes, he should feel interested, pleased, and eager to begin. If he feels nothing like this but merely that a routine duty is to be fulfilled, or a monotonous necessity is to be endured, the chances for success are reduced.

280

One important error made too often by beginners is to sit down to their exercise in the wrong frame of mind. They come to it demanding, wanting, or expecting a mystical experience, that is, a bestowal of Grace. They will get a better result if they reverse this attitude and replace it with a giving of themselves, a loving offering of their heart and a feeling of joy at being able to sit down with the thought of the Beloved without interference by any other activity. If they will only give before they try to get, they will have much less cause to complain of their failures in meditation.

281

If your meditations are barren and dry, one or more of several different reasons may be the cause, and consequently one or more of several different remedies may be needed. Among these, a useful but neglected remedy is to pray for, or meditate on, the inner welfare of others, either specific persons or humanity in general. In that case, do not confine yourself exclusively to those in your family dearest to you, for they are extensions of yourself, and your interest in them is egoistic. To help others in this secret way will bring others to your help in your own time of need.

282

Meditation that is not accompanied by a deep and warm feeling of reverence will take much longer to reach its goal, if it reaches it at all.

283

The belief that reality can be touched only in the trance state implies that its attainment is an intermittent condition and that a man would have to spend twenty-four hours every day to sustain it if he wished to remain perfectly enlightened. This is an error, a case of confusion between the end and only *one* of the means to this end. It is the love which he brings to the task which really matters. Prolonged trances, set meditations, and formal reflections are, after all, only instruments, whereas such love is the dynamic power that wields them.

284

The exercise must be approached reverently, and its central idea lovingly, if it is to yield its full fruit.

285

In time he will always enter this room or approach this hour with reverence.

286

Feeling may and indeed will always accompany his meditation but it should be delicate, sensitive, and quiet, not a violent, highly personal, or anxious emotion. For the latter disturbs the effort to reach contact with the higher self or distorts the resultant message and experience after it is reached.

287

It is a matter of transferring attention for this brief period from the ego and fixing it lovingly on the Overself. For while thought dwells in and on the ego alone, it is kept prisoner, held by the little self's limitations, confined in the narrow circle of personal affairs, interests, problems. The way out is this transfer of attention. But the change needs a motive power, a push. This comes from love and faith combined—love, aspiration, longing for Overself, and faith in its living ever-presence within.

288

If he is responsive to music, he may employ its help to stir spiritual feelings as a preparation for the actual period of meditation.

289

Come to the meditation seat as reverently and as gently as you would come into a noble and ancient cathedral.

290

It is advisable to preface the period of meditation with brief, reverent, devotional worship. This may be addressed to whatever interpretation of the Higher Power most appeals to the individual—his own Higher Self or a truly advanced Spiritual Guide or the Infinite Presence.

291

There is a practice which can bring the concentration into heart-consciousness. Cultivate a feeling of warm, devoted love for the Overself, along with an indrawing into the heart. Concentrate the attention there physically. Also, the breath should be held with an air of expectancy in the same way that you hold your breath during the moment before a famous lecturer, say, starts an important public speech, or, like a hen when she's trying to hatch an egg, giving it warmth and expectancy and concentration.

As attentiveness deepens, you will feel a drawing-in from all directions. When you get a feeling (which may come during meditation or at any time) that you are at the centre of a circle, this will indicate that you have touched the heart-consciousness. The exercise requires you to think less and feel more.

It helps markedly if you think of the heart as a cave. You as a conscious being have to enter this cave, pass through its entire length, until you gradually see a tiny gleam of light at its other end. This light grows stronger and stronger as you approach it. (But this can be actually done only after the mind and emotions have been sufficiently quieted, so the preliminary phase of concentrating must first be gone through.) Fasten all your attention unwaveringly upon this gleam until it expands and envelopes you in a great light. Think of it as the Overself seen and felt. A later exercise and stage is to *feel* it only, to banish *seeing* it altogether.

292

The wisdom of Jesus warned men not to let the sun come down on their wrath, for their prayers would be profitless, their God unhearing. For the same reason, do not approach meditation with hatred towards someone in your heart. If you cannot get over the sense of injury he has created, practise some relaxation exercises first, slow and deepen the breath-cycle, make it even and rhythmic. Stretch the body out flat on a couch and let it lie still for five minutes. Only after all these preliminaries have cooled your indignation may you begin to meditate.

293

It is an obstacle to success in meditation if he times himself by a watch or a clock. This will create a subconscious pressure diverting his attention intermittently towards the outer world, towards his affairs and schedules in that world, towards the passage of time—all things he had better forget if he wants to remember the Overself and reach its consciousness.

294

The practice of meditation is not to be a mere daily routine. It should be, and if properly sincerely persistently done, does become a joyous eagerly-looked-forward-to holy ritual.

295

A spirit of reverential worship should infuse meditation, if it is not to become a mere psychological exercise.

296

The more love he can bring into this practice, the more he is likely to succeed with it. If he cannot yet feel any love for the Overself, then let him bring joy into it, the joy of knowing that he is on the most worthwhile journey in life.

297

Love gives real force and renewed fire to meditation. Without it the struggle is much harder, and the successful result much slower to attain.

298

He should approach the meditation seat with gentle reverence, with subdued delight in the opportunity it gives him.

299

It is an act of self-discipline to make up for a period lost by practising at the earliest possible time after it. This bespeaks devotion and appreciation.

300

Knowing that the Overself awaits him, the proficient meditator will come with eager anticipation to the place reserved solely for this purpose.

301

Meditation is not only a lost art among the Occidentals: it is also a difficult art for all of us, Orientals included—so difficult that a man may strive through the years and think that he has gained nothing.

302

Until one has become adept in the art, invoking the presence of the Overself through sitting in meditation calls for considerable patience and the capacity not to stop through depression or irritation because good results are not immediately apparent. In this point, the art is likened by the ancients to sitting in the antechamber of a palace while waiting for an audience with a reigning monarch. A man may have to wait the monarch's pleasure for hours, perhaps, before he is able to see him. Or he may not. But if during the waiting period he rises in annoyance or despair or impatience and goes away, then he will certainly lose the chance of seeing the king, whereas by curbing these emotions and sticking to his aim, he may eventually succeed in it. Again, the practice of meditation is like the digging of a well. You keep on boring downwards into deeper and deeper ground. Yet although the work is arduous and irksome, you see no water until you are nearing the end. In just the same way, you meditate day after day apparently without results; but lo! one glorious day the water of spiritual life suddenly appears. Every time he sits for meditation and faithfully sticks out the allotted period despite its dryness and despite its apparent barrenness of result, the student is working on deep-rooted materialistic habits, tendencies, complexes, and extroversions within himself. The advance which he makes is consequently slight and slow at first, but it is there. If it is so inconsiderable in the early stages, the cumulative effect begins to show itself as considerable in the later stages. In the end, it will be as difficult for him not to meditate—or even to bring each individual period of meditation to an end—as it was difficult to continue it during the novitiate. However, to overcome this problem of dryness and barrenness pertaining to the earlier stages, it will be wise for the beginner to remember that it is unnecessary for him to tax his strength and patience by over-long practice. He may begin with a fifteen-minute period and should increase this only when the desire, the urge, and the encouraging feeling of progress inspire him to do so. Even then the increases should be quite small and at intervals, so that if he rises to a three-quarter-hour period it may happen only after a whole year's daily effort. When the aspirant is sufficiently advanced he will, however, do better by dispensing altogether with the thought that he should limit himself to a particular length of time for his practice. The fact that he is seeking what is ultimately a timeless consciousness should now begin to affect his practical approach and mental attitude, should now free him from any feeling he unconsciously assimilated from the breathless haste and restless tumult of modern conditions.

303

No thought of the time that is passing, or of the engagements that are to be kept later in the day, or of the duties and labours that are pending, should be allowed to intrude. This is the correct attitude, and the only one, which can bring meditation to any success at all.

304

The process of meditation resembles the letting down of a bucket into a well. If the bucket is not let down far enough, the water is not reached. In that case all the time given and trouble taken achieve nothing. If there is no patience in the meditator, there will be no success in getting to the calmer depths of the mind where lives its godlike essence.

305

Any feeling of fret over results, hurry to finish the session and resume normal work activity, strained effort which makes meditation depend entirely on your own will and your own concern—as if the higher self had nothing to do with the matter—any of these things impede the practice and reduce the chances of bringing the meditation to success.

306

If the wrong mental attitude is brought to the practice of these meditation exercises, if tension is introduced in the beginning and frustration later, then how can the further stage of contemplation ever be reached? If the ego is tightly clung to all the time, if its motive and desire in undertaking the practice is to acquire more powers for itself, more status in the human situation, more results of being "spiritual" without paying the price involved, then the merger of self into Overself in the final stage cannot be attained. For the ego will either fail to stop its thinking activity or, succeeding, will be lulled but not mastered, will enter a psychic not a real spiritual condition, will achieve pseudo-enlightenment. While trying to follow the usual instructions on meditation, what is actually done defeats its ultimate purpose and prevents its getting beyond a certain point. For the mind is being used wrongly simply because it is *habitually* used in that way. By "wrongly" is meant: "for the purposes of meditation," however right and long-established it may be for all other and ordinary purposes. The alternative to this predicament is to take to a different road from the start, to do at the beginning what will anyway inescapably have to be done at the end. The easiest method for this is to "affirm the divine Presence, Reality," and not to let go of the affirmation. This turns attention away from the ego and directs it to the thought-free Infinity which can swallow it.

307

If the effort in meditation is intense and long-continued, its results must eventually appear.

308

The life of meditation is hard for most people and not accessible to them. It requires such a reversal of all their ways of living—this complete leap from total activity at the other—that the incorporation of the meditation hour in the day-to-day program requires a real battle of the will.

309

Who could do anything but succeed if he started meditating with the attitude that no matter how long he has to wait for the feeling of contact with the Overself, he will continue to sit there?

310

If he comes to the practice holding the attitude that here is a duty which is tiring and monotonous and which he is to get over and done with as soon as possible, he defeats it from the start and ensures its failure. Better not to come at all, than in this negative way.

311

The first secret of successful meditation is patience—and still more patience.

312

The longer a sitting meditative position is held and the boredom resisted, the more effective becomes this preliminary work.

313

A certain firmness of decision is required to quit promptly whatever one is doing and withdraw into the meditation period.

314

What the beginning learner has to do is to let his practices take him on until he is willing to pursue his meditations *in depth*.

315

If a man is really serious and really determined, he needs to work every day or evening on his aspirations. First, he should seek to be able to keep thoughts under a measure of control; second, to be able to get absorbed in *deep* meditation, not stopping the work until he can let attention fall away from its physical surroundings.

316

The pressure of worldly duties awaiting his attention will try to insert itself into his mind and stay there, the strain of being punctual—like a good Occidental—in performing them will introduce impatience, unease, and even tension. Such feelings are quite destructive to the work of meditation.

317

If he finds that the meditation period has not been fruitful, nevertheless let him be assured that it has not been wasted. The *habit* of sacrificing a part of every day to it has been kept. It is its own reward for such loyalty.

318

Quite a number of those who say they entirely lack the capacity to meditate are committing a mistake. They are simply indolent, in this particular matter, however eager and active they may be in other matters.

319

From the stumbling efforts of the beginner to master meditation to the sure swift passage into stillness of the adept, there is a long path of industrious practice.

320

No one can go beyond the first stage without forcing himself to endure irksomeness, to hold on, to wait patiently, determinedly, and to hope cheerfully for eventual success.

321

Neither the intuitive voice nor the mystical glimpse will answer to your call if you demand an instant, clear, and powerful response. But if you are patient, co-operative, and meditative, there is a better chance of successful result.

322

The higher self is there every time he sits down to meditation, but he should not let impatience pull him away from the possibility of realizing its presence. Success may need time, often plenty of time; and he must learn to wait in patience on the Lord.

323

When this daily withdrawal becomes a congenial part of the program involved in living, as natural and necessary, as satisfying as any other human need, meditation will be successful sooner or later.

324

To keep up the habit of daily meditation until we love it, is the way to success.

325

In his beginning experiments he may meet with little success. He need not blame himself or find fault with his procedures. This result is common enough and to be expected.

326

Time, and plenty of it, is needed for this mystical operation. The deeper you go into yourself, the longer it takes to arrive there.

327

It is pathetic to contrast the hard, disciplined training of the Tibetan lamas with the feeble efforts of many Westerners who abandon trying to learn meditation if the ten or fifteen minutes a day they give to it do not yield striking mystical experiences within a few weeks or months. First, its very start is a test of endurance—the red-robed monks being compelled to sit in one position hour after hour without stirring and without fidgeting. They are not even allowed to flicker an eyelash.

328

If it were an easy practice, many more Westerners would be engaged in it than the relatively few who are to be found doing it today. But it is not. Beginners too often complain that they cannot centre their thoughts, nor tranquillize their minds, nor get any response from divine being within.

329

If facility can come only after many years of constant practice, even that is not too high a price to pay for it.

330

He needs patience to work his way through the first layers of boredom, distraction, and frustration. But once this has been achieved, he can begin to thrust attention more surely, more quickly, towards the higher goal.

331

The attitude that you have all the time you need is not only a necessary one but also a delightful one.

332

So much depends on to what depth within himself he is willing to go, on how far he can carry his mind's search for an awakening to a newer consciousness. It is there, it is there, though he does not see it yet. He must not let go but rather must push himself to the limit until exhausted. The promise is that it will not be in vain.

333

There is no doubt that the delightful experiences which may come in the earlier stages of learning to meditate often pass away, and life becomes very ordinary again, while the practice itself seems unrewarding. Here the right word to be uttered is patience; the right truth to be learned is that in the end it is not you who are doing the work but the Higher Power, which is drawing you inward to Itself. What you have to do is to let go of the concept that you are managing it all and let God be regarded as the primary agent in the whole of life.

334

They have worked at meditation exercises, but without successful result. Apart from the inherent difficulty of these exercises, there is another likely cause of this failure. It is the inevitable wrong use of the mind while doing them, in the absence of knowledge to the contrary. They continue to carry into the new work the same egoistic approach that they carry into the day's general work as a whole.

335

Of what avail will it be to sit there, travelling round and round in self-centered thought, closeted with his ego and still held tightly in its embrace? Only by breaking out of this closed circle will the new awareness, the higher life, become a realizable possibility.

336

The thoughts and emotions of the ego, no less than the sense reports of the body, are outside the true self. In meditation he must make himself absent to them and present only to what wells up from within, if he is to become aware of the true self.

337

The ego must begin its meditation by turning away from the thoughts of its own affairs to the thought of the Overself.

338

The ego is so taken up with itself that the time of meditation, which ought to be its gradual emptying-out, remains merely another field for its own activity.(P)

339

It is a giving-away from oneself from the little ego to the large cosmic being.

340

There are many widely different kinds of meditation. All are useful for their particular purposes and in their proper places. But in the end the ultimate degree to which they must lead is to think of nothing but the Overself, not even of his own reactions to or relations with it.

341

The meditator seeks to penetrate the various strata of mental consciousness, all of which are tinted with ego-love, until he reaches That which lies hidden beneath them all.

342

Whether he kneels in the prayer of adoration or squats in the meditation on truth, his face is turned in the right direction—away from the little self—and this is of first importance.

343

What happens is that he takes his ego with him into the meditation, even to its deeper layers, and only in the very deepest where Grace takes hold of him is he able to lose it.

344

Relax from your own selfhood, let the ego go, and discover the peace which can then well up from within. It is yours, a covered hidden part of your being, unknown before because ignored and unsearched for.

345

If he is to become aware—however briefly—of his spiritual self as it really is on its own level, then he must become unaware of his lesser self for a time. This is to say philosophically what the Old Testament says in a different way: "No one hath seen the face of God."

346

That alone may be called the fulfilment of meditation, and its real practice, which shuts out of the mind everything except the Overself.

347

Meditation requires a positive, aggressive attitude of mind at its beginning. Because the mind may be tired at the end of the day, it cannot be forced. This is one reason why meditation requires patience. If the student waits for a while, the mind will refresh itself and get its second wind, so to speak, but most students give up before this point is reached. When the mind has refreshed itself, one is then conscious of this hitherto dormant energy and his thoughts are automatically stilled. The point has then been reached where he may release all further effort and humbly wait for the Overself to reveal itself. Warnings and voices may be experienced. Remember what the Psalmist said: "Be still and know that I am God."

Sometimes the Overself reveals itself in other ways: it may use another person, or other persons; it may appear in a sentence in a book opened at random.

One should never try to grasp the Overself. One must learn how to wait humbly for its self-revelation. With practice, this comes in a shorter time. It may last only a few minutes. After it has revealed itself and silently left, there is no need to continue or prolong meditation, except to remain for a while in the ineffable sense of peace it usually leaves behind.

It is because of the effort in mind-concentration required that morning meditation is usually recommended. Thoughts are like unruly horses: it is easier in the morning, when the mind is fresh, to control them than at the end of a day's work when the mind is fatigued.

348

He is learning to walk in a new world—that of mental purity, of mind-in-itself unadulterated by thoughts—and both time and practice are required to develop sufficient stability in the new consciousness.

349

If he proposes to wait until outer conditions arrange themselves more perfectly in his favour, providing sufficient privacy and adequate silence, he may do well. But meanwhile the months and years which pass ought to be utilized and not wasted.

350

The spiritual wealth within him is hidden so deep that unless the shaft is sunk far enough down and worked for a long enough time, the end may be disappointment.

351

Skill in the art of meditation, as in all other arts, comes from training—whether by one's self or by a qualified teacher—or from trial and error in constant practice.

352

The more time you give yourself for these exercises, the less hurried you will feel. And this in turn will allow you to express more successfully the qualities of patience and reverence which an approach to the Overself must necessarily have.

353

The seeker who is willing to take up his position in the same seat at the same hour every day and then sit still while he waits for truth or beauty to appear, rejecting boredom or dissatisfaction, will achieve good results by this patience in time.

354

If the effort brings no immediate response, but the thoughts continue their usual race, do not let that be a source of discouragement. For regular persistent practice, even when it yields no satisfactory result, is contributing towards eventual success.

355

A tremendous patience is needful here, a willingness to come to the meditation room as if he is going to sit there forever. The Overself may not be hurried.

356

The feeling of eagerly waiting for something to happen gives birth to impatience. This frustrates the very purpose of meditation, for it creates in its turn a sense of hurry, tension, nervous agitation—the extreme opposites of inner stillness. They shut it out.

357

If the session is to be really profitable, in the highest sense, it should be approached with the utmost patience. He should be prepared to wait, and to go on doing so, for the inner light to manifest itself, without giving way to restlessness disappointment or frustration. This is the Hall of Waiting in occult terminology.

358

If thoughts cannot be kept out of the mind, patience can be kept in it.

359

The dilettantes soon tire of the hard work, unremitting patience, and regular practice which meditation calls for.

360

Although the overdoing of meditation is unlikely by most Westerners and unprofitable by philosophic standards, yet to practise it by the clock is uncouth and undesirable. For it is an attempt to touch the eternal, to lift the meditator to a region which no watch-dial and no pendulum-movement can measure.

361

It may help him to bear this patient waiting if he learns and remembers that it is an essential part of the actual procedure of meditation exercise.

362

At times he will feel baffled completely while trying to teach himself the technique. He will be unable to acquire a mastery of it despite all his efforts.

363

Meditation is not achieved cheaply. For one thing, it asks you to yield some measure of patience. Give it enough time to let your agitations calm down, your pressures subside, and your muscles get rested. Twenty minutes is a minimum need, half an hour would be better.

364

"Little by little, and by constant practice," as the *Gita* says, this act of sitting *mentally* still is learnt.

Regularity of practice

365

Whoever wishes to pluck the fruits of meditation in the shortest time must practise with both perseverance and regularity. This advice sounds platitudinous, but it happens to be true within the experience of most students. Such is the law of subconscious mental unfoldment and it is by understanding and applying it that success can be attained.

366

He is not asked to devote more than a short part of the day to these exercises. If he advances to a stage where it may be necessary to desert active life for a time, the Higher Self will bid him to do so by inward prompting and will arrange his circumstances in a way which will make this possible for him. But until it happens it would be a mistake on his part to anticipate it by premature action or impulsive emotionalism.

367

The practices are to be done in daily sessions, each lasting from fifteen minutes in the case of beginners, to sixty in that of sufficiently advanced persons.

368

Meditation will obtain its ultimate objective if it is not only deep but also long.

369

How can a few feeble minutes produce great results? We need to take more time, to sacrifice some non-essential activity, and to fill in the many momentary interludes during and between the essential ones with spiritual recollection.

370

He should fully understand and accept the importance of being punctual in keeping his unwritten appointment when the meditation hour comes round. If he is careful to honour his word in social or professional engagements, he ought to be at least not less careful in honouring it in spiritual engagements. Only when he comes reverently to regard the Overself as being the unseen and silent other party with whom he is to sit, only when he comes to regard failure to be present at the prearranged time as a serious matter is the practice of these exercises likely to bear any of the fruits of success. It is a curious experience, and one which happens too often to be meaningless, that some obstacle or other will arise to block the discharge of this sacred engagement, or some attractive alternative will present itself to tempt him from it. The ego will resent this disturbance of its wonted habits and resist this endeavour to penetrate its foundations.

He must resist this resistance. He must accept no excuse from himself. The decision to sit down for meditation at a stated time is one from which he is not to withdraw weakly, no matter what pressure falls upon him from outside or arises from inside. It may require all his firmness to get away from other people to find the needed solitude or to stop whatever he is doing to fulfil this promise to himself, but in the end it will be worthwhile.(P)

371
In this matter take no excuses from yourself. The practice *must* be regularly done.

372
Once he has set them, he ought to try to keep place and time sacred for this special purpose. That will convert the one into a shrine and the other into a sacrament.

373
By appearing regularly every day at the place, he is proving his earnestness, demonstrating his faith, and showing his patience. These three qualities will support his appeals or prayers to the Overself in a solid way. The response of Grace may be an eventual reward. Now this response may not necessarily manifest itself during the actual meditation period. It may come the next day—sometimes even the next week. The line of connection must be traced by his intuitive feeling.

374
It is not necessary to make a full-time job of meditation. Specific daily intervals will suffice.

375
Ignatius Loyola, founder of the Jesuit order, wisely restricted mystical exercises to certain times. They should not be overdone.

376
What is important is that if the pressure of other matters or meetings compels him to forego work at the regular meditation hour, he should try to make up for it at a later hour. Only by holding himself to this disciplined effort can he gain the best fruits of this exercise in the shortest time.

377
He could do worse than to take a vow to practise meditation daily, and to honour it faithfully. This will not be easy. The temptation to disregard the vow when tired in body or strained in mind will be strong. Pressures from outside circumstances are also likely to arise to hinder him from carrying it out. Yet great will be his reward if he habituates himself to drop everything else at the appointed hour, or as soon after as he can possibly arrange, to turn his attention inward and devotion Godward.

378

In the intermediate stage, it would be unwise to set any time limit for the duration of each exercise. It would be better to be intuitively guided from within by the experience itself and governed by its conditions as they develop. The soul and his own inner needs will be better directors than his watch.

379

It is better in most cases not to meditate for more than about sixty minutes at each session because one may develop a dreamy, languid temperament and find it more difficult to cope with the necessary activities of ordinary life. Monks however are in a different situation and this advice is not given to them.

380

We need certain times and a special place for meditation because their association with the exercise helps us to drill the mind and body. The habit thus created becomes a source of power.

381

Even if the mind resists these efforts to induce a meditative condition, it will usually break down if a longer time is allowed for the efforts. Like the inhabitants of a besieged fortress, if the besiegers can wait outside long enough they will be starved into surrender.

382

The number of times he is to practise each day will depend on the strength of his aspiration and the circumstances in which he lives. It may be once; it may be twice or thrice. The length of time he is to give to each single practice-period will depend on the degree of skill he has reached.

383

It is important to note that the two (or even more) hour meditation period which is the rule in most Zen monasteries is prescribed for their particular milieu and not for the world outside it. Thus a modern Zen master told his American disciple that a third to a half of an hour daily would suffice for meditation when back in his own country.

384

Once the meditator begins to feel the peace and stillness, let him seek to prolong it as long as possible.

385

The ego not seldom finds all sorts of excuses for avoiding regular practice of meditation. Nevertheless, such practice is necessary. The ego's resistance is due partly to the difficulty of re-adjusting to new habits and partly to an inherent knowledge that its own tyrannical reign is thereby being threatened. To render the practice easier and less irksome, it is best to start with short periods and to increase their length of time only when an inner prompting to do so comes of its own accord.

386

In your attempts at meditation your intellect is still busy; it's hard for you to keep the thoughts out. What you should do is to gradually lengthen the time allotted for practice, but don't overdo this or you will get psychic results. Be patient. The mind will give up its struggle eventually.

387

He must let higher matters accompany his ordinary occupation, his family obligation, his necessary worldly activities. For this he needs to organize his time so that a few minutes at least, a half hour (or more) if possible, are surrendered to them, to studies, reflection, meditations, and silences.

388

It is absurd to believe that men—except very exceptional ones—can spend all day meditating on God: this is one of the criticisms of monkish existence. For while they are supposed to do this, others have to work to support them.

389

Because the most effectual way to learn meditation is to practise it every day, the effort should be persistently and regularly made. Human sloth is proverbial and the time-tested way to overcome it is by sternly using the power of will to set and keep a pattern of daily living. A strict rule must be laid down in this matter, a deliberate habit must be created, an order must be given and obeyed.

390

Few have sufficient strength of concentration for exercises lasting longer than twenty minutes.

391

We must pay homage to the Overself, and pay it daily. Anything less is at our peril.

392

His observance of this self-set daily program for retiring into the solitude of his room will be frequently tested. Unless he forms the habit of promptly withdrawing from work or the companionship of the hour, he may lose the precious opportunity with which time presents him.

393

Not by casual meditations can meditation itself be mastered.

394

It is very strange how time alters its values during meditation. Twenty-five minutes of actual clock time may feel like a whole hour of meditation time.

395

It is most important to practise regularly, for every lapse throws success farther away quite disproportionately to the time lost.

396

Experience in meditation confirms this truth, that if the practitioner persists in continuing through the initial phase of fatigue, he will find his "second wind" and be able to remain absorbed for a long period.

397

The spiritual hour must be accepted as a fixed part of the daily regime, as fixed as the dinner hour. This is the first momentous step to the restoration of real peace inside man, and consequently outside him too.

398

Mechanical engineers tell us that it takes six times as much power to start a fly-wheel from a dead stop as it does to keep it going once it is in motion. In other words, it takes only one-sixth as much effort to keep on the move, once you have steam up and are on the way, as it does to stop a bit to rest and then start over again.

399

In this matter of attending to his exercise, he should be strict with himself. If he is faithful, he will develop slowly to the degree where habit will lead him to the meditation room at the appointed hour even if he has forgotten his duty.

400

Whenever the fixed hour is indicated by the clock but not by his memory, or whenever it is overlooked under the press of business, the invitation to meditate will silently and sweetly be delivered to his conscious mind by the subconscious.

401

Regularity of practice, sitting at the same time every day, will enable him to benefit in various ways by the automatic tendency of the mind to follow habit patterns.

402

The practice of meditation during any one day may allowably be intermittent and irregular but not from one day to another.

403

An intense quest will naturally lead to more regularity in meditation. It is a skill, and like all skills, developed by regular practice.

404

Constant practice is more important for success in meditation than any other single factor.

405

The time to break off his meditation will be determined by the circumstances of his life or by an inner urge.

406

Formal exercises in meditation done at set hours are more useful to the beginner than to the proficient.

407
The period can begin with only five minutes but it should be increased within a few weeks or months according to individual capacity. The aim should be to build it up to a half hour.

408
This period ought to become the central attraction of the entire day every day of the week. That it seldom does is our loss where we might have a gain. This perhaps is where the imposed discipline of an ashram, monastery, or other organized spiritual retreat may have an advantage over the loose freedom of a layman's life.

409
If he is unable to do so at regular hours let him meditate when he can at irregular ones.

Ending the meditation

410
Never introduce any particular problem or personal matter for prayer or for consideration until after you have gained the peak of the meditation, rested there for a while, and are ready to descend into the deserted world again.(P)

411
First seek in your meditation for the Overself, then, when you feel something of its presence, then only, may you make any effort to help other persons by the powers of thought and prayer.

412
This is not to say that the higher condition of meditation should never be used for any other idea than God alone. For when God has been served in this world, instead of leaving the finished meditation and returning to the ordinary activities, the thoughts can be restirred to serve and help enlighten or simply touch others.

413
Always close your meditation or end your prayer with a thought for others, such as: "May all beings be truly happy."

414
Rise from the meditation seat slowly and gently, not jerkily and abruptly. This is so as not to break off this finer delicate awareness which makes the Spirit real and not a mere word.

415
A vital point that is often overlooked through ignorance is the proper re-adjustment to ordinary routine activities just after each time a meditation exercise is successfully practised or an intuition-withdrawal is genuinely felt. The student should try to carry over into the outer life as much

as he can of the delicately relaxed and serenely detached feeling that he got during those vivid experiences of the inner life. The passage from one state to another must be made with care, and slowly; for if it is not, some of the benefits gained will be lost altogether and some of the fruits will be crushed or mangled. It is the work done in the beginning of this after-period that is creative of visible progress and causative for demonstrable results.

416

Every time he has attained a really successful meditation he should, afterwards, study every detail of its course, analyse all its important experiences, and observe carefully what ideas and feelings came to him by themselves out of the deeper unconscious level. Above all, he should apply the same studies to the moments when the feeling of inner stimulus, contact, and inspiration made itself known. They require special attention.

417

If after a meditation period the body is too stiff and the muscles of the limbs too inactive, it will be easier to get up if the trunk is moved from side to side for a little while.

418

Sitting there in the quiet dusky room, coming out of his deep meditation into a world soon peopled by remembered faces, passing them with a benedictory smile and upward-pointing call, he returns to a different kind of atmosphere and has to adjust himself to its unpleasantness, its materialism, and its turmoil.

419

It is highly important that in those minutes immediately following the period of meditation the person should not move too abruptly into his active everyday life, but rather gently and slowly, and certainly without any stress whatever. An easy transition from the one state to the other is best.

3

FUNDAMENTALS

Stop wandering thoughts

The longest book on yoga can teach you nothing more about the practical aim of yoga than this: still your thoughts.

2

One of the causes of the failure to get any results from meditation is that the meditator has not practised long enough. In fact, the wastage of much time in unprofitable, distracted, rambling thinking seems to be the general experience. Yet this is the prelude to the actual work of meditation in itself. It is a necessary excavation before the building can be erected. The fact is unpleasant but must be accepted. If this experience of the first period is frustrating and disappointing, the experience of the second period is happy and rewarding. He should really count the first period as a preparation, and not as a defeat. If the preliminary period is so irksome that it seems like an artificial activity, and the subsequent period of meditation itself is so pleasant and effortless that it seems like a perfectly natural one, the moral is: more perseverance and more patience.

3

If the turning wheel of thoughts can be brought to a perfect standstill without paying the penalty of sleep, the results will be that the Thinker will come to know *himself* instead of his thoughts.

4

Meditation is admittedly one of the most difficult arts to learn. The mind of humanity in its present-day condition is so restless, so wandering, and especially so extroverted, that the effort to bring it under control seems to the beginner to meet with disheartening results. Proper patience, right technique, and the mental help of an expert are needed. In most cases it takes several years, but from experience and knowledge there may come the skill and ease of the proficient meditator.

5

A rabble of thoughts pursue him into the silence period, as if determined to keep his mind from ever becoming still.

6

It is useful only in the most elementary stage to let thoughts drift hazily or haphazardly during the allotted period. For at that stage, he needs more to make the idea of sitting perfectly still for some time quite acceptable in practice than he needs to begin withdrawal from the body's sense. He must first gain command of his body before he can gain command of his thoughts. But in the next stage, he must forcibly direct attention to a single subject and forcibly sustain it there. He must begin to practise mental mastery, for this will not only bring him the spiritual profits of meditation but also will ward off some of its psychic dangers.

7

Do not miss the object of your meditations and lose yourself in useless reveries.

8

The moral is, find the object that makes most appeal to your temperament, the object that experience proves to be most effective in inducing the condition of mental concentration.

9

The first quarter-hour is often so fatiguing to beginners that they look for, and easily find, an excuse to bring the practice to an abrupt end, thus failing in it. They may frankly accept the fatigue itself as sufficient reason for their desertion. Or they may make the excuse of attending to some other task waiting to be done. But the fact is that almost as soon as they start, they do not want to go on. They sit down to meditate and then they find they do not want to meditate! Why? The answer lies in the intellect's intractable restlessness, its inherent repugnance to being governed or being still.

10

Command your thoughts during this first period of meditation; direct them by the energized will towards a definite and specific subject. Do not let them drift vaguely. Assert your mastery by a positive effort.

11

In your meditations, stop thinking about the things that ought to have been left outside the door and start thinking about the Overself.

12

The mind will rush off like a wild bull from the discipline he seeks to impose on it. If this fails, it will use temptations or diversions or pessimism.

13

Think of the lama sitting in long and sustained meditation in the freezing cell of a Tibetan monastery and be ashamed of your own weakness.

14

If the meditation is not to lose itself in empty day-dreaming, it must be alert.

15

If meditation were to stop with ruminating intently over one's own best ideas or over some inspired man's recorded ideas, the result would certainly be helpful and the time spent worthwhile. It would be helpful and constructive, but it would not be more than that. Such communion with thoughts is not the real aim of meditation. That aim is to open a door to the Overself. To achieve this, it casts out all ideas and throws away all thoughts. Where thinking still keeps us within the little ego, the deliberate silence of thinking lifts us out of the ego altogether.

16

The essence of yoga is to put a stop to the ego's mental activities. Its ever-working, ever-restless character is right and necessary for human life but at the same time is a tyrant and slave-driver over human life.

17

One of the hindrances to success in meditation, to be overcome with great difficulty, is the tendency of the intellect—and especially of the modern Western intellect—to think of the activity to which it could be attending if it were not trying to meditate, or to look forward to what it will be doing as soon as the meditation ends, or to project itself into imaginations and predictions about the next few hours or the next day. The only way to deal with this when it happens is forcibly to drag the mind's attention away from its wanderings and hold it to the Now, as if nothing else exists or can ever exist.

18

Catch your thoughts in their first stage and you catch the cause of some of your troubles, sins, and even diseases.

19

The thoughts which intrude themselves on your meditation in such multitudes and with such persistence may be quelled if you set going a search as to where they come from.

20

If the wandering characteristic of all thoughts diverts attention and defeats the effort to meditate, try another way. Question the thoughts themselves, seek out their origin, trace them to their beginning and reduce their number more and more. Find out what particular interest or impulse emotion or desire in the ego causes them to arise and push this cause back nearer to the void. In this way, you tend to separate yourself from the thoughts themselves, refuse to identify with them, and get back nearer to your higher identity.(P)

21

The first part of the exercise requires him to banish all thoughts, feelings, images, and energies which do not belong to the subject, prayer, ideal, or problem he chooses as a theme. Nothing else may be allowed to intrude into consciousness or, having intruded by the mind's old restlessness, it is to be blotted out immediately. *Such expulsion is always to be accompanied by an exhaling of the breath. Each return of attention to the selected theme is to be accompanied by an inhaling of the breath.*(P)

22

When thoughts are restless and hard to control, there is always something in us which is aware of this restlessness. This knowledge belongs to the hidden "I" which stands as an unruffled witness of all our efforts. We must seek therefore to feel for and identify ourself with it. If we succeed, then the restlessness passes away of itself, and the bubbling thoughts dissolve into undifferentiated Thought.(P)

23

He must first work at the cleansing of his mind. This is done by vigilantly keeping out degrading thoughts and by refusing entry to weakening ones.

24

He must wait patiently yet work intently after he closes his eyes until his thoughts, circling like a flock of birds around a ship, come gently to rest.

25

We habitually think at random. We begin our musings with one subject and usually end with an entirely different one. We even forget the very theme which started the movement of our mind. Such an undisciplined mind is an average one. If we were to watch ourselves for five minutes, we would be surprised to discover how many times thought had involuntarily jumped from one topic to another.

26

The first problem is how to keep his interest from drying up, the second how to keep his attention from wandering off.

27

When he has previously purified his character, he will naturally be able to sustain long periods of meditation without being distracted by wayward emotions.

28

The passage in consciousness from mere thoughts to sheer Thought is not an easy one. Lifelong ingrained habit has made our consciousness form-ridden, tied to solids, and expectant of constant change. To surrender this habit seems to it (albeit wrongly) quite unnatural, and consequently artificial resistances are set up.

29

To keep up the meditation for some length of time, to force himself to sit there while all his habitual bodily and mental instincts are urging him to abandon the practice, calls for arousing of inner strength to fight off inattention or fatigue. But this very strength, once aroused, will eventually enable him to keep it up for longer and longer periods.

30

As the mind slowly relaxes, the number of thoughts is reduced, the attentiveness to them increased.

31

Whenever the meditator notices that he has lost his way and is no longer thinking of his chosen subject, he has to start again and rethink the subject. This process of refinding his way several times may have to be repeated during each session of meditation.

32

It will be a help to meditate more successfully if, at the beginning, the breathing rhythm is equalized so that the inbreath and the outbreath are roughly of the same length and if one draws the air in a little more deeply than normally and lets it out a little more slowly than normally.

33

The so-called normal mind is in a state of constant agitation. From the standpoint of yoga, there is little difference whether this agitation be pleasurable or painful.

34

If a student is not purified enough, nor informed enough, it is better not to endeavour to reach the trance stage. He should devote his efforts to the control of thoughts and to the search for inner tranquillity along with this self-purification and improvement of knowledge.

35

The thought-flow may be stopped by forcible means such as breath control, but the result will then be only a transient and superficial one. If a deeper and more durable result is desired, it is essential to conjoin the breath control with other kinds of self-control—with a discipline of the senses and a cleansing of the thoughts.

36

The aim is to work, little by little, toward slowing down the action of thinking first and stilling it altogether later.

37

If the initial period of distracted, wandering, overactive, or restless thoughts irks him by its length, he should remember that this shows the state of his mind during most of the day.

38

It is a custom among the yogis, and one laid down in the traditional texts, to begin meditation by paying homage to God and to the master. The purpose of this is to attract help from these sources.

39

The mind is dragged hither and thither by its desires or interest, dragged to fleeting and ephemeral things.

40

The undisciplined mind will inevitably resist the effects needed for these exercises. This is a difficult period for the practiser. The remedy is to arouse himself, "summon up the will," and return again and again to the fight until the mind, like a horse, begins to accept its training and learns to obey.

41

In this interim waiting period nothing happens, only the thoughts bubble along as they usually do during an idle time, except that there is some strain, some constriction whenever he remembers that there is a purpose in his sitting here, a control needed to achieve it.

42

He is to begin by giving a disciplined attention to the workings of his own mind.

43

The body soon begins to protest against the unaccustomed stillness suddenly enforced on it: the mind soon starts to rebel against the tedium and boredom of the early stages, and the habitual unrest of both will have to be faced again and again.

44

It is difficult, often impossible, to stop thinking by one's own effort. But by grace's help it gets done. With thinking no longer in the way, consciousness ceases to be broken up: nothing is there to impede movement into stillness.

45

If the innate capacity is lacking, as it usually is, then the aspirant requires some skill gathered from repeated experience to shut out sounds which bring the mind back to physical situations.

46

It is not only thoughts that come up in the form of words that have to be brought under control, but also those that come up in the form of images. So long as consciousness is peopled by the activities of imagination, so long does its stillness and emptiness remain unreached. That certain yoga exercises use either of these forms to reach their goal does not falsify this statement. For even there the method practised has to be abandoned at a particular point, or stop there by itself.

47

The intellectual type tries to analyse what he does and sees in the attempt to understand it more fully. But the end result is that the transcendent part of the experience is lost; one set of thoughts succeeds only in producing another. He must be willing and ready to stop intellection at the start of the exercise. This is essential to success in meditation.

48

Whatever method blocks the wandering of thoughts or the practice of intellectualism, whether random or continuous, may be useful so long as it assists concentration and logical examination is avoided. It could be a mantram, but not a devotional, intelligible, or meaningful one. It could be a diagram, a dot on the wall, or a door-handle.

49

He must try to keep his mental equilibrium undisturbed by the hardships and unbroken by the pleasures which life may bring him. This cannot be done unless the mind is brought to rest on some point, idea, name, or symbol which gives it a happy poise, and unless it is kept there.

50

It is not enough to achieve control of the body, its urges and its drives and its passions, splendid though that certainly is. His advance must not stop there. For he has yet to deal with his *thoughts*, to recognize that they come from his ego, feed and nurture it, and control of them must also be achieved.

51

The first law of the disciple's life is to bring his own thoughts under law.

52

"To stop thinking is as if one wanted to stop the wind" is an old Chinese statement.

53

The control of thought and its consecration to exalted themes will bring him more peace and more power.

54

He must give himself a sufficient length of time, first to attain the concentrated state and second, to hold it.

55

He finds that, however willing and eager he may be, he can sustain the intensity of struggle against this restlessness of mind only for a certain time.

56

Imagination is likely to run away with his attention during this early period. At first it will be occupied with worldly matters already being thought about, but later it may involve psychical matters, producing visions or hallucinations of an unreliable kind.

57

He must give his thoughts a decisive turn in the chosen direction every time they stray from it.

58

Even when he is meditating, the aspirant may find that feelings, thoughts, memories, or desires and other images of his worldly experience come into the consciousness. He must not bind himself to them by giving attention to them, but should immediately dismiss them.

59

Experiences and happenings keep attention ever active and ever outward-turned, while memories, although internal, direct it back to the physical world. So a man's own thoughts get in the way and prevent him from a confrontation with pure Thought itself.

60

The ability to bring the mind to controlled one-pointedness is extremely difficult, and its achievement may require some years of effort and determination. He need not allow himself to become discouraged but should accept the challenge thus offered for what it is.

61

The mind flutters from subject to subject like a butterfly from flower to flower, and is unable to stay where we want it.

Blankness is not the goal

62

A mere emptiness of mind is not enough, is not the objective of these practices. Some idiots possess this naturally but they do not possess the wisdom of the Overself, the understanding of Who and What they are.

63

Philosophy does not teach people to make their minds a blank, does not say empty out all thoughts, be inert and passive. It teaches the reduction of all thinking activity to a single seed-thought, and that one is to be either interrogative like "What Am I?" or affirmative like "The godlike is with me." It is true that the opening-up of Overself-consciousness will, in the first delicate experience, mean the closing-down of the last thoughts, the uttermost stillness of mind. But that stage will pass. It will repeat itself again whenever one plunges into the deepest trance, the raptest meditative absorption. And it must then come of itself, induced by the higher self's grace, not by the lower self's force. Otherwise, mere mental blankness is a risky condition to be avoided by prudent seekers. It involves the risk of mediumship and of being possessed.(P)

64

Vacuity of mind is not to be confused with perception of reality.

65

It is only a limp, semi-mesmeric state, after all, and yields a peace which imitates the true divine peace as the image in a mirror imitates the flesh-and-blood man. It is produced by self-effort, not by Grace, by auto-suggestion rather than by the Overself.

66

"No more serious mistake can be committed than considering the hibernation of reptiles and other animals as illustrating the *samadhi* stage of Yoga. It corresponds with the *pratyahara*, and not the *samadhi* stage. *Pratyahara* has been compared with the stage of insensibility produced by the administration of anesthetics, for example, chloroform." —Major B.D. Basu, Indian Medical Service

67

To seek mental blankness as a direct objective is to mistake an effect for a cause. It is true that some of the inferior yogis do so, trying by forcible means like suppression of the breath to put all thoughts out of the mind. But this is not advocated by philosophy.

68

To attempt the elimination of all thoughts as they arise, with the aim of keeping consciousness entirely empty of all content, is another method which some yogis and not a few Occidentals try to practise. It is not as easy as it seems and is not frequently successful. Philosophy does not use this rash method, does not recommend making the mind just a blank. There are two perils in it. The first is that it lays a man open to psychic invasion from outside himself, or, failing that, from inside himself. In the first case, he becomes a spiritualistic medium, passively surrenders himself to any unseen entity which may pass through the door thus left open, and risks being taken possession of by this entity. It may be earthbound, foolish, lying, or evil, at worst. In the second case, he unlooses the controls of the conscious self and lets into it forces that he has long outgrown but not fully eliminated—past selves that are dying and would be best left alone, subconscious impulses that lead into evil or insane hallucinations masquerading as occult perceptions or powers. Now it is correct to say that the mind must be completely mastered and that a vacuum will arise in the process, but this is still not the way to do it. The better way is to focus the mind so unwaveringly on some one thing, thought or image or phrase, so elevated that a point will be reached where the higher self itself suddenly obliterates the thoughts.

69

The silence of meditation is a dignified thing, but the silence of a stupid empty mind is not.

70

Merely being thought-free by itself may lead to psychic results. One has to sink back to a dynamic *positive* mental silence by starting meditation with a dynamic positive attitude.

Eliminating thoughts and eliminating the ego during meditation are two different things. You should experiment with the various methods given in the books if you want to know which would help you most.

71

Su Tung Po: "People who do not understand sometimes describe a state of animal unconsciousness as the state of *samadhi*. If so, then when cats and dogs sleep after being well fed, they too do not have a thought on their minds. It would obviously be incorrect to argue that they have entered *samadhi*."

72

Zen Patriarch Hui-neng: "It is a great mistake to suppress our mind from all thinking . . . to refrain from thinking of anything, this is an extreme erroneous view . . . your men are hereby warned not to take those exercises for contemplating on quietude or for keeping the mind in a blank state."

73

The drowsy torpor of a lazy mind is not the true void to be desired and sought.

74

The feeling of peace is good but deceptive. The ego—cause of all his tension—is still hidden within it, in repose but only temporarily inactive.

Practise concentrated attention

75

Meditation has as its first object an increasing withdrawal of the mind from the things of this world, and also from the thoughts of this world, until it is stilled, passive, self-centered. But before it can achieve any object at all, attention must be made as keenly concentrated as an eagle's stare.

76

The aim is to achieve a concentration as firm and as steady as the Mongolian horseman's when he gallops without spilling a drop of water from a completely filled glass held in his hand.

77

Each exercise in meditation must start with a focal point if it is to be effective. It must work upon a particular idea or theme, even though it need not end with it.

78

The genius is the product of intense concentration. All those who lack this quality, will also lack genius.

79

When it is said that the object of concentration practice should be a single one, this does not mean a single thought. That is reserved either for advanced stages or for spiritual declarations. It means a single topic. This will involve a whole train of ideas. But they ought to be logically connected, ought to grow out of each other, as it were.

80

Exercise: When wholly absorbed in watching a cinema picture or a stage drama or in reading a book with complete interest, you are unconsciously in the first stage of meditation. Drop the seed of this attention, that is, the story, suddenly, but try to retain the pure concentrated awareness. If successful, that will be its second stage.

81

These concentrations begin to become effective when they succeed in breaking up the hold of his habitual activities and immediate environment, when they free his attention from what would ordinarily be his present state.

82

He is able to reach this stage only after many months of faithful practice or, more likely, after some years of it. But one day he will surely reach it, and then he will recognize that the straining, the toil, and the faith were all well worthwhile.

83

The first thing which he has to do is to re-educate attention. It has to be turned in a new direction, directed towards a new object. It has to be brought inside himself, and brought with deep feeling and much love to the quest of the Soul that hides there.

84

The mind can be weaponed into a sharp sword which pierces through the illusion that surrounds us into the Reality behind. If then the sword falls from our grasp, what matter? It has served its useful purpose.

85

There is an invisible and inaudible force within us all. Who can read its riddle? He who can find the instrument wherewith to contact it. The scientist takes his dynamo and gathers electricity through its means. The truth-seeker concentrates his mind upon his interior and contacts the mysterious Force back of life. Concentrated thought is his instrument.

86

The effort needed to withdraw consciousness from its focal point in the physical body to its focal point in a thought, a mental picture, or in its own self, is inevitably tremendous. Indeed, when the change is fully completed, the man is often quite unaware of having any body at all.

87

Patanjali points out that inability to hold a state of meditation after it is reached will prevent the arisal of spiritual consciousness as much as inability to reach the state at all.

88

The mind must be emptied first of all content save this one paramount thought, this fixed focus of concentration.

89

Let it be granted that the practice of concentration is hard to perform and irksome to continue for weeks and months without great result. Nevertheless, it is not too hard. Anyone who really makes up his mind to master it, can do so.

90

When this concentration arrives at fixity and firmness which eliminates restless wandering, intrusion, and disturbance, the need of constantly repeating the exercise vanishes. It has fulfilled its immediate purpose. The aspirant should now transfer his attention to the next ("Constant Remembrance") exercise, and exert himself henceforth to bring his attainment into worldly life, into the midst of attending to earthly duties.

91

The practice of yoga is, negatively, the process of isolating one's consciousness from the five senses and, positively, of concentrating it in the true self.

92

With it maximum moral and mental consciousness is induced. There are two separate phases in this technique which must be distinguished from one another. The first involves the use of willpower and the practice of self-control. The second, which succeeds it, involves redirection of the forces in aspiration toward the Overself, and may be called the ego-stilling phase.

93

All exercises in concentration, all learning and mastery of it, require two things: first, an object or subject upon which attention may be brought steadily to rest; second, enough interest in that object to create some feeling about it. When this feeling becomes deep enough, the distractions caused by other thoughts die away. Concentration has then been achieved.

94

Concentration practice advances through stages. In the first stage that which is concentrated on is seen as from a distance, whereas in the second stage the idea tends to absorb the mind itself. In the first stage we still have to make hard efforts to hold the idea to attention whereas in the next stage the effort is slight and easy.

95

Quietening the mind involves, and cannot but involve, quietening the senses.

96

Just as we get strong by enduring tensions in the varied situations of life, so we get strong in concentration by patiently enduring defeats one after the other when distractions make us forget our purpose while sitting for meditation.

97

The body must stop its habitual movement. The attention must take hold of one thing—a metaphysical subject or physical object, a mental picture or devotional idea. Only after proficiency is reached in this preliminary stage should the intellect seek an unfamiliar stillness and an expectant passivity—which mark the closing section of the second stage.

98

If any light flash or form is seen, he should instantly concentrate his whole mind upon it and sustain this concentration as long as he is able to. The active thoughts can be brought to their end by this means.

99

It is possible for a perfectly concentrated yogi to imagine away the whole world out of his existence!

100

If the reverie attains the depth of seeing and feeling hardly anything outside him, being only faintly aware of things before him or around him, that is quite enough for philosophical purposes. A full trance is neither necessary nor desirable.

101

He concentrates daily on the image which he desires to create and sustain in his mind.

102

This work of pushing attention inwards, back to its very source, and the sense of "I-ness" back with it, is to be accompanied by thinking only until the latter can be stopped or itself stops. This work is then continued by a stilled and steady search. When the need of search comes to an end, the searcher vanishes, the "I" becomes pure "Being," has found its source. In these daily or nightly sessions, it is his work to turn away from the diffused attention which is his normal condition to the concentrated attention which is indispensable for progress, and to sustain it.(P)

103

It is not advisable to listen to music whilst working at a typewriter, doing creative writing, or reading to learn. The only exception is reading light, unimportant, or entertaining material—although even then it is still not advisable. This is because it leads to a divided mind; it creates tension, and what one is doing must necessarily suffer to some extent while trying to attend to the music.

104

Reading a noble book helps because it concentrates the thoughts along a single track. It is thus an exercise in concentration.

105

If his lower emotions and earthly passions are to be brought under proper control, will and reason, intuition and aspiration must be brought into the struggle against them. If his acts are to be his own, and not the result of environmental suggestion, if his thoughts are to arise from within his own mind, and not from other people's minds, he must learn the art of fixing them on whatever he chooses and concentrating them whenever he wishes.

106

Give questers this order of Daily Exercise: (1) Prayer in posture; (2) Breathing in posture; (3) Affirmations in mantra—semi-meditation; (4) Full meditation.

107

Because he needs to generate enough power to concentrate his mind on this high topic, a certain economy of energies is required and an avoidance of distractions.

108

The same power of directing attention and concentrating thought which binds him to the worldly existence can be used to free himself from it.

109

The cultivated and concentrated faculty of attention becomes the tool wherewith he carries on his inner work upon himself.

110

The preliminaries of meditation must not be mistaken for the actual meditation itself. They are merely occupied with the *effort* to brush off distractions and attain concentrated thought whereas it is effortless, continuous mental quiet. They carry the meditator through the initial period of search; it is the higher state of consciousness which they induce.

111

Such intense concentration can abolish time and annihilate space in it; thus reveries demonstrate their relativity and their mentalness.

112

A useful exercise to help acquire concentration is to shut the eyes, direct attention toward some part of the body, and hold it there.

113

We make use of conscious efforts only in order to attain subconscious effort; we fix one thought in meditation only in order to arrive at a state beyond all thought.

114

The mind's great creative potency reveals itself in proportion as the mind's concentrativeness develops.

115

Nuri the Dervish was an adept in meditation. When asked from which master he had learnt such skill, he said that a cat watching a mouse had been his guru.

116

There are two different gazing practices used by the yogis. The first requires them to fix their eyes steadily on the end or tip of the nose; the second requires them to fix it on the root. The first leaves the eyelids closer together than the second. There is a third practice of a related kind in which the gaze is directed to the centre of the stomach, or navel.

117

Meditation Exercise on Pulse-Beat: Take hold of the left wrist between thumb and forefinger of right hand. Locate the artery where the circulation of the blood can be felt. Concentrate attention on this pulse-beat undividedly.

118

The state of concentration acquired during a worldly pursuit differs from that acquired during mystical meditation in that the first is usually directed toward outward things and the experience of sense-pleasures, whereas the second is directed toward inward being and rejects sense-pleasures. Thus the two states are at opposite poles—one belonging to the ego-seeking man, and the other to the Overself-seeking man.(P)

119

Whereas ordinary concentration keeps the attention still turned toward outward things and situations, that concentration which attains its third stage is transformed into contemplation. Here the attention is entirely inward-turned and toward the heavenly being, the holy of holies that is the Overself.

120

There are two ways in which concentration is practised. The first is unconscious and is used by many persons to get their work done whether they be engineers or artists. They have to hold their mind to the job, the matter, or the duty in hand. The scientist may practise it, too, in analysing or in logically developing a theory or in linking up different ideas. The meditator uses concentration in a different way if he is at the first stage, which is the conscious and deliberate practice of concentration. It is then used without analysis, without discursive thought. It is simply held to a single object or idea. The attention is not allowed to wander away into developments of that idea or object. In short, the connections to other things are not made.

121

Concentration, from the standpoint of mystical development, may be regarded as achieved when attention is kept on one idea all the time, without being divided up over several different ideas. It is *not* achieved if kept on one subject all the time through considering several related ideas—that is, ordinary concentrated thinking.

122

He must train himself to possess the power to concentrate: first, on a single line of thoughts to the exclusion of all others and second, on a single thought.

123

With the gradual settling down of thought and body, the mental stiffness which resisted concentration diminishes. He will be distinctly and vividly aware of this turning point because of the ease, and even delight, with which his mind will now feel its own exalted power.

124

The spiritual life of man at this juncture is a battle against the outward-running tendency of the mind. To perceive this in oneself is to perceive how weak one really is, how feeble a victim of worldly activities, how lacking in the ability to concentrate perfectly even for five minutes, and how unable to hold the attention for the same length of time in the impersonal embrace of a philosophic theme.

125

The Samurai of old Japan embodied a yoga technique in the fencing instruction. The novice had to develop the power of mental concentration, and then use it by picturing himself during meditation wielding the sword to perfection. Thus the body was broken gradually to the will of the mind, and began to respond with rapid lightning strokes and placings of the sword. The famous Katsu, who rose from destitute boy to national leadership of Japan's nineteenth-century awakening, went night after night to an abandoned temple—where he mingled regular meditation with fencing practice in his ambition to become one of Tokyo's master swordsmen.

126

This power to sustain concentrated attention upon a single line or objective for a long time—a power so greatly admired by Napoleon—comes in the end to those who persevere in these practices.

127

The fixed statue-like posture of the hunter watching a prey close at hand, refraining from movement lest he disturb it, eyes and mind completely intent on the animal, gave the yogi seers another object lesson in the art of concentration.

128

He makes the novice's mistake of assuming that what is good for him, necessary for him, is equally good and necessary for others. But what is essential for mystical experience is one thing and one thing only—the faculty of fixing one's attention within and sustaining it.

129

Through it you effect a change in your entire mental make-up. The mind becomes increasingly one-pointed. It is able to form quick decisions. Those decisions are usually correct because all the facts of the case are seen at once, as in a flash. It will give you an air of definite purpose, simply because in your external life you are merely working according to the purposes planned in quietude. Your every act becomes more real and vital. You gather self-confidence because you concentrate your mind on the one thing you are doing.

130

His purpose must be utterly unified, absolutely single-minded.

131

The attainment of reverie passes through two stages also. In the first, the mind is like a little child trying to walk but often falling, for the abstracted mood is intermittent only and soon lost. In the second stage, the mind is like an adult walking steadily and continually, for the abstracted mood remains unbroken and undisturbed.

132

When the meditator tries to keep out all other thoughts except the chosen one, he puts himself up to a tension, a strain—because in most cases he simply can not do this and the failure which is finally admitted after repeated efforts then has a depressing and discouraging effect upon his Quest. Therefore, other and easier methods have been devised for beginners as a preliminary to the more difficult practices of concentration. Such methods include the steady gazing at a physical point, object, or place; use of a mantram, which is the constant repetition of a word or phrase or formula; Short Path affirmation which is the dwelling mentally and constructively on a metaphysical truth or ethical quality of character; and, finally, the practice of certain breathing exercises.

133

When the capacity for concentration is intensified and prolonged, the man is then ready for the further phase which is meditation as such.

134

It is a useful practice, when the thoughts during meditation refuse to be concentrated, to turn them, too, over to the Higher Power—no matter to what event or person, situation or place they stray.

135

He imagines a point upon the wall and concentrates all his being upon it until he is aware of nothing else but the point. All other thoughts have to be emptied out of his mind, all experience of the physical senses other than this sight of the point has to vanish.

136

A simple technique for meditation which has been used in Asia since the most ancient times avoids the use of any human being or any sacred mantram as the object of meditation. This technique in its most primitive form is to take a piece of charcoal and to draw a circle or a square on the wall of a room and then in the centre of the pattern to put a dot. The student is then told to concentrate his gaze upon the dot and to think of nothing else. The pattern is usually large enough for him to see it quite plainly when sitting a yard or two or even three from the wall. Nowadays, the same technique is used by making the diagram on plain white thick drawing paper and pinning the paper to the wall.

137

The practice of using a physical object upon which to gaze in order to concentrate attention during meditation makes it much easier for those who are attracted to it. A metaphysician of Konigsberg, Immanuel Kant, used the same practice when working out his metaphysical theories. Sitting in his study, he would look through the window and fix his sight on a particular fir tree which was growing outside. One day it was cut down and removed and for some time thereafter Kant found difficulty in holding his line of thought without the accustomed fir tree to gaze upon. Indeed, Kant was such a creature of habit that every evening punctually at five o'clock he would take his walk. People in the city of Konigsberg used to time their watches by his appearance in the street, because he was invariably punctual in starting his walk.

138

For those who have set up a high spiritual ideal and moral character for themselves and who have acquired sufficient knowledge through study or lectures about the principles and fundamentals of yoga, there is an excellent exercise which will help them through the elementary phases of development; but to others who are highly neurotic, mentally disturbed, approaching or under psychosis, it is not only not recommended, but would be dangerous. This exercise is to concentrate all the attention upon one object in the surroundings and to keep it there. All associated ideas, analysis, and thoughts about the object should be thrown out. It is not a matter of reflecting about the object, but of holding it in the view and in the mind to the exclusion of everything else.

One can begin with very short periods of practice and go on slowly to longer ones, but when some amount of success has been established by the rigorous use of willpower the object should be chosen from some things elevating to the mind such as beautiful music or beautiful landscape. For the elementary phase, about fifteen minutes should be the maximum, but for this uplifting phase one may go on longer.

139

The practice of one-pointed concentration of attention for any purpose of an ordinary or worldly character or professional or technical nature can be carried to such a far point that it will influence the mind generally, so that when in the course of time the person evolves to higher aims and worthier goals he has ready to use and to bring into his efforts to attain those goals this concentrated power of the mind which is so valuable and so necessary for his inner growth.

140

To squint lightly at the root of the nose is another form of concentration. It is a help towards withdrawing from the physical senses and entering either the psychic or the spiritual planes. The psychic pictures may be seen as symbolic or literal, and clairvoyance may develop. If these manifestations are rejected, and attention is drawn deeper into the void of space, freedom and joy may be felt. But if they are accepted, the creative faculty of the artist is unfolded.

141

Meditation exercise (Lama Drati): Imagine a white dot in centre of forehead and keep attention held unmovingly on it for one hour. Or you can place it in heart. Better still, imagine the figure of Buddha projected in front of you, radiating white light. Or place the Buddha miniature-sized on your head. All these are called exercises to attain one-pointed mind. Only after this attainment can you properly do the more advanced exercises.

142

What concentration means to the artist is what it means to the mystic. Only its object is different. The late Sir Henry Wood, conductor of the London Queen's Hall Concerts, told how, during the First World War, he never heard, whilst conducting, the sirens warning the metropolis of impending air raids. This is what rapt absorption means.

143

It is important to give the mind a definite idea to hold and mull over or a definite line to follow and concentrate on. It must be positive in this early stage before it can safely become passive in a later stage.

144

The art of fixing the mind in free choice, of holding thoughts as, and when, one wills, has yet to be valued and practised as it ought to be among us. Overlooked and disregarded as it has been, it is like buried treasure awaiting the digger and the discoverer.

145

The mind can be influenced by the five senses only when it attends to them.

146

At a certain depth of penetration into his inward being, pain of the body and misery of the emotions are unable to exist. They disappear from the meditator's consciousness.

147

During the first period, which may extend to half an hour, when nothing seems to happen and the line of thought or awareness is wobbly and uncertain, discouragement irksomeness and impatience quite often overcome the practiser. They may induce him to abandon the session for that day. Such a surrender to defeatism is unwise. Even in the case of those who have practised for some years the tedious initial waiting period may still have to be endured. For it is the period during which thoughts settle slowly down just as a glass of muddy water slowly clears as the mud settles to the bottom. The proper attitude to hold while this process continues is patience. This is quite indispensable.

148

How can a man unify his consciousness with the Overself without first putting his mind under some sort of a training to strengthen it, so that he will not let go but will be able to hold on when a Glimpse comes?

149

Where attention is being fixedly held on a single topic by the power of a strong interest in it, there will be little regard given to the passage of time.

150

Thoughts will drift past in ever changing variety, but he will learn to give them no attention even though he is aware of them.

151

The act of continuous concentration—if carried on for some time— draws an extra and unusual quantity of blood to the brain. This causes pleasurable sensations which may increase to an ecstatic degree.

152

The nasal gaze meditation exercise is both easy and quieting. It is mentioned in the *Gita*. The half-closed eyes look down on the tip of one's nose. They must not wink during the gaze or be closed. When tired, close them and rest. Avoid strain, staring, and popping the eyes wide open. The action should be one of relaxation, restful. All attention of an alert and concentrated mind should be fixed on the gazing. This exercise gives control over the optic nerve and contributes towards steadiness of mind.

153

With sufficient, well-directed practice, he should fix the ideal of being able to attain a capacity of withdrawing attention from the world and concentrating it within himself without losing a single minute.

154

His progress into the deeper state is retarded if, while trying to hold his attention on the chosen theme, he lets some of it remain *self-consciously* alert at the same time to what he is doing and what his surroundings are like.

155

Any method which settles the mind upon a fixed subject, or concentrates attention upon a single object, may be used. But the result must be elevating and in accord with his ultimate purpose.

156

With all attention gathered in, listen to the beating of the heart.

157

When the mind is too active and thoughts succeed each other too quickly, as in the case of very nervous or very intellectual persons, physical methods are indicated for practice. These may be breathing exercises, repetition of a sound or listening to music of a repetitive nature, gazing at a landscape, figure, work of art, or symbolic pattern.

158

Meditation succeeds to the extent that attention is controlled and turned inward. When this control becomes so intensive that neither sounds nor lights can break it, its concentration is complete.

159

How beautiful is that detachment from unpleasant surroundings which the capacity to intensely concentrate bestows. And this is only one of its rewards. Efficiency in studying a new subject is another.

160

The secret of concentration is . . . practise concentration! Only by arduous effort and persistent, diligent endeavours to master his attention will he finally succeed in doing so. No effort in this direction is wasted and it may be done at any time of the day.

161

One can turn a mystical experience of as much as twenty years ago, or longer, into focus for attention in meditation, and thereby assist the memory to recall every detail of it.

162

It is not essential for the meditator to be so sunk in his practice as to become entirely heedless of his surroundings.

163

The mental detachment needed for this study permits him to shake off personal worries and pettier distractions. When he can fully concentrate in his thinking, sustained and unwandering absorption is possible.

164

The practice of isolating consciousness and remaining centered in it, can be followed whether we are in solitary meditation or active in the world. In meditation it becomes the object of thoughts; in activity it becomes their background. The eyes cannot look at themselves, neither can consciousness: it is itself the subject and cannot be its own object. If the thoughts let themselves slip back into it—their source—the stillness of being is experienced. Staying in it is the practice.

165

His attention should, in theory, be wholly concentrated on this single line of thought. But in practice it will be so only at broken intervals.

166

Yoga demands that the mind occupy itself with one thought or one coherent line of thought, that attention be held fast to it, whether it be the thought of something abstract like God or the thought of something concrete like the cross.

167

Through such concentrative thinking, we may reach peace. It is hard, certainly, and the handcuffed intellect will struggle in your grasp like a reluctant prisoner newly arrested. You must continue with your effort to develop conscious concentrated thought no matter how fumbling your first forays may be.

168

The aim is to sit there totally absorbed in his thought or, at a more advanced level, rigidly concentrated in his lack of it.

169

The word "centre" is a purely mystical term: it is unphilosophical. Where is the possibility of a central point in the mind which is so unlimited? But for practising mystics seeking to retire within, the centre is an excellent goal to aim at.

170

Could one of these yogis practise his meditation while assailed by the deafening noise of a steel-girder rivetting machine operating outside his cave? Is it practicable to follow the advice of the Maharishee, which I heard him give a would-be meditator complaining about being bitten by mosquitoes, to ignore them? Let it be noted that no person who is trying to practise this art could be distracted if he did not attend to the sense affected, whether it be hearing aroused by a machine or feeling aroused by a mosquito.

171

Shutting the eyes is only the first step toward shutting all the senses. That in its turn is only a step towards the still harder task of shutting out all thoughts and all ordinary everyday feelings.

172

The five senses serve us well in the ordinary hours of actual life but tyrannize over us when we try to transcend it and enter the spiritual life.

173

Within a few minutes of starting the exercise they feel exhausted. The effort to concentrate the mind is hard enough but to concentrate and introvert it at the same time is too much for them.

174

The ancient yoga texts enjoin concentration of a steadfast gaze upon a small object until the eyes begin to shed tears. The result of such practices is a cataleptic state in which the mind becomes fixed and unmoving while the body becomes stiff as wood.

175

It is not enough to carry the concentrated awareness away from outward things: it must then be kept there. This also is hard, because all tendencies rebel at first.

176

His attention must be absolute and perfect if it is to be effectual and creative in producing this result.

177

Concentration requires a capacity for continuous attention.

178

Attention must not waver, thought must not wander. This is the ideal, of course, and is not approached, let alone reached, until after long practice.

179

To keep the attention away from any other than the chosen subject is the work of this first stage. The better this is sustained, the deeper is the penetration into the subject.

180

Whatever distracts attention openly and violently, like the passions; or subtly and insidiously, like curiosity; or preoccupies it with cares and anxieties, like business, is likely to interfere with the mind during practice sessions either in concentration or exaltation.

181

The stage of concentration is evaluated as having been established when it can be sustained long enough to let attention become sufficiently abstracted from surroundings, sufficiently absorbed in the mental object, and for the practice itself to be easy, unhindered, attractive.

182
Some of the old Buddhist monks, the histories say, reached *samadhi* simply by steadfast gazing upon the floor.

183
All that lies on the margin of attention may remain there.

184
There is no doubt that, in its early phases, the art of meditation makes demands for more concentration than most persons possess, that they soon tire unless their enthusiasm continues.

185
Fixing the gaze upon a spot marked on a wall or an object near or far, is only a preliminary to fixing the mind on a thought.

186
When consciousness is deliberately turned away from the world and directed inward to itself, and when this condition is steadily maintained by a purified person, the result is a real one.

187
Again and again he will have to collect his thoughts and bring his attention to the central point.

188
To achieve this kind of concentration where attention is withdrawn from the outer world and held tightly in itself, a determined attitude is needed of not stopping until this sharply pointed state is reached. All other thoughts are rejected in the very moment that they arise. If at the start there is aspiration and devotion toward the Overself, and in the course of the effort too, then eventually the stress falls away and the Stillness replaces it.

189
He who is unwilling to endure concentration sustained to the point of fatigue will not be able to penetrate to the deep level where truth abides. But when he does succeed, the fatigue vanishes, an intense exhilaration replaces it.

190
When he is going to practise any exercise—whether mystical or physical—his mind should be thoroughly concentrated on it and not on anything else. All thought and energy should go into it, if it is to be successfully done.

191
When concentration attains its effective state, the ever-tossing mental waves subside and the emotional perturbations become still. This is the psychological moment when the mystic naturally feels exaltation, peace, and super-earthliness. But it is also the psychological moment when, if he is wise, he should turn away from revelling in personal satisfaction at this

achievement and, penetrating yet deeper, strive to understand the inner character of the source whence these feelings arise, strive to understand pure Mind.(P)

192

To bring his scattered thoughts to heel, to give undivided attention to the intuitive feeling which would lead to the secret spiritual self—this is the first task.

193

If it is to profit him, the student must not allow his meditation to become nebulous and vague.

194

The will, driving the attention to a fine pinpoint of concentration, sinks through layer after layer of the mind till it reaches the noblest, the wisest, and the happiest of them all.

195

It would be a serious error to believe that he is to continue with any particular exercise or chosen theme, with any special declaration or analysis or question, no matter what happens in the course of a session. On the contrary; if at any moment he feels the onset of deeper feelings, or stronger aspirations, or notable peace, he ought to stop the exercise or abandon the method and give himself up entirely to the interior visitant. He ought to have no hesitation and no fear in considering himself free to do so.(P)

196

When this gentle inward pull is felt, concentrate all attention, all feeling, and all desire upon it. Give yourself up to it, for you are receiving a visitation from the Lord, and the more you do so, the closer He will come.

197

This is the stage of adoration, when the Overself's beauty and tranquillity begin to take possession of his heart. He should then cease from any further thinking discursively about it or communing verbally with it. It is a time for complete inner silence. Let him engage himself solely in beholding, loving, and eventually uniting with the gracious source of these feelings.

198

There is a crucial time in the meditation session when the meditator goes into reverse as it were—instead of intensifying his attention on the idea or object, imagery, or sound, he lets go in surrender and rests. But it is not a rest in egocentricity. All has been handed over to the higher Self to whom he now feels close. Only at this point is he concentrated, calm, ready, and receptive to the Divinity.

199

When that delicate feeling comes over him, he should hold on to it with all his concentrativeness and all his collectedness.

200

There is a distinct feeling of something like a valve opening in the region of the heart.

201

The moment he feels the beginnings of any movement towards the indrawing of thought and feeling away from externals, he should at once respond to it and let attention fall deeper and deeper into himself, even if for only five minutes. This is important because of the currents of Grace which are being telepathically transmitted to him in fulfilment of the existing relationship.

202

If he is willing to submit to the Overself's gentle drawing, he must first be able to recognize it for what it is.

203

The sensation of being drawn gently inside will be felt.

204

He is to push attention from outside himself to inside. He is then to push away extraneous thoughts while he concentrates on the feeling-search for his innermost self.

205

Better than any other practice is this deep in-searching.

206

Consciousness must focus itself inward upon ascertaining its own source to the exclusion of everything else.

207

The more he internalizes his attention, and the less he responds to the sense-impressions, the nearer he draws to the spiritual presence in his heart.

208

The divine atom is that part of the body with which the Overself is most directly associated, and that is why it is placed in the heart, but of course, the Overself is associated with the whole body. There is a scientific explanation why the heart is the spiritual centre of the body and why the brain is the mental centre, and this is given in *The Wisdom of the Overself.*

209

His determined, one-pointed attention keeps going down deeper and deeper into his own being.

Varieties of practice

210

There are various practical methods of achieving the combined aim of remembering the divine and concentrating on the divine. Mantram-repetition is one of them. They are mostly elementary and well-suited to aspirants who are at an early stage of development. But these aspirants cannot stay there always. The time comes when they must seek and struggle for a higher stage. Full enlightenment can come only to the fully developed.

211

Although there are some general features common to most techniques, there is also in each case something which is personally needed to suit the particular temperament, character, and status.

212

Each method is merely a point of departure, not a place or arrival. It is a focussing of thoughts upon a special object or subject with a view to travelling later beyond all thoughts into the stage of contemplation.

213

Most of these techniques are preliminary, intended to bring the mind into one-pointed concentration. They do *not* lead to the real enlightenment.

214

There is no objection to elementary methods of learning to concentrate, that is, to mantram, affirmation, and breath control—provided it is recognized that they *are* elementary and therefore have their limitations. But when, as is so often the case, this is not known, not understood, or not thought to be correct, then illusions and deceptions are fostered. One of the illusions is that enlightenment, Truth, reality, has been attained. One of the deceptions is that this technique is all that needs to be done.

215

We have tried to formulate methods and to adapt exercises which will enable the modern man to come into this transcendental consciousness without deserting the world and without becoming a votary of asceticism.

216

It is a valuable exercise for those who are repelled by all exercises, to reach back in memory and imagination, in surrender and love, to some grand rare moment of mystical insight. They will not be repelled by this one, for it is so simple that it can hardly be classified among the exercises. And yet it is, with a value immensely disproportionate to its simplicity.

217

The student should not feel bound to follow rigidly a devotional-meditational program laid down, as it needs must be, on general lines to suit a variety of people. He should feel free to express his individuality by improvising additions or alterations in it should a strong prompting to do so come to him.

218

All these rules and suggestions are for beginners. In the end he will have to learn to be able to practise in any place and at any time.

219

Let him experiment with many different exercises and so learn which ones suit him best and help him most.

220

All these methods are simply mechanical devices for throwing the conscious mind out of gear.

221

None of the elementary methods of yoga such as breath control and mantram lead to a permanent control of the mind, but they prepare the way and make it easier to take up those practices which do lead to such a result.(P)

222

So far as meditation is affected by their hidden operation, the tendencies draw one person by one way and others by another. There is no single road. Those who fail to advance in, or are unattracted by, discursive meditation, may use mantrams, symbols, and forms instead.

223

Whether the seeker uses a Tibetan *mandala* (spiritually symbolic picture) to concentrate on, or an Indian *mantram* (continuous mental or muttered repetition of a verbal formula), the end result will be an indrawn state of consciousness, abstracted from the outside world, or else a deeper and more sustained remembrance of God. Like the other yoga methods, they are devices to achieve one-pointedness of mind.

224

When selecting an exercise for practice it is well to begin with one that comes easiest to him.

225

A new exercise, theme, or practice in meditation will naturally need more time than an old familiar one.

226

The method of the Maharishi Mahesh Yogi can not lead to enlightenment by truth, but it can lead to a very pleasurable temporary quieting of the mind.

227

Explanations of the yogic chakras: He should treat them for just what they are, points in the physical body upon which to concentrate the mind. As he progresses inwardly, he moves up to the next higher chakra; but this kind of concentration yoga is not ordinarily recommended. It belongs to a special yoga which seeks the awakening of the spirit fire and that is a risky undertaking.

228

In Tibetan Buddhist initiations of certain schools, the master uses his sceptre to touch those centres which are specially sensitive to receive the mystic power he is transmitting among them. After touching the head and breast, the importance of the nerve centre at the nape of the neck is recognized by receiving the third touch.

229

After some practice, he will less and less consciously think of the technique and more and more instinctively follow it.

230

The most balanced procedure is to alter the themes and exercises from time to time to meet the different requirements of his all-round development as well as the different intuitive urges and passing moods which may manifest themselves.

231

The advocacy of meditation in a nonspiritual medico-psychological form would probably meet the situation of a number of individuals. However, there ought to be, side by side and along with it, another effort to advocate meditation in a religious and aspirational form for the sake of other individuals who are ready to emerge from narrow orthodoxy, but still wish to keep their religious faith. In both cases, it is necessary to point out that all kinds of meditation must be safeguarded by some effort at self-purification and at strengthening intellectual balance. Otherwise it may do harm as well as good.

232

Even the large range of possible meditations upon spiritual principles, mental ideas, imagined pictures and physical objects does not exhaust the list. He may use his own body, too. The gaze may be concentrated between the eyebrows, down the nose, or upon the navel. The process of breathing may be closely watched.

233

The instructions and directions which are of first importance must be separated from those which are merely second in importance, or confusion will result.

234

Discussion of the methods of meditation, and critical scrutiny of its nature and results can only be of value, if not of interest, to the handful of initiates who have practised one of the methods and experienced some of the results. All others will be dependent on what they have heard or read about meditation. To them such discussion and such scrutiny will be either incomprehensible or unprofitable or bewildering.

235

A continuous ringing of large heavy old church bells, if intently concentrated upon, may produce in a person appreciative of the music in them, a suitable starting point for introverting attention.

236

The methods used to induce this absorbed trance-like state have been as many as they are varied, from the loud bull-like roars of the Pasupata yogis to the aesthetic whirlings of the Mevlevi dervishes.

237

The witch-doctor who, or whose assistant, beats out a rhythm on his drum accomplishes a concentration of mind—a lulling of the senses and a recession from the world for his hearers, to a farther extent than they would have been able to accomplish for themselves alone.

238

There are exercises which lead to this higher consciousness. By the power of will they concentrate attention; by pursuing an elevated topic they bring the latter to meditation; by patiently and perseverantly dropping the will which served so well, they attain the stillness of contemplation.

239

Some of these techniques make the mind numb and thus arrest thinking: they are not only very elementary but also inferior. But for numbers of people they are the easiest ways and the most resultful. They have to be used by such persons as stepping-stones, not as permanent homes.

240

There are various ways used by various seekers of putting the conscious mind out of ordinary action. The way of those dervishes who twirl around on their feet and, at the same time, spin around in a larger circle, is one of them. They eventually get vertigo and fall to the ground. They swoon, and thereafter may get a glimpse.

241

The true inner use of the koan is correct and laudable. The mistake is to make its practice a cause of anxiety and stress. No. It should develop smoothly, thinking harmoniously and even logically, and thus reach the inevitable recognition that intellect can go no further. So the intellect stops working, resigns itself, and lo, *acts no more* (Wu Wei—inaction). The man then waits patiently and peacefully and acceptantly. The result is no longer in his hands. It must be now entrusted to the higher power.

242

Where meditation uses thoughts or images—logical sequential thoughts, or symbolical or realistic images—it is still the work of the man himself and therefore within the ego.

243

As to whether meditation should begin with mental concentration or mental stillness, each practice is advisable at different times or during different phases of one's development. In the course of a year, the student may devote his work during some months to beginning with the first and during other months with the second. It is not possible to generalize about which one is better during any particular period; this depends entirely on individual circumstances. The best way to find out is to make an impersonal self-examination, and then follow one's own intuition.

244

The creator of the Order of Whirling Dervishes used the gyratory movements and dance concentrations, with reed-pipe musical accompaniments, to bring them into the mystical experience. This is possible because body and mind react upon each other. To a lesser extent but in a different way, the same principle is used in hatha yoga. Both methods are intended to reach and awaken people who would find the solely mental, physically immobile meditation too difficult.

245

They complain about the noise outside their meditation room but the noise of their ego inside it is louder. Their techniques are useful and preparatory but unless accompanied or followed by discrimination, knowledge, understanding, they fail to root out the ego, only lulling it and tying them to the espoused system, dogma, or credo.

246

The different yogas are transitory phases which the seeker must develop and then outgrow.

247

Those who feel the need of outward ritual and sacramental service should satisfy it, but those who find simple meditation with nothing added more attractive may progress in their own way.

248

If some of the disciplines are no longer practical under the conditions of present-day living, others are still useful.

249

There is available for us all a technical method in which may be found the means to achieve the refulgent moods of mystical inspiration.

250
Technique should suit temperament.

251
The well-known helps to concentration such as rosaries, mandalas, geometrical diagrams, candle flames in the darkness, and, most popular of all, a mantram may be used by beginners but they are not necessary to fairly advanced students.

252
It is neither right nor wrong to try to suppress thoughts in meditation exercises: what matters is to fit what is attempted to the particular object of the particular exercise. So there are times to let thoughts move and times to rein them in.

253
The practice of *tratak* [continuous gazing] is intended to make the yogi blind to external scenes by attending to a single object; the practice of *shabda* yoga is intended to render him deaf to external sounds by attending to a single sound; and with sights and sounds cut off, he is well nigh cut off from the whole external world. Thus these systems of yoga are no other than techniques for inducing a concentrated inward-turned state.

254
Dalai Lama on Tibetan tantra: "You push up Force through spine then lean backward mentally to meet it."

255
To the alternatives of thinking with the head and thinking with the heart, the Japanese Zen master offers a third choice: "Think with the abdomen," he advises the practiser of koan meditation exercises. The Tibetan Tantrik masters offer even a fourth choice: "Think with the generative organ and sublimate its feelings." The Advaita Vedantins go still farther. "Think quite abstractly, not of the body at all," they counsel. Should all this not show that no method is of exclusive importance?

256
The Eastern Church used, among other Hesychastic methods of making meditation more successful, the pressing of the chin against the chest.

257
Once a professor at leading Indian universities, and then on attainment of independence a minister in the Indian government, the late Radhaku-mud Mukerjee was a co-disciple of the same guru who sent Yogananda, founder of S.R.F., to America! Once when we meditated together, Mukerjee swayed as he sat, moving head and shoulders from left to right in a circular fashion. At first this rotation was quite slow, but it picked up a little speed as it went on.

258

Voodoo musicians and African witchdoctors use the rhythmic beating of drums to induce either the trance state or emotional crescendos.

259

The desert fathers, the Egyptian eremites, have their Indian equivalents. Meditation without philosophy, without instruction, without knowledge, produces widely and strangely different results in different people.

260

Some of these old yogas were curious, some alluring, and others horrible. Thus one required him to let his body enter regularly into sexual intercourse but to think all the time about the act's animal ugliness and evil consequences. He was to do this until the sight of a naked female body aroused revulsion, its white gleaming limbs seemed more hideous than attractive, and its invitation to coitus filled him with disgust. Another method required him to sit on a fresh corpse in the pitch darkness of a cemetery at midnight and think solely of the quality of fearlessness. These apparently were Indian versions of the attempt to take the kingdom of heaven by violence. In Bengal and Tibet they are still practised by some fanatics. Yet more aspirants are likely to fail with them than succeed. In the one yoga, such failures would result in greater sensuality than before and in the other in greater fear than before. Nevertheless their effectiveness may be granted. But, we ask, is it not better for civilized modern seekers to use more refined and less drastic methods?

4

MEDITATIVE THINKING

The path of inspired intellect

The next type of meditation is the analytic. It may deal with personal experience, general events, universal laws, the nature of man, and the reality of soul, but always it seeks by analysis and reflection to understand.

2

In this type of reflective meditation, critical thinking is not banished but is illuminated by the Overself's light. It is the path of inspired intellect. It is extremely valuable because it can reveal the right path to take in practical affairs and the right course to take in moral ones. It is equally valuable for extracting the lessons out of past experience.

3

The topic selected for practice may be quite personal to begin with, provided that it is suitable to help bring about self-improvement of a positive kind such as removing faults and cultivating virtues. But this is only preparatory, since it is still concerned with the ego and designed to improve concentration. When experience and regular practice have reached a sufficient development, then the topic should be one which makes him feel highly reverential and should be directed to the OVERSELF not to the ego, not even for the ego's improvement spiritually.

4

A clear distinction has to be made between thinking about God and the experience of God. Each has its place. Thinking and evaluating take place on the intellectual level; one should not limit oneself to that but should try to arrive at the inner stillness, the experience of the Overself during meditation. There should be a clear sense of the difference between these two. The piling up of thoughts, however reasonable they are, acts only as a signal; they point out which way to go, but at the end drop them.

5

It is not merely an intellectual exercise. All the piety and reverence and worship gained from religion are needed here too. We must pray constantly to the Soul to reveal itself.

6

When thinking has done its best work, reached its loftiest point, it should relax and cease its activity. If all else has prepared the way, the mind will be ready to enter the silence, to accept a take-over by the Overself.

7

In this type of meditation, the intellect must think, first about itself and second about what is beyond itself. This change of thought becomes a stepping-stone to a change of consciousness.

8

The old Quaker family morning custom of reading aloud a passage from the Bible, and following it by a period of meditative silence, is a useful pointer. Any book that inspires may be read vocally then shut and pondered quietly; any sentence that holds and exalts attention may be made the subject of slow, grave utterance followed by silent concentrated rumination. Any word, attribute, name, or phrase that enshrines spiritual truth may be affirmed in speech and afterward contemplated in hush.

9

Vichara means discursive thinking, so *atmavichara* means thinking one's way into the real self.

10

To shorten the period of reincarnations, thought is needed: first, analytic reflection about the past; second, imaginative reflection about the future.

11

All possess the power of reflection but few use it. When this power is turned outwardly, we look upon the physical body, its organs and senses, as our self and so plunge into the bustling activity of this world without hesitation. But if this same power of reflection be turned inwardly, we begin to forget our activities and to lose knowledge of the physical body and its environment. For we become so deeply indrawn into the world of thought that for the time being this inner world becomes for us the real world. Thus we are led gradually by repeating this practice to identify ourselves with the mind alone, to look upon ourselves as thought-beings.

12

In this type of meditation the activity of thinking is not rejected. On the contrary, it is deliberately accepted, for its character undergoes a marked change. At a certain stage, when concentration thoroughly establishes itself, some force that is deeper than the familiar personal self rises up from within itself and imposes a continuous stream of sequential, illumined thoughts upon the consciousness.

13

Our richest moments are those spent in deep reverie upon the diviner things.

14

Deep reflective thinking is present behind deep impersonal thinking.

15

What a relief for a man, harassed by anxieties and frustrated by burdens, to turn towards these great impersonal verities and consider them in the serene mood of the twilight meditation or the sunrise worship.

16

At different periods in his career there will be the need of—and consequently the attraction to—different subjects for meditation. Thus: the beauty of a flower, the ugliness of a corpse, the attributes of a sage, the infinitude of space, the changes of adolescence, middle, and old age.

17

This habit of persistent daily reflection on the great verities, of thinking about the nature or attributes of the Overself, is a very rewarding one. From mere intellectual ideas, they begin to take on warmth, life, and power.(P)

18

The Overself takes his thoughts about it, limited and remote though they are, and guides them closer and closer to its own high level. Such illumined thinking is not the same as ordinary thinking. Its qualitative height and mystical depth are immensely superior. But when his thoughts can go no farther, the Overself's Grace touches and silences them. In that moment he *knows*.(P)

19

The books which live are those written out of this deep union with the true self by men who had overcome the false self. One such book is worth a thousand written out of the intellect alone or the false ego alone. It will do more good to more people for more years. The student may use such a work, therefore, as a basis for a meditation exercise. Its statements, its ideas, should be taken one by one, put into focus for his mind to work on.

20

An inspired writing is more than something to be read for information or instruction; it gives a man faith, it becomes a symbol to which he can hold and from which he can draw a renewal of trust in the universe. It is this trust which makes him deny himself and inspires him to reach beyond himself. For his mind to fasten itself to such a writing, therefore, and to use it as a focus for meditation, is unconsciously to invoke and receive the grace of the illumined man who brought the writing to birth.

21

In these inspired writings, we may look for two distinctive qualities: the power to stimulate thought and the power to uplift character. In the first case we shall find them a seed-bed of ideas which can bear ample fruit in our minds; in the second case there is imparted to reading some flavour of the unshakeable moral strength which the inspired writers themselves possess.

22

Let him dwell upon some piece from an inspired writing or think out the meaning of some eternal verity. Let him do this with the utmost attentiveness. Such meditation will not only enable him to advance in concentrativeness but will also profit him mentally and morally.

23

If he can respond to these great inspired utterances, if he can let his thought work over them in the right way and let his emotion be susceptible to their inner dynamism, his intense concentration will enable him to share at least the reflected light behind their creator, the light itself.

24

There is a sensitivity and a depth in such works which are truly remarkable, a power, a light, and a heat to inspire their readers which is born from genius.

25

When thought is thus trained to its uttermost point and when it is etherealized by dwelling on the most abstract topic, it leaps out of itself, as it were, transcends and transforms itself and becomes intuition.

26

Paragraphs that are born and written in this higher consciousness are lasting ones, like many of the vigorous scriptural sayings.

27

The meditations on the "I," on transiency, on good and evil, and on suffering are but for beginners. They do not require the subtlety needed for ultra-mystic meditation.

28

The thought of the Overself may easily open the gate which enters into its awareness.

29

The difference between the first stage, concentration, and the second stage, meditation, is like the difference between a still photograph and a cinema film. In the first stage, you centre your attention upon an object, just to note what it is, in its details, parts, and qualities, whereas in the second stage, you go on to think all around and about the object in its functional state. In concentration, you merely observe the object; in meditation, you reflect upon it. The difference between meditation and ordinary thinking is that ordinary thinking does not go beyond its own level nor intend to stop itself, whereas meditation seeks to issue forth on an intuitional and ecstatic level whereon the thinking process will itself cease to function.

30

The better kind of thinking is that which is directed to the idea of the Overself. It reaches a culmination when the thinker is absorbed so fully into the idea that he and the thought slip away into, and remain undistracted from, the actual consciousness of the Overself.

31

Thoughts may be a hindrance to meditation merely by their presence or, if of the proper kind, a help to it. And the only proper kind is that which leads them to look toward the consciousness which transcends them.

32

The search for first causes, when done only intellectually and metaphysically, may become a shadow, or a looking-glass image of the real search. For this must, and can only be done, on a deeper level—the intuitive. The process to be used is meditation.

33

In meditation one should follow the path pointed out by his temperament. He should strive to think his own thoughts and not always echo those of others.

34

It is not enough to learn these teachings by study and analysis of them. They should also be allowed to work unhindered upon passive, receptive, still moods of the silenced intellect.

35

Upon those who are sensitive to truth at a high level, these statements have a strong and peculiar effect. There is deep awe, as if standing before a mystic shrine, reverential joy, as if beholding new mosaic tablets. There is, indeed, a feeling of being about to receive staggering revelations.

36

That a theme for meditation should be formulated in the interrogative is at once an indication that the kind of meditation involved is intellectual. *What am I?* is a simple question with a complex answer.

In this exercise you will repeatedly think of what you really are as distinct from what you seem to be. You will separate yourself intellectually, emotionally, and volitionally—so far as you can—from your flesh, your desires, and your thoughts as being objects of your consciousness and not pure consciousness itself. You will begin by asking yourself "Who am I?" and, when you comprehend that the lower nature cannot be the real you, go on to asking the further question: "What am I?" By such frequent self-studies and self-discriminations, you will come closer and closer to the truth.

37

Is the experiment too difficult? How can a man stop thinking? I remember now that it is not suggested that one should deliberately stop thinking. No, it is taught, "pursue the enquiry, 'What am I' relentlessly." Well, I have pursued it up to this point. I cannot definitely pin down my ego either to the body or the intellect. Then who am I? Beyond body and intellect there is left only—nothing! The thought came to me, "Now pay attention to this nothingness."

Nothing? . . . Nothing? . . . Nothing? . . . I gradually and insensibly slipped into a passive attitude. After that came a sense of deepening calm. Subtly, intangibly, quietness of soul invaded me. It was pleasant, very pleasant, and soothed nerves, mind, and heart. The sense of peace which enveloped me while I sat so quiet gently swelled up into bliss ineffable, into a marvellous serenity. The bliss became so poignantly keen that *I forgot to continue thinking*. I simply surrendered myself to it as ardently as a woman surrenders herself to the man she loves. What blessedness was not mine! Was it not some condition like this to which Saint Paul referred when he mentioned "the peace which passeth understanding"? The minutes trickled by slowly. A half hour later found my body still motionless, the face still fixed, the eyes still indifferent to, or oblivious of their surroundings. Had I fathomed the mystic depths of my own mind? Impatience might have reared its restless head and completely spoilt the result. I saw how futile it was to attempt always to impose our habitual restlessness in such unfamiliar circumstances.(P)

38

In one sense all attempts to meditate on spiritual themes are attempts to awaken intuition. For they achieve success only when the activity of the thinking intellect is stilled and the consciousness enters into that deep silence wherefrom the voice of intuition itself issues forth.

39

To use these sublime ideas in and for our hours of contemplation, is to use definite potencies.

40

During these meditations, he is to dwell aspiringly and lovingly upon the ideal at times and to reflect calmly and rationally about it at other times. Thus he will learn to achieve imaginatively an effective self-government.

41

My use of the term "reverie" may mislead some to think I mean idle, drifting, purposeless, languid thinking. I mean nothing of the sort.

42

Only after a long, long search can he trace these thoughts to their final source in the pure stream of Mind.

43

Work on such themes inspires a writer, a thinker, or a teacher, as work on the higher levels of art must inspire the creative artist.

44

The practice of self-inquiry begins with the self's environment and ends with its centre. It asks, "What is the world?" Then, "What is the Body?" Next, "What is the Mind?" Then, "What is the source of happiness?" And finally, "What am I?" at the threshold of its innermost being.

45

He should sit down by the seashore or on a hillside or on the roof of a tall building or in any other place where he can get a long, uninterrupted view of ocean and sky or sky alone. If no other place is available, let him lie on the ground and gaze at the sky. Then let him think of the Spirit as being like this vast expanse in its freedom and uniqueness, but infinite and boundless where the other is not.

46

Ordinarily our minds have too limited and too ego-centered a range. It is needful to broaden them by reflections and meditations which are highly abstract and totally impersonal. "The universe is infinite and unmeasurable. How tiny and insignificant is this planet Earth in relation to it! How trivial and unimportant are earthly things, if the planet itself is such! How ridiculous to let oneself be captured and imprisoned by momentary sensual pleasures which have not even the duration of most of these things!" Such is one sample of how this exercise could begin.

47

Those who have tried it know how much harder real meditation is than mere thinking. The two are not the same.

48

If he finds only ignorance, bewilderment, or ordinariness, then he needs to go farther into himself. The revelation is there but at a deep level.

49

In these earlier stages, what matters is how deeply absorbed his attention becomes in the subject, how strongly held is his control over the thoughts which come into the area of awareness, how far away he withdraws from activity of the body's senses.

50

Every time a thought rears its head, evaluate it for what it is and then push it aside. Every time an emotion rushes up, recognize it, too, for what it is and detach yourself from it. This is the path of Self-Enquiry, for as you do these things hold the will directed towards finding the centre of your being. Do them with dogged persistence. Do them in your consciousness and in your feeling.

51

Some imaginative minds can make profitable use of the vastness of the ocean or the immensity of space as topics on which to meditate in the advanced stages.

52

If the utmost benefit is to be extracted from this kind of exercise, he should, at the end and before he rises to resume the ordinary daily life, briefly repeat to himself its leading points and then sum up in concentrated emphasis its final lesson.

53

Although he may collect together only those thoughts which refer to the chosen subject, he may take different sides of it by turns.

54

Whatever thinking is done during the exercise, one ought to strive for the utmost clearness and the fullest alertness in it.

55

He may deliberately choose a fresh subject each day or let the spontaneous urge of the moment choose it for him. Or he may take again one that has served him well before.

56

The kind of meditation in which the meditator ponders persistently what his source is, what the "I" really is, has the eventual effect of dehypnotizing him from these false and limiting identifications with the body, the desires, and the intellect.

57

It must be a topic very distant from, and quite unconnected with, his ordinary occupations of the day. He must release himself altogether from their problems and pleasures.

58

The more he practises at such times a thinking that is sense-free and beyond the physical—that is, *meta*physical in the truest sense—the better will he be prepared to receive the intuitive influx from the Overself.

59

The pursuit of the self comes at last to an irreducible element. The analyser cuts his way through all intermediate regions of the mind.

60

When intellect lies exhausted and prostrated, at the end of its self-directed efforts, and gives up, it may then be ready to *receive* what, earlier, it could not.

61

The ordinary kind of meditation seeks to escape from intellectualism at the very beginning, whereas the metaphysical kind uses it from the beginning. Even though it is analytic, it does not limit itself to cerebral activity; it conjoins feeling also, since it seeks an experience as well as understanding. Therefore, in the "Who Am I?" work it moves with the whole being and with all its intensity.

62

Concentration keeps the mind implanted on a particular thought, or line of thought, by keeping off the other ones. Meditation removes the single thought and keeps the mind quiet. This is an excellent state, but not enough for those who seek the Real. It must be complemented by knowledge of what is and is not the Real.

63

The whole collected force of his being is brought to this idea.

64

In these exercises he thinks of God's nature, qualities, and attributes; he meditates on God's infinity, eternity, and unity.

65

After he has entered on the Short Path, fit themes for his meditation will be those which turn him away from the personal ego. He can meditate on the glorious attributes of God, or on the essential perfection of the cosmos, or on the utter serenity of his Overself, for instance.

66

Most students can profitably meditate on such fragments of the World-Idea as they can glean from different and varied sources: from the texts of mystical seers, philosophic sages, religious prophets, and even their own personal intuitions.

67

The more we use our thoughts to get the deep understanding of ourselves, of God, and the world, and the more we still the thoughts to get them out of the way when the divine is ready to speak to us, the more successful will our search become, and the more will we awaken from the dream of an unreal materiality.

68

But unless the point is surrendered and silenced, it will not be possible to go beyond the intellectual stage of understanding. And it is only a minority who can achieve this silence and yield capacity for deepening their experience to what amounts to a realization of the truth. The silence has another name: either meditation or contemplation.

69

If he has had a spiritual experience in which first-hand direct knowledge of his own spiritual nature and its non-materiality and immortality became evident to him, let him take that memory and cherish it as a basis for his present meditations.

70

When we take up a book that throws light before our feet, that day becomes a starred event in the calendar of our life. It is not to be easily forgotten, because the planets of Truth and Beauty are hard to find amid the panoply of rival lights in the sky.

71

When one carries intellect to its highest exercise, which is *right* reasoning, he comes near to the finest function of nature—intuition. Yet the gulf between them remains impassable unless he is willing to perform the vital and supreme act of stilling it altogether. In the intellect's complete silence the voice of divine intuition may be heard.

72

The goal of enlightenment can be reached by thought alone—despite the contrary assertion of the English medieval hermit who wrote *The Cloud of Unknowing*—but only when thought is so finely sharpened that, seeing precisely where its limits lie, it is willing to cease its own activity and surrender to the higher power. But it must be wise enough to believe in the existence of such a power, to know that It is unthinkable and unsearchable and therefore must be allowed to take over where thinking stops. Yet the medieval author is quite right to this extent—that where thought is wrapped in love and warmed by it, the enlightenment is that much more attainable.

73

Pythagoras had seen that the universe was built on number, Spinoza that the number of possibilities was infinite: both men worked with a mathematically trained mind whose borderland merged into intuition, in the same way as it does with a metaphysically trained mind; but it must be purified and strengthened, too, if the required concentration is to be sustained and if its course is to be straightened and not distorted. Then the intuitive *experience* of infinity comes with the intuitive *notion* of it. This must be so because the Mind which conceived the universe is itself infinite.

74

Select a sentence from psalm, prayer, gospel, or book which epitomizes for you the entire quest, or uplifts you nearer to the goal of the quest. Murmur it to yourself slowly and repeatedly. Ponder over its meaning.

75

The names of God traditionally used in the Orient, such as the Compassionate, the Guide, the Answerer of Prayer, the Pardoner, the Patient, are helpful as objects of prayer or subjects of meditation.

76

It is only when the ideas of a book live in your memory and thinking long after you have put away the book itself that the author's purpose has really been achieved.

77

Another excellent and always useful theme for meditation is to read a few sentences from an inspired book and then let your thought dwell upon what you have read.

78

Such books set the mind groping for the mysterious source whence it has arisen.

79

The theme may be one of those great truths of philosophy which lift the mind to an impersonal and eternal region, or it may be one of those apt sentences from an inspired book or bible which lift the feelings to adoration of the Overself.

80

Take any of these great ideas by turns, or as they suit you at different periods, and subject them to intensive meditation.

81

At each of these daily sessions, he will be ever watchful for any inner leading toward a special topic to engage his musing.

82

When you get a great thought—chain it. Hold it.

83

The more he can lose himself in the abstract thought, the mental image, the chosen ideal, the quicker he will find himself in the Soul's presence.

84

The practice of self-quest eliminates the opposition of the intellect in a marvellous manner and brings the mind up to the very borders of the transcendental, where it is taken up and put to the service of the Divine.

85

When he is so sunk in abstraction that he does not notice even the presence of another person, his meditation has gone as deep as it ought to.

86

As he meditates on these sacred sentences, every word will become more alive and more significant.

87

When concentration comes without difficulty and can be practised with ease, he should go on to meditation.

88

Bringing the same line of thought into the focus of attention again and again, holding it there sustainedly, is a path to realizing it.

89

He must study these inspired sayings as a lapidary might study a gem— with loving care and joyous feeling.

90

If the meditation attempts prove completely arid, they may be prefaced by slow, thought-out reading punctuated by reflective pauses when the book is to be put aside. It is during such pauses that the impetus to the inner movement may be felt. The book's work is then done.

91

A useful exercise is to meditate on the wisdom written in the book of the universe.

92

The kind of meditation called discursive tries to think actively about an idea or a truth until it is fully penetrated.

93

The end of all this thinking is to be not-thinking, mental quiet. This state comes hard to everyone; it leads many to utter boredom, but a few to utter peace.

94

The materials for these analytic meditations will come directly out of his present circumstances and past experiences, out of the lives of other people he has known, out of the pages of books he has read.

95

He is to take such a mighty spiritual truth or philosophic maxim into deepest consideration and deepest feeling.

96

Whatever topic will interest him soonest, engage his attention more firmly, and absorb it more fully is the best topic to meditate upon.

97

"Meditate on the mind as Brahman" (the Supreme Being), counsels an ancient Indian text.

98

Too often does he lose his way and leave the high subject of his meditation for thoughts about personal affairs and worldly topics.

99

We need to meditate more often on these reminding statements of the sages, to become more concerned with our higher interests.

100

Take a concept of God into your meditation and try to stay with it as long as you can. This itself is a form of worship, as true a form as any that you will find in a church.

101

It is a valuable, important, and fruitful topic of meditation to think of the Divine Principle as it is in its real nature and essential being, not as theologians have thought it to be or visionaries have imagined it to be.

102

Meditation is not achieved if the concentrated mind is directed toward a subject of personal and worldly nature. Reflecting on the subject will give a deeper knowledge of it and a fuller perception of its meaning, but it will not give anything more. However concentrated the mind may become, it will not escape from the ego, nor does it seek to do so. Meditation is achieved if the concentrated mind is used to reflect on the Overself or the way to it.

103
Let thinking examine itself, always with a view to penetration of its hinterland.

Self-examination exercises

104
Meditation must be accompanied by constant effort in the direction of honest self-examination. All thoughts and feelings which act as a barrier between the individual and his Ultimate Goal must be overcome. This requires acute self-observation and inner purification. Hate, jealousy, anger, greed, spite, and so on, form many an inner Mount Everest which each seeker must scale and conquer for himself before he can hope to see What Is Beyond.

105
The student must avoid falling into the snares of self-flattery. An excellent means of doing this is to review the facts of his past life to pick out his sins and blunders, his slips and falls.

106
The form into which his life-theory is molded is itself a product, or rather a projection, of the unconscious side of his mind, where a host of complexes maintain their existence remote from his criticism, examination, or even discussion.

107
It is important for him to know correctly whence his leading ideas, impulses, intuitions, and even dreams come from. He must accurately measure the heights and depths of the various levels from which they descend or ascend to his ordinary consciousness.

108
It is not easy for the student to assess correctly the motives which actuate his inner and outer life, for an important group of them does not ordinarily reveal itself to his conscious mentality.

109
He should from time to time pass in analytic review the important events, the experiences, and the attitudes of his past. It is not the good but the evil emotions and deeds, their origins and consequences, that he should particularly attend to, mentally picture, and examine from the perspective of his higher self. But unless this is done with perfect honesty in an impersonal unconcerned detached and self-critical spirit, unless it is approached with a self-imposed austerity of emotion, it will not yield the

desired results. It is not enough to mourn over his errors. He should carefully learn whatever lessons they teach.

110

In reviewing his past, he may discover how the ego has cunningly sought to preserve itself, how it has led him into logical deceits and made him believe it was absent when in reality it was very much present, how it has played subtle tricks of every kind upon him.

111

He ought to study his past errors intently, not to reproach himself emotionally but to reform himself constructively.

112

He must watch his thoughts daily and examine his actions nightly. He must apply the lancet to his motives periodically. He must analyse and re-analyse himself impersonally.

113

This does not mean that he should be forever solemnly examining his moods, analysing his feelings, and making himself the object of his own attention. It means that he should do this only for a while, at certain times, or on regular occasions.

114

Self-examination requires him to find out and identify the positive qualities as well as the negative ones, if he is to give himself a fair picture.

115

A delicate balance is needed here. If he becomes overly critical of his own self, of his character, decisions, choices, and attitudes, he may find himself becoming morbid and his will to action paralysed.

116

His past is a matter for analytic consideration, not for melancholy brooding. He must gather its fruit in the lessons it yields, convert its sufferings into virtue and wisdom.

117

He must be on his guard against the falsifications, the rationalizations, and the deceptions unconsciously practised by his ego when the self-analysis exercises become uncomfortable, humiliating, or painful. Nor should he allow himself to fall into the pit of self-pity.

118

During this half hour he must suspend the personal way of looking at life. He must stand aside from the ego for the time being and regard impersonally and impartially its acts and emotions as well as the events and fortunes with which it meets. He must examine all these experiences as if they had happened to somebody else. He collects the materials for his meditation from all the chief incidents and episodes, doings and feelings of the whole day. His reflection upon them must take a twofold course: in the first, he simply gives up errors, illusions, and complexes; in the second, he learns truths, principles, and virtues.

119

In looking back over the past, he humbly perceives his mistakes and sadly apportions the blame for his failure to himself. He no longer wastes his time in hunting alibis or in criticizing other people for his troubles. Nor does he complain of fate. He now sees that in aspiring for spiritual growth and praying for spiritual help, those very experiences which exposed his weaknesses and brought out his faults were the answers to his prayer, the grace shed upon his aspirations.

120

His memories of the unhappy past or the mistaken present must be converted into lessons in wisdom. Otherwise his meditations over them will only turn them into breeding-grounds of resentment and other negative thoughts.

121

He should develop the sense of self-criticism to a high and even painful degree. He cannot any longer afford to protect his ego, as he did in the past, or to seek excuses for its sorry frailties and foolishnesses.

122

What he will think feel or do in any given circumstances will be most largely determined by these past tendencies. How important then the need of such critical self-examination exercises.

123

He will need to develop the ability to stand back periodically from the personal self and survey its life, fortunes, character, and doings quite impartially. During this exercise, he should adopt the attitude of a disinterested spectator seeking to know the truth about it. Hence, he should study it calmly and not take sides with it emotionally.

124

This is to say, nearly the whole of your life can be steered managed and controlled by the simple process of taking stock once a day.

125

We must not seek to escape the consequences of our deeds merely by handing them over to the Overself. We must not hand them over before we have tried earnestly to master their lessons. If we hand them over prematurely, be assured they will never reach the Overself at all.

126

Another purpose which he must keep in view when recalling the past and seeking the lessons which stand out from it, is the discernment of karma's working in some of these experiences.

127

Where passions, appetites, and desires of an unworthy kind are the repeated themes of these critical analyses, they tend to become weaker and weaker as the process, with its corrosive effect, extends into a long time.

128

What is to be sought for during this short period and in this exercise is detachment from his own experiences and separation from his own habitual egoism.

129

His meditations on this subject of self-improvement must be constantly repeated and unremittingly pursued. He must look relentlessly at the ugly truth about himself face to face and then zealously foster thoughts that counteract it until they become habitual.

130

When we develop the habit of critically reflecting upon our experiences, we find it needful to revise our ideas and alter our outlook from time to time.

131

It may be easy to get the worldly, the practical message of particular experiences, but it is not so easy to get the higher, the spiritual message they contain. This is because we habitually look at them from the ego's standpoint, especially when personal feelings are strongly involved. Truth calls for a transfer of the inner centre of gravity.(P)

132

If, however, an effort is not made to purify themselves by undergoing the philosophic discipline, then even this analysis of the past will yield little or no value to them. Experiences will be viewed not as they really are but as the viewer wishes to see them. The troublesome or painful consequences of their own blunders, weaknesses, or sins will not be interpreted as evidence of such, but as evidences of other people's faults. Their personal emotions will dominate and hence misread every situation. The sources of their own difficulties not being seen, the necessary changes in thought and behaviour will not be made.

133

It is the business of the disciple who is in earnest to pry beneath the surface of his actions and discover their real motivating forces, to examine his feelings and impulses and ascertain their hidden character, and not to interpret them falsely at his ego's bidding. He has to probe into his attitudes and discover what they spring from; he has to learn to analyse his feelings impartially and coolly—a task which few men like to do or can do; he has to achieve a clear understanding of the cause of his failures and errors.

134

For some it is a useful practice to write out a self-arraignment, listing the most glaring faults first and the most hidden ones later. This helps them to keep constantly aware of what they have to avoid. It calls to them quietly but insistently.

135

To observe himself correctly, a man must do so impartially, coolly, dispassionately, and not leniently, conceitedly, excitedly. He must also do it justly, with the whole of his being and not psychopathically, with only a single part of it.

136

It is easy for troubled persons to fall into a neurotic self-pity, to brood tensely over the picture of their personal miseries. They are doing what is right in a way which is wrong. It is right to analyse troubles so as to understand how and why they have arisen. But this should be done casually, impersonally, and with special reference to the faults or weaknesses which have caused or contributed to the arising. The lesson should be learnt, the resolve to do better in future taken. Then the absorption in such a gloomy topic should be brought to an end. The light of hope and faith and surrender should be let in.

137

A warning is needed: When it lacks humility, moral self-examination often goes astray and yields a misleading result.

138

Those who are not completely honest with themselves, who prefer attractive delusion to repulsive truth, merely defer the moment of humiliating confession.

139

He has to search out and rid himself of phobias and prejudices, inhibitions and neuroses, obsessions and other mental ills. He has to see himself not as his admirers do, but as his enemies see him.

140

He must constantly examine his actions and observe his feelings. But he is to do so impartially, critically, and by the standards of the ideal for which he is striving.

141

He who has not the courage to face himself as he is, to look at his weak points along with his better ones, is not fit for philosophy.

142

To unwrap his inner self of thoughts, emotions, desires, motives, and passions; to decide what is worth keeping and what needs cutting out in it, this is his first task.

143

He should keep on probing into his weaknesses and thinking about them constructively, their causes and consequences. The improvement of character and the elevation of moral condition are the foundation of all spiritual work.

144

This unending probe into the meaning of his own life and humanity's life, this constant self-examination of character and motive, leads to a swifter development of his mind and growth of his ego, a faster realization of himself and unfolding of his inner potentialities.

145

There must arise an awareness of his hidden defects, of those distorted emotional and intellectual factors, those subtly warped purposes, which have grown up with his past and now dominate his subconscious being. He must open up the covered places of his heart and he must do it ruthlessly and fearlessly.

146

He notes his characteristics as if they were outside him, belonging to another man and not inside him. He studies his weaknesses to understand them thoroughly. They do not dismay him for he also recognizes his strengths.

147

If the results of such an examination disturb his self-confidence and shake his vanity, so much the better for his quest.

148

He is to try to be aware—first at specified times and later at all times— of his inner state, of his thoughts and feelings, his motives and desires. That is, he is to watch himself. There are two forms of this exercise. In the passive one he watches without passing judgement or making comment. In the other and active one, he measures his state against the ideal state— not, however, by intellectually formed standards but by a mind-quietening waiting for intuitive feeling.

149

At this stage of his inner life, the disciple will find himself being led more and more in the direction of his own past. He will find himself considering its various phases but especially those which were marred by ignorance, error and sin, wrong decisions, and foolish actions. These broodings will inevitably take on a melancholy saddening character. That, however, is no reason for avoiding them. Those super-optimists who would have men gaze only at the present and future, who deprecate all remembrance of the blundering past, seek a transient pseudo-happiness rather than a truly durable one. For, in the disciple's case certainly and in other men's cases perhaps, it is by frank confession of these mistakes and misdeeds and by gloomy recognition of their chastening consequences that their valuable lessons are distilled and their useless recurrence avoided. The disciple should search thoroughly for his weaknesses of character and faults of intellect, and having thus detected them as well as humbled himself, be constantly on his guard against them until he has succeeded in eliminating them altogether.

150

The hour for retirement at night should also be the hour for recalling the day's happenings, deeds, and talks in memory, at the same time making an appraisal of their character from the higher point of view. But when the exercise has come to an end, the aspirant should deliberately turn his mind utterly away from all worldly experience, all personal matters, and let the hushed silence of pure devotional worship fall upon him.

151

This exercise is particularly suited to those periods when he is able to retire from social life and worldly business, when he can go into retreat for a while. There he can reflect with profit upon the faults on his past conduct.

152

He must begin to practise introspection. This may be given a morbid turn, as is so often done by those not engaged with the quest, or it may be given a healthy one. If he uses the practice to examine the causes of his mistakes and to discover the weaknesses in his character, and then takes the needful steps to eliminate the one and overcome the other, it can only benefit and elevate him.

153

Such retrospective analyses, critical evaluations, and impersonal interpretations of his past must be attempted only in calm periods if the results are not to be emotionally distorted. Against this rule there is nevertheless an exception. When he feels bitter self-reproach about his bygone mistakes or misdeeds, it is well to take advantage of such an anti-ego attitude while it lasts.

154

During this passive and receptive phase of meditation, various events, happenings, and objects return to consciousness again and in this way the meditator has an opportunity to deal with them from a higher standpoint or from a fresh and different one. He may also receive information or knowledge in this way about the thing psychically or intuitively which he did not have before.

155

The tough, harsh analysis of one's own errors should not end there, should not terminate in agonized self-torment. It must be counter-balanced by positive attitudes.

156

It is possible to watch, by introspection, the happenings in the mind. But to do this accurately and adequately, the detachment fostered by the witness-attitude must be present. Part of his consciousness must stand aside, cool, untouched by emotions, and independent of ego.

157

To search around inside oneself may be a morbid or a dangerous affair, if it has no high objective.

158

He should try to put himself into the future and look back on this present period.

159

The unconscious motives may be only half-hidden from the conscious mind and deliberately ignored or may be completely sunk.

160

In order to unmask his sensitivities and recognize them for the hidden motives that they usually are, the seeker must deliberately subject himself to the most intensive and gruelling self-analysis. Every disguise must be stripped bare. Every stumbling block must be penetrated. Every form of self-deception must be uprooted. His highest aspirations must undergo the same examination and treatment as his lower characteristics. The results—if he perseveres and is strictly honest—are more than likely to shock him, or, at least, to lead to some startling discoveries. Such self-analysis will naturally lead to the seeking of a humbler, more selfless, and more worthwhile way of life.

161

Recognition of mistakes is essential but should not be dwelt on in a purely negative fashion. The Teacher may indicate that recognition alone is not enough; more effort should be put forth to overcome them. But if he were to set down all the faults and defects still observable, his student might become so dejected that he would throw away his opportunities. On the other hand, if the student is earnest, certain virtues and favourable tendencies would also be evident, and these, set down fully, might cause him to become so elated that he would overestimate his possibilities.

162

An analytical remorse may be helpful in uncovering faults or deficiencies, but a morbid remorse will hinder betterment and paralyse aspiration.

163

The habit of dissolving his customary egoistic regard for himself is well worth cultivating repeatedly for a period. For several reasons it is good to learn this art of detachment, to practise becoming a second and separate person, to watch himself and note the different reactions to the day's events. During this exercise, he should place his attention upon some decisive event from his past which meant much to him at the time. He is to consider it as impartially and coolly as if it had happened to another man. He must keep out personal emotion from this special survey as he analyses the whole happening from beginning to end, from causes to results. He is to judge it critically and where he finds his former attitude or acts faulty, reshape it or them mentally to the correct form.

164

You will face a moment in your mental self-analysis when fear will descend upon you, when the dread of disintegration will shadow you—for you will reach for the bottom.

165

If his past mistakes were made out of ignorance but in utter sincerity, he need not spend the rest of his life tormenting himself with vain reproaches.

166

He must search himself for the real motives behind his conduct, which are not always the same as those he announces to other persons or even to himself.

167

He alone knows what the real man is like behind the image which others have of him. But he knows it only under the colouring of extenuations, justifications, and repressions, with which he tints it.

168

It would be easy for him to comb through the surface of his character during this self-examination and yet miss the real motivations lying beneath it.

169

A true appraisal should list both the good and bad qualities of a seeker. It should invent nothing, hide nothing.

170

This scrutiny must penetrate his character deeply. It must look first for the psychological causes of his dismal failures—the faults, the indisciplines, and the inadequacies.

171

To recognize our guilt in tracing the source of certain troubles is always hard—so blinded by egoism are we. The philosophic discipline aims at creating the requisite personal disinterestedness in us.

172
Remember that in examining yourself it is unlikely that you will be impartial.

173
Introspective self-examination of this kind, done in this way, is not morbid and unhealthy. On the contrary, it is helpful and healthy.

174
If he studies past experience in this impersonal and analytic way, what he learns will help him begin a self-training of character and intellect that will stop the commission of further mistakes or sins and eliminate the fallacies of belief or habit.

175
Such self-examination will be fruitful if it suppresses nothing and reveals everything, more especially if it seeks out failings rather than virtues.

176
Philosophy does not encourage a morbid dwelling over past sins, lost opportunities, or errors committed. That merely wastes time and saps power. The analysis finished, the lesson learned, the amendment made, what is left over must be left behind. Why burden memory and darken conscience with the irreparable if no good can be done by it?

177
The result of this unflattering examination will be that he will pass for a while from self-love to self-despising.

178
He must scrutinize motives and find out to what extent they are pure or impure, sincere or hypocritical, factual or deceptive.

179
He must regard his faults with sincerity and without flinching. He should be too much in earnest to hide them from himself or to seek plausible excuses for them.

180
He must practise severe self-judgement and ruthless self-criticism by looking at his imperfections with courage and honesty, subordinating smug vanity until the revelation of himself to himself comes out clearly and truthfully in the end.

181
He will find that undoing his past mistakes will be hampered or helped by his capacity to recognize them for what they really are.

182
By searching himself and studying his past, he may be able to determine at what point he deviated from the correct path of living or right thinking.

183

When the impact of the truth about his own underlying motives is first felt, he is likely to sink into grave discouragement.

184

It may be disheartening to review from time to time the present state of his own failings but it is better than pretending they are not there and getting tripped by them in consequence.

185

He should not refuse to recognize his own deficiencies, but he need not either exaggerate or minimize them while doing so.

186

He must explore his own past and glean the lessons from it. He must analyse the personal and environmental factors which composed each situation or influenced them, and he must do all this as adequately and thoroughly as possible.

187

He should study his brilliant successes and sorry failures for the different lessons which both can teach him.

188

When, at long last, he is able to burrow beneath the very foundation of his ego, the meditation approaches its best value.

189

He has to stand aside from himself and observe the chief events of his life with philosophic detachment. Some of them may fill him with emotions of regret or shame, others with pride and satisfaction, but all should be considered with the least possible egoism and the greatest possible impartiality. In this way experience is converted into wisdom and faults are extracted from character.

190

It is out of such reflections that we now learn what fools we made of ourselves just when we believed we were doing something clever, what fallacious ideas we held just when we believed the truth within our grasp.

191

Each separate recollection of these past errors is in itself a repeated punishment.

192

Let him throw all his experiences into this scrupulous analysis. It does not matter whether, on the surface, they are important or not. So long as there is some instructive significance to be distilled from them, some moral lesson, philosophic principle, practical guidance, or metaphysical truth, they are grist for his mill. Most events and episodes that he can remember, the trivial as well as the tragic, are to be reconsidered from this strictly impersonal point of view and made to serve his spiritual development.

193

To make the mind acquainted with itself by watching its thought while in a state of detachment, is a main purpose of such spiritual exercises.

194

It is in such relaxed periods, when the panorama of his own personal history filters through his mind, letting the events pass but keeping back their lessons, that he can practise an impersonality which profits his future lives.

195

A technique of remembrance is necessary to discover what lessons are still needed by constantly analysing one's whole past life, judging all major decisions and actions in the light of the results to which they led, and of the effects which they had both upon himself and upon others. Such reflection should be done not only in the form of meditation, but also at odd times when the mood comes upon him, no matter what he is doing.

196

It is an experience when not only known mistakes, moral or worldly, stand out sharply before his mind's eye but others, hitherto unrecognized as such, are seen for the first time.

197

Every aspirant knows that when this self-examination reveals the presence of wrong attitudes he must fight them.

Moral self-betterment exercises

198

In early periods of development, it is necessary to include in the meditation period exercises for the constructive building of character. They will then be preparatory to the exercises for mind-stilling.

199

The imagination which sports with personal fancies and plays with egotistic fictions may be harmful to philosophic pursuit of truth, but the imagination which creatively sets out to picture the further steps in development is helpful to it.

200

The philosophical use of meditation not only differs from its mystical use in some ways but also extends beyond it. A most important part of the student's meditations must be devoted to moral self-improvement. When he has made some progress in the art of meditation, he has acquired a powerful weapon to use in the war against his own baser attributes and personal weaknesses. He must reflect upon his own mistaken conduct of the past and the present, repent its occurrence, and resolve to rid himself of the weaknesses which led him into it. He must contemplate the possibility of similar situations developing in the future and picture himself acting in them as his better self would have him act. If, instead of using meditation periods only for lolling negatively in the emotional peace which they yield, he will reserve a part of those periods for positive endeavour to wield dominion over those attributes and weaknesses, he will find that the fortified will and intensified imagination of such moments become truly creative. For they will tend to reproduce themselves successfully in his subsequent external conduct. That which he has pictured to himself and about himself during meditation will suddenly come back to his consciousness during the post-meditative periods, or it will even express itself directly in external deeds when their meditative stimuli have been quite forgotten.

201

Creative Thought: This exercise makes use of one of man's most valuable powers—spiritualized imagination. Everyone possesses the image-making faculty to some degree and artists to an extraordinary degree. The student must strive to get something of the artist's imaginative capacity and then ally it with the illuminating and dynamizing power of his higher self. But this can only be successfully and perfectly achieved if, first, the images are harmonious with the divine will for him and if, second, he has developed to the second degree of meditation. But not many can fulfil these conditions. Nevertheless, all may attempt and benefit by the exercise, even though their attempt will be halting, their benefit partial, and the results imperfect. For even then it will be greatly worthwhile. This is the right way to make imagination serve him, instead of letting it evaporate in useless fantasies or harmful daydreams.

202

This exercise accepts and utilizes the power of imagery, the faculty of visualization, which is one of the features distinguishing the man from the animal. It places desirable patterns in the mind and places them there regularly and persistently, until they begin to influence both the way we approach fortune and the fortune which approaches us. These patterns concern the self's character and the self's future, portray the ideal and predict the morrow.

203

Meditation directed towards the reform and improvement of character should have a twofold approach. On the one hand, it should be analytic and logical self-criticism, exposing the faults and weaknesses, the unpleasant results to which they lead both for oneself and for others. On the other hand, it should be creative and imaginative picturing of the virtues and qualities which are the contrary opposites of the faults and shortcomings exposed by the other approach. The meditator should picture himself expressing these traits in action.

204

In the meditational work upon eradicating the fault, he may begin by trying to remember as many occasions as he can where he showed it, and express repentance for them.

205

The act reproduces the picture he had painted of it in his imagination. His ideal character, his perfect pattern of conduct need no longer remain unrealizable or frustrating.

206

The labour on himself does not mean a moral labour only: although that will be included, it is only preparatory. It means also, and much more, giving attention to *his* attention, noting where his thoughts are going, training them to come back *into himself* and thus, at the end, to come to rest at their source—undisturbed Consciousness.

207

He is able to rise above his own limited experience by imaginatively absorbing other people's experience.

208

The evil consequences of yielding to certain desires forms a fit theme for this kind of meditation exercise.

209

We must bring our questions and problems to the silent hour with the desire to know what is really for our own good, rather than for our personal gratification.

210

He who develops along these lines through the creative power of meditation, will eventually find that his instinct will spontaneously reject the promptings of his lower self and immediately accept the intuitions of his higher self.

211

There are two factors which retard or accelerate, prevent or consummate the result he seeks to achieve by the creative use of thought. The first is his individual destiny, preordained from birth. The second is the harmony or disharmony between his personal wish and the Overself's impersonal will for his own evolution. The more he can take a detached view of his life, separating his needs from his desires, the more is his wish likely to be fulfilled by the use of this method.

212

From these sessions he can draw attractive qualities—strong in will-power, relaxed in nerves, and ever-smiling in face. From them, too, he is likely to renew more courageously than before his personal commitment to the Quest.

213

He should analytically study, warmly admire, and imaginatively possess the characteristic qualities of Sagehood. They form an excellent topic for dwelling on during the meditation period.

214

These rare natures who dispense goodwill and radiate tolerance, who rise calmly and without apparent effort above anger-provoking situations and highly irritating persons, represent an ideal. It is not an impossible one and may be realized little by little if he faithfully practises constructive meditation upon the benefits of calmness as well as upon the disadvantages of anger.

215

The exercise deals with persons, things, situations, and problems which exist only in imaginary circumstances inside his own mind. But otherwise he is to give it all the reality he can, to see, hear, touch, and smell internally as vividly as if he were using these same senses externally. Except for any special modification which the philosophic discipline may call for, every act is to be done mentally just as he would do it in real life.

216

He is to picture to himself the exact quality he seeks to gain, just as it feels within himself and expresses through his actions.

217

A useful meditation exercise is to create in advance through imagination, any meeting with others likely to happen in the near future or with those he lives with, works with, or is associated with, which may result in provocation, irritability, or anger. The student should see the incident in his mind's eye before it actually happens on the physical plane, and constructively picture himself going through it calmly, serenely, and self-controlled—just as he would like himself to be, or ought to be, at the time.

218

Meditation is more fruitful if part of it is devoted to reflection on ideals, qualities, and truths needed by the student at the time.

219

Meditation should be begun with a short, silent prayer to the Overself, humbly beseeching guidance and Grace. This may be done either by kneeling in the Western fashion or by sitting in the Oriental fashion. After offering his prayer, the aspirant should sit down in the position he customarily uses in meditation, close his eyes, and try to forget everything else. He may then form a mental picture of his own face and shoulders, as though he were looking at himself from an impersonal point of view. He should think of the person in the picture as a stranger. Let him first consider the other's faults and weaknesses, but, later, as a changed person, endowed with ideal qualities, such as calmness, aspiration, self-mastery, spirituality, and wisdom. In this way, he will open a door for the Higher Self to make its messages known to him in the form of intuitions. He should be prepared to devote years to intense efforts in self-examination and self-improvement. This is the foundation for the later work. Once the character has been ennobled, the way to receiving guidance and Grace will be unobstructed.

220

The student must earnestly try to learn the lessons of his own experience by considering situations as impersonally and unemotionally as he can. By meditating on them in a cool, analytical way—ferreting out past blunders and not sparing himself—he may uncover some of the weaknesses impeding his progress. He should then make every effort to correct them.

221

The problem of trying to control temper is one that is frequently presented. It can only be solved slowly under ordinary circumstances. During meditation, he should picture himself in a temper and then deliberately construct an imaginative scene wherein he exercises more and more discipline over himself. These mental pictures when sufficiently repeated and with sufficient intensity will tend to reappear before his mind's eye at the moment when he does actually fall into a temper.

222

The method of visualizing what you wish to materialize may only serve to fatten the ego and block spiritual advancement, which is what happens with most of its practisers. But if it is resorted to only when the mind has been harmonized, even for a few moments, with the Overself, it will not only be harmless but also successful. For at such a time and in such a condition, nothing will be wished for that will not be conformable to the higher welfare of the individual.

223

Although an uninformed, unchecked, and unguided imagination can carry him into dangerous places or on useless journeys, can bog him down in utter self-deception or influence him to delude others, nevertheless when it has the right qualities the imaginative faculty can carry him far along the spiritual path. It can help him to create from within himself good qualities and bettered attitudes which, ordinarily, the discipline of painful events would have created from without. It is needed for visualizing the Ideal, for acquiring virtues, and for holding the Symbol in meditation. Hence the old Rosicrucian adept, Mejnour, who is one of the leading characters in that interesting occult novel, *Zanoni*, says: "Young man, if thy imagination is vivid . . . I will accept thee as my pupil." And Bulwer Lytton, the author, himself an experienced occultist, remarks: "It was to this state that Mejnour evidently sought to bring the Neophyte. . . . For he who seeks to discover, must first reduce himself into a kind of abstract idealism, and be rendered up, in solemn and sweet bondage, to the faculties which contemplate and imagine."

224

Analyse, understand, and confess the sin; express remorse, resolve to act rightly in the future and finally *throw yourself on God's mercy*.

225

There is no psychic danger for the worthy in the pre-visioning exercises, but there would be for people dominated by low motives and expressing unpurified emotions.

226

It is possible by the power of such meditations, creatively to shape the character and deepen the consciousness of oneself.

227

It is not enough to visualize oneself living the ideal; one must also learn to retain the picture.

228

Creative Thought Exercise: He visualizes possible events, pre-examines his behavior on meeting them, and re-shapes these anticipated thoughts and deeds on higher principles.

229

Creative Meditation Exercise: He may think of probable meetings during the next day, if he is practising at night, or of the coming day if at morn, of events that are likely to happen then, and of places where he may have to go. Alongside of that he may imagine how he ought to conduct himself, how to think and talk under those circumstances. And always, if the exercise is to prove its worth, he should take the standpoint of his better, nobler, wiser self, of the Overself.

230

He must train himself during solitary hours in the qualities he seeks to express during active ones. Creative imagination and concentrated thinking are the means for this self-training.

231

All dominant tendencies and ruling ideas which are of an undesirable character constitute fruitful sources of future action. If, by such creative meditation, we eradicate them we also eradicate the possibility of undesirable action in the future.

232

Out of these quiet moments there will emerge into active day-to-day life those controls of character, those disciplines of emotion, which elevate the human entity.

233

When you have climbed the peak of this meditation, you have entered into your most powerful creative moments. It is well therefore at such a time to make your first step in descent to ordinary consciousness a step in self-improvement. Take some defect in character that needs to be overcome and imaginatively treat yourself for it like a doctor treating a patient.

234

Every helpful self-suggestion given at this point of contemplation will germinate like a seed and produce its visible fruit in due time.

235

The meditation practices of the Jesuits were based on the same principle. Their exercises transformed men's character. The student had to experience imaginatively what he hoped to realize one day physically. The duality which is affirmed and pictured intensely in meditation becomes materialized in time.

236

Such constructive meditation on positive qualities will help to eliminate wrong fears from a man's life and increase his strength to endure the vicissitudes of modern existence.

237

By constantly meditating upon the Ideal, the creative power of imagination gradually implants the likeness of its qualities, attributes, and virtues in him. It becomes, indeed, a second self with which he increasingly identifies himself.

238

The work of meditation may eventually become a transforming one. If the meditator, while resting in this creative quietude, earnestly strives to re-educate his character, impersonalize his attitude, and strengthen his spirituality, he can develop an inner life that must inevitably bring marked and deep changes in his outer life.

239

And it is through such persistent reflections upon experience that his character slowly alters, thus confirming Socrates' saying: "Virtue can be learned." The ideal pictures for him the sort of man he wants to be.

240

It is a useful exercise to spend time recollecting the previous day's actions, situations, and happenings in the same order in which they manifested. Those persons who appear in them should be recalled as vividly as they were then seen, and their voices heard as clearly.

241

Right reflection about past experiences, together with determination to take himself in hand, will lead the student to a more worthwhile future and smooth the path ahead.

242

This exercise requires him to review the day just past from the hour of waking out of sleep to the hour of going back to bed at night.

243

The value of taking this kind of a backward look at the day just finished is far more than it seems. For everything in him will benefit—his character, his destiny, and even his after-death experience.

244

The exercise is practised when he retires for the night and is lying in the dark. He goes backward in time and recalls all that has happened during the day—the persons he has met, the places he has visited, and what he has done. The picture should be made as fully detailed as possible and cover the entire field from the moment he awoke in the morning until the moment he lay down to begin the exercise. If he has talked with others, he notes the particular tone and accent of their voices, as well as hearing the sentences themselves. He tries to insert as many little items into his visualization as will render it sharp, realistic, and convincing. Out of this background he selects those of his actions and words, as well as those of his feelings and thoughts, which call for amendment or correction or discipline. He is to cull out of the day's episodes and happenings not only what his conscience or judgement tell him call for corrective work in meditation but also what is most significant for his spiritual purpose and what is likely to prove most fruitful for his creative work in meditation.

245

All will come under review periodically—the management of his relationships with others, his personal, social, and professional activities, the management of his life. But all this scrutiny is to be done from a standpoint higher than the ordinary one, less ego-governed and more impersonal. Therefore it should be done only and preferably at such times as this mood is upon him, if it is to be effectively done.

246

He should, for the purposes of this exercise look back a number of years to the points in his personal history where opportunity was missed or decision was wrong or action could have been better. Then, using his imaginative faculty, he should reconstruct the situations and mentally, correcting his past errors, do what he ought then to have done. From there, he should proceed to trace the probable consequences down through the years.

5

VISUALIZATIONS, SYMBOLS

The type of meditation called discursive—by which is meant the kind which rambles on in reflective or logical thinking—does not suit every student. Several who have essayed it without success after repeated attempts are really temperamentally unsuited for it, yet they need not abandon hope. There is another method of meditation which is actually easier, worth trying, and possibly better suited to their temperament. During a wide experience with dealing with Western students, I found that those who have failed with discursive meditation are not necessarily more lacking in good potentialities than those who have succeeded. It is simply that they have found the method which will draw out the potentialities that they possess.

Visualizations

2

Meditation exercises whose method is to visualize a form, pattern, or happening appeal to, and are easier for, some people.

3

The philosophic mode of meditation makes use of imagination as much as it makes use of reason. Through the use of these faculties, when directed toward abstract themes and high objects, it leads the meditator to universal spiritual intuitions that in their own turn will conduct him to philosophic experiences. Thus mental picturing and mental thinking, when rightly used, assist his liberation just as when wrongly used they retard it.

4

There are two faculties worth developing. They are the faculty of observation and the faculty of imagination or visualization. We look, but see little, for we do not notice much of the detail. We are unable to imagine clearly, sharply, and vividly. We lack the ability to recreate a physical scene purely in the mind.

5

Those persons who are unable to "see" and hold these symbolic pictures through their mind's eye with sufficient vividness, may still take heart. The capacity to do so can develop itself as a result of repeated practice in this exercise. Even if at first the picture seems far-off, faint, blurred, and vague; even if it appears only fitfully and fragmentarily; by degrees the persistent effort to hold it will be rewarded with the ability to do so continually as well as clearly.

6

As a support for the beginning period of practice itself, as a means to fix attention, a particular physical object or sound may be chosen. He may gaze at a chink of light shining in a dark room or listen to the pendulum-swing of a metronome. Whatever is thus isolated from the outer world for concentration, is used merely as a jumping-off platform from which to enter the inner world.

7

Tratak is a technique for focusing the eyes, as unblinkingly as possible on a special point—this could be a black dot inside a black circle on a white sheet or wall—until tears fill them.

8

Some yogis try to tranquillize the mind by practising the gazing exercise. They mark a black point on a white wall, or draw a black circle on the wall, and then sit down opposite it so that their eyes are exactly opposite. The body is kept quite still and they continually stare at the mark for as long as their experience or their teacher prescribes.

9

The gazing exercise can be suitably applied to the empty sky by day or night, to a star, a tree, etc.

10

A single colourful flower placed in a slim vase may be used for the gazing exercise.

11

Among physical objects a flower, a stick, or a flame have traditionally been used.

12

To quieten thoughts, it is helpful to some practitioners to visualize a globe of blue light—the so-called Wedgewood or powder blue—and to concentrate on it as fixedly as they can.

13

Meditation may also be made on a colour which, if harmonious to the meditator, will lead him by deepening concentration into a mystical state.

14

The lovely colours brought into the sky by the fall of eventide make a fit object for meditation.

15

A properly directed imagination may be as much a help to his progress as an improperly directed one is a certain hindrance to it. During some exercises for meditation it can be creatively used in a particular way. For instance, the aspirant thinks of his master, if he has one, or of a scriptural personage, if he believes in him, or of an unknown, ideal, beneficent, perfected Being in the angelic world, and imagines him to be "the Gate" to a deeper order of existence. The aspirant then implores him for admittance into this order, for strength to make the passage, and for Grace to become worthy of it. In this curious situation, he has to play a double part. On the one hand, he is to be the person making the request; he must feel intensely, even to the point of shedding tears over what he is mentally crying out for; on the other hand, he is to see him doing so, to be a mere witness of what is happening. Thus at one time he will be part of the scene, at another time merely looking at it. Every detail of it is to be vividly pictured until it carries the feeling of veridical reality.

16

He is to take complete possession of this image, to take hold of it inch by inch.

17

Imagine and believe that the Master is here in your room, sitting in his accustomed chair or position. Then behave and meditate as you would do if in his presence.

18

This exercise requires him to retract his attention inwards until, oblivious of his immediate surroundings, he intently projects certain suggestive mental images into this blankness and holds them determinedly yet calmly. The result will appear later in his ordinary state when the wakeful consciousness will seize these images abruptly and unexpectedly and effectively act upon their suggestions.

19

Imagine a brilliant white light shining forth in the heart and spreading into the entire body.

20

Any visualized form, especially of a living or a dead master, may be used as a focus of concentration.

21

Visualization Exercise: It will help him if, for a few minutes, he stops whatever exercise he is engaged with and projects the mental image of himself doing it successfully.

22

A remarkable, unusual, and excellent exercise in self-perception is to *imagine* himself sitting down to the work of meditation, and going through with it to successful fulfilment of his purpose, all obstacles seen, fought, and eventually pushed aside. *All* this is to be done in his mind, his own person, and its doings becomes the object of concentration. In short, he paints a mental portrait of a meditating man, who is himself.

23

Exercises: Visualize a lovely quiet landscape scene, either from memory or pictures, and think of yourself being there. Feel its peacefulness. Visualize the face of some inspiring person; feel you're in his presence.

24

A suggested theme for this pictorial concentration is that of a spiral pattern like a staircase. The meditator must choose whether it seems to go up or down, guided by intuition.

25

When the mental form on which he is meditating vanishes of its own accord and the mind suddenly becomes completely still, vacant, and perfectly poised, the soul is about to reveal itself. For the psychological conditions requisite to such a revelation have then been provided.

26

It is easier for almost all people to think pictorially rather than abstractly, to form mental images rather than mental conceptions. Although the more difficult feat is also the superior one, this fact can be utilized to promote meditational progress. The mental picture of a dead saint whom the aspirant feels particularly drawn to or of a living guide whom he particularly reveres, makes an excellent object upon which to focus his concentration.

27

I mentioned in *The Quest of the Overself* that radiations from a photograph had been discovered by a scientist I met long ago, Mr. Shrapnell-Smith, and also by another English investigator at that time whose name I can not now remember. Many readers of the book have since then sought for photographs of their gurus and used them as objects for concentration. Not only so, but somewhat later the idea was adopted by healers who used photographs of patients living at a distance to give them absent treatment at a fixed time of the day, the patient himself putting himself in tune with the healer passively and receptively. In connection with these usages of photographs by disciples of gurus and healers of patients, it ought to be pointed out that more effective than using the material object of the photograph is the implantation of the picture in the mind, the mental image itself. In other words, the thought of the guru without any external physical aid or the thought of the patient gives a better connection for the purpose desired. Centuries ago, before photography was invented, gurus knew this principle and many of them told their disciples that wherever they were living the remembrance of the guru would give a link and that the emotional attitude, devotion, reverence, and so forth, linked with the remembrance, would bring back some benefit from the guru.

28

The picture must be perfectly vivid and sharply formed. It must be held for a little while. Then let it slowly fade away into the still centre of your being, absorbed by its light and love.

29

Withdraw attention from everything outside and imagine a radiant, shining Presence within the heart. Visualize it as a pure golden sunny light. Think of it as being pure Spirit.

30

He should study the figure well, note every one of its details carefully, close his eyes, and then try to reproduce the figure again mentally.

31

To place the drawing before you is the first stage. To hold it in your mind is the second one. Hold the mind immobile upon it until a slightly hypnotic state is induced.

32

The mandala is a diagrammatic representation, used by Tibetans and Jains for concentration, usually featuring a square enclosing a circle. Each side of the square has an opening. At the centre of the circle is a figure which is the important part of the picture and to which attention must find its way through the openings and put to rest there, until the deeper mind is reached.

33

No man has complete freedom to use his creative thought-power to its most magical extent, for all men have to share it with the Overself which, being their ruler, also rules the results of their efforts. In a divinely ordered world it would be anarchical to vest full power in unredeemed man.

34

The trained meditator can make any episode of his own past seem as real and near as the present. He is able to create distinct and vivid images of it after so long a time as even several years.

35

These image-building powers can be expanded until mere thoughts seem external things.

36

The gazing exercise may be alternated by simply looking towards a point midway between both half-closed, half-opened eyes and keeping them fixed in this position.

37

Visualized figures can be concentrated on with such intensity as to make them seem like real ones. Such an experience which is sought in certain meditation disciplines is used as an illustration of the tenet that everything known is, in the end, a mental experience.

38

The meditator should sustain the chosen mental image for as long as his power allows.

39

The first stage of this exercise consists in withdrawing attention from the object or landscape at which he is looking, and using it instead to observe the eyes themselves; they remain open. The second stage is to withdraw attention still further and try to become aware of the observing mind alone.

40

The eyes look out on the landscape in a vague general way, without focussing on any particular object. This belongs to the second stage, whereas specific concentration belongs to the first and more elementary one.

41

It may help the meditator to picture the world along with his body dissolving into space until all distinctions stop.

42

The use of imagined forms, scenes, and persons is only for beginners in meditation: it is to be left behind when the object has been sufficiently achieved. As Saint John of the Cross says, "For though such forms and methods of meditation may be necessary in order to inflame and fill their souls with love through the instrumentality of sense, and though they may serve as remote means of union, through which souls must usually pass to the goal of spiritual repose—still they must so make use of them as to pass beyond them, and not dwell upon them forever." Such a use of pictured forms must include the master's too. Saint John of the Cross even includes Christ's. For many this practice is a step forward, but aspirants must not linger all their lifetime on a particular step if they really seek to climb higher.

43

It is a common practice for religious or mystical Indians to meditate upon their favourite deity until they get the experience of being completely identified with it of becoming one with it. This experience is then considered a grace given by the deity itself. But what else is it to the outside observer, however sympathetic he may be to such practices if he is at all critical at the same time, than a process involving the creative imagination and what is the end result but an imaginary one?

44

In the end the symbol must be dropped; the reality it points at must alone be held by the mind when it seeks a deeper level of meditation.

Symbols

45

The Spiritual Symbol represents in a symbolic language what is usually represented in spoken or written words.

46

The Spiritual Symbol serves a threefold purpose. It is an aid to concentration of attention. It expresses and teaches a universal truth or law. It evokes an intuitive perception of this truth or law. Moreover, it may even bring about a certain moral effect upon the character provided the foregoing three purposes have been successfully realized.

47

The cross is a symbol given to man by the creative imagination of his race's early seers. Its flat crossbar is his ordinary everyday life which he shares with all other men. Its upright bar is his higher spiritual life which he shares with God. The entire figure tells him that crucifixion of his ego is resurrection of his spirit—normally and daily dead in the material life.

48

If the paper photograph of a living sage or the bronze statue of a departed one helps to remember his achievement, to realize his ideas, or even to touch his aura, why should we not use it? It is only when we put it to superstitious uses that we then degrade the sage's name and harm our own progress.

49

Just as a photograph contains certain magnetic radiations which link it with the person pictured thereon but which vanish with his death, so the book of a living author offers an activated link between his mind, which is incarnated in its pages, and those readers who look to him and his writings for help. Although at his death the contact with his actual mind is broken, the contact with the way in which it worked is not.

50

The Spiritual Symbols are given to pupils who are highly intellectual, professional, or active-minded as a means of (1) allaying mental restlessness; and (2) constructively working on the inner bodies, since these forms are in correspondence with the actual construction of (a) an atom, and (b) the universe.(P)

51

The Cross symbolizes personally the utter surrender of the ego in desiring and willing impersonally. The vertical line means consciousness transcending the world, the horizontal one means consciousness in the world: the complete figure shows the perfect balance needed for a perfect human being.

52

The geometric designs which appear in the stained glass windows of so many churches, on the painted frescoes of so many tombs, and in the architectural plans of so many temples are sacred symbols useful for this purpose. They have not been selected by chance but by illumined men, for their number is very small compared with the hundreds of possible group-ings and arrangements also available. The measurements of the different parts of each geometric symbol follow certain proportions which are not fixed by personal whim but by cosmic order. This is why Pythagoras declared that number is the basis of the universe. The same proportions of 1-4-7-13 exist in the distances of the sun to its planets and asteroids, in their movements. They were used in Stonehenge, in the Greek temple, and in the Gizeh Pyramid. Each symbol corresponds to some cosmic fact; it is not arbitrary or imaginary or accidental. Its value for meditation practice does not end with promoting concentration but extends beyond that. Its power to affect man derives also from its connection with the divine World-Idea, whose perfection and beauty it reflects.

53

The purpose of using the symbol has been achieved when the user actually feels the luring presence, the inspiring force of the spiritual quality it symbolizes. He should then put it aside and concentrate on the feeling only.

54

A practical rule which applies to all the pictures, diagrams, and designs is to visualize them as standing vertically upright, not as lying flat as when drawn on paper.

55

The artists who drew these spiritual diagrams in the first instance belong to far-off antiquity. They were mostly holy men, monks, or priests. Cen-turies ago, as they meditated on the mysteries of God, the universe, and man, they entered a state of mystical revelation and saw eternal truths, hidden realities, laws and forces of the universe. When they tried to communicate their intuitive knowledge to others, they felt guided to do so in the form of the symbolic pictures. Even today these visions sometimes arise of their own accord, offering themselves spontaneously to the mind's eye, when the intuition is trying to find another form of expression than the verbal one for what it knows or what it seeks to communicate.

56

The spiritual emblem combining a circle and some other form stands for reconciliation of the Overself and the ego, for integration of man's higher and lower nature.

57

There are used in India, Tibet, and China meditation symbols of a purely geometric kind. They may be quite simple or quite intricate in design. They are drawn in black ink on white paper or parchment, or they are embroidered in coloured silk panels on tapestries, or they are painted directly on monastery walls. The designs include completed circles, perfect arcs, equilibrated triangles, rigid squares, pyramids, pentagons, sexagons, octagons, and rhomboids. It is believed that by concentrating on these geometric diagrams, with their straight undeviating lines, some help is obtained toward disciplining the senses, balancing the mind, and developing logicality of thought.

58

The Pyramid is a perfect symbol of both spiritual balance and spiritual completeness.

59

Symbols are diagrams or paintings on paper pertaining to the chosen Ideal or deity worshipped.

60

The concentration of attention on the chosen symbol must occupy itself with reflections which rise above their merely pictorial value.

61

Colours enter into the composition of a Spiritual Symbol. Each is significant, each corresponds to a cosmic or a human force.

62

The spiritual diagram takes the shape of a square combined with a circle when it stands for a reconciliation of opposites, for the equilibrium of their forces and the balance of their functions.

63

Manjusri is depicted with sword in hand, meaning that he cuts away one's illusions.

64

Whether it be called a mandala, as with Tibetan Buddhism, or a yantra, as with Tantrik Hinduism, it consists of a geometrical design, or a linear diagram, or some non-human, non-animal, non-pictorial representation by a drawing which is taken as a symbol of God, or of the higher self. Concentrated attention upon it is supposed to lead man closer to this self, like any other form of worship.

65

At the apex of a pyramid there is only a single point. At its base there are innumerable points. The tenet of the One appearing as the Many is well symbolized by this ancient figure.

66

When the spiritual emblem takes the form of a circle, it represents the Wholeness which is the ideal state of the fully developed and equilibrated man.

67

The higher self should be invoked at the beginning of the deliberate work done on these affirmations and symbols. The latter may then become its channels, if other conditions have been fulfilled.

68

The gesture of right thumb tip joined in circular form to the forefinger tip represents, in Hindu-Buddhist statues, giving a blessing of the truth. The same gesture also appears in some Greek Orthodox Christian icons as a blessing.

69

The Rising Sun was originally a symbol of the Overself in relation to man's conscious development.

70

The Swastika originally had two meanings: as a wheel revolving clockwise it was the symbol of the unfolding World-Idea; as a radiant circle it was the pictograph of the invisible Sun behind the sun, which was the proper object of human worship.

71

The symbol is intended to create a corresponding mood, or to arouse a latent force.

72

The highest of all symbols is that which expresses God.

73

The thought-form whose reverence helps him to keep concentrated, the mental image whose worship holds his attention quite absorbed, justifies a place for itself in the meditator's method. Only at an advanced hour may he rightly put them aside. But when that hour arrives, he should not hesitate to do so. The devotional type of meditation, if unaccompanied by higher metaphysical reflection, will not yield results of a lasting character although it will yield emotional gratification of an intense character. Overself is only an *object* of meditation so long as he knows it only as something apart from himself. That is good but not good enough. For he is worshipping a graven image, not the sublime reality. He has to rise still higher and reach it, not as a separate "other," but as his very self.

74

Philosophy recognizes that the human mind cannot even grasp the concept of the Void that is a Spirit save after a long course of study and reflection, much less realize it. Therefore it provides for this situation by offering a Symbol of that Void, a picture or an idea of which the mind can easily take hold as a preliminary until he can make the direct attempt.

75

This Symbol will become a focal centre in his mind for all those spiritual forces which he has to receive intuitively. From it he will get inspiration; to it he must give veneration.

76

Thus the symbol becomes equated with the Soul, with entry into and memory of it. The indefinite and formless, the remote and abstract Reality takes on a nature which, being approachable, comprehensible, and visible, can help him seek, worship, and love that Reality in a personal and human way.

77

The portrayal of Gautama as a seated meditating figure symbolizes his basic message. This was really, and quite simply, "Be still—empty yourself—let out the thoughts, the desires, and the ego which prevent this inner stillness."

78

What is the inner significance of the rosary? At the time of meditation, the worldly man is harassed by worldly thoughts. The rosary teaches that until unimpeded meditation becomes possible, the aspirant should persevere, leaving behind thought after thought. The beads represent thoughts and they are pushed back. The thread passing through the beads represents "the all-pervading ideal." With patience and perseverance, thoughts are subdued and, as a result of unimpeded meditation, the ideal is realized. The head bead which is bigger than the rest represents the point of realization, that is, God, in whom the universe has its birth and in whom it ends.

79

There is a difference between the symbol which only tells us that a higher reality exists and the symbol which not only tells us that but also inspires, leads, informs, and helps us to its attainment.

80

The symbol is to be no mere abstraction, no formal usage, but a living presence.

81

When a Buddha figure has its palms turned upward with the thumbs touching, this symbolizes unwavering faith.

82

The strength which he cannot find in himself, he may draw from the Symbol. In that is release from self-weakening doubts, is the power to achieve greater things.

83

The Swastika is an ancient symbol used in Tibet, in India, and in China. It is closely related to another symbol, the Cross. The Swastika bespeaks the fixed unmoving and everlasting centre of a circle whose circumference is the ever-changing, ever-moving world-process.

84

The Swastika is both a meaningful symbol and a picture of what actually happens. The ever-moving vibration of the ultimate atom goes forward and right in a circle to bring a world into being and to maintain it, but it moves backward and left to deteriorate and eventually destroy it. (This is mirrored in the big dipper, too.)

85

The circle is also used as a symbol of complete self-mastery.

86

There have been many opinions about the symbolism of the Pyramid. The Freemasons, the Theosophists, and others have put forward their views. Since the actual structure of the Pyramid stood upon a temple built like a cube, at least in the case where the famous Sphinx and the Great Pyramid are concerned, the whole figure should be taken into account when analysing its symbolism. The base, cubically shaped, represents both balance and stability: the visible pyramid, triangular in form, represents aspiration and the Quest.

87

If men cannot find a human channel in whom they can believe as mediating the higher power to them, then they usually feel the need of finding one in whom they can believe as a symbol of it.

88

A symbol is a message from his higher self to his personal self. It is intended to give him hope and faith for the future as well as to encourage him to fresh efforts in developing a new life out of the ashes of the old one.

89

A figure or photograph may give off a vibration of attained peace. If we are sensitive enough to respond, we begin to share it.

90

Men who cannot absorb the subtle concept of the Spirit, who cannot grasp the idea of infinite and eternal being, may yet absorb, and therefore be helped by, the concept of its human Channel, may yet visualize and be inspired by its human *symbol*.

91

What the mantra does for sound, the yantra does for sight. It is a graphic representation, pictorial or geometrical, full of philosophic significance about the vanity of earthly existence. In shape, it is either square or circular (when it is renamed *mandala*). It is used first to fix the mind and then to pass beyond it.

92

The Polynesian and Hawaiian traditions wove sacred symbolic patterns into cloths in certain combinations and hung the cloth as a tapestry to gaze upon. The results, spread over time or spectacularly swift, were inner peace and spiritual uplift.

93

The practical use of the Spiritual Symbol requires it to represent himself, or the relation between the different parts of himself, or the whole Cosmos.

94

What are these symbols but attempts to make use of art for man's loftiest purposes—the transforming of his consciousness?

95

The Far Eastern symbols are divided into two classes: simple geometric diagrams and elaborate pictures of Nature or of Enlightened Men. The first class appears also in the Near Eastern traditional patterns.

96

The image of the Magic Circle or globe expresses the goal of Wholeness as exemplified in the true, complete, fully developed, individualized, "redeemed" man.

97

Jung found that certain symbols were present in the ceremonial art of primitive religions as well as in the dreams of contemporary persons. He concluded that they were universal and archetypal, projected by the collective inner being of humans.

98

Rama Prasad writes: "The tantrik philosophers had symbols to denote almost every idea. This was necessary because they held that if the human mind were fixed on any object with sufficient strength for a certain time, it was sure by the force of will to attain that object. The attention was secured by constantly muttering certain words and thus keeping the idea always before the mind. Symbols were used to denote every idea. 'Hrim' denotes modesty. 'Klim' denotes love."

99

The superior type of aspirant can dispense with symbols, but this type is much less frequently found.

100

In the animal kingdom we find that boa constrictors can practise union with their mates for a longer period than other creatures. Why does the Hindu religion honour the serpent as a symbol of the highest knowledge? Why did Jesus say, "Be ye shrewd as serpents?" And why did Gautama the Buddha receive the cobra as his protector against the sun's fierce rays when he sat in the final session of meditation before attaining Nirvana?

101

The symbol is to be remembered and revered daily.

102

The first value of the symbol is that it at once focuses attention, concentrates thought, arouses love, and strengthens faith. The second is that it automatically reminds the aspirant of the higher state, being, and power.

103

The sign made by joining the thumb to the tip of the forefinger of the right hand so as to form a circle shows that the person knows the highest truth. It appears in both Hindu (atman is one with Brahman) and Greek Orthodox sacred pictures.

104

Many members of a group use their master's face for the purpose. Many Hindus choose the deity they worship for the mental image to be meditated on. Jesuits choose Christ's figure, the Rosicrucians a rose.

105

The image, thought, or name of a spiritual giant gives a point of concentration and helps to settle the wandering mind.

106

The exponents of some yoga methods have minutely described, in their books, seven centres or "lotus-flowers" or "whirling wheels" as they are termed, which are situated in the "soul-body" at intervals from the base of the spine up to the crown of the head but which work in intimate relation with similar places in the physical body. Elaborate diagrams have also been drawn to make plainer their claims about this remarkable feature of spiritual anatomy.

On its practical side, the system affords a basis for redirecting attention, a method of providing useful points for concentrating it as a yoga exercise. It is easier for undeveloped minds, which are unable to entertain abstract metaphysical ideas or to meditate upon them for any length of time, to picture the "centre" in the throat, for example, and fasten their attention upon that. To encourage these novices to undertake such meditations they are lured with the bait of miraculous powers, a different power being associated with each "centre," or with that of visions of gods and goddesses, a different deity being associated with each centre. If the novice practises, he will gain some tranquillity, even if he fails to unfold any powers.

Guru yoga

107

The practice of meditating on the mental image of the master is helpful at the proper time, but the meditator should understand that it is not the most advanced practice. If at any time during it, or after attempting it, he feels drawn to the Void exercise, or to any of the exercises dealing with the formless spirit of Mind, he ought to let himself slip away from the pictorial meditation and pass up into the pure contemplation. He need have no reluctance or hesitation in doing so.

108

There is hope and help for those among the masses who are tired of moribund, orthodox religion but who are not able to make the grade of mysticism. Let them repeat in their heart again and again, day after day, the name of a Spiritual Guide in whose attainment they earnestly believe, who is known to have dedicated himself to service and in whose saving power they are prepared to trust. He may be a man long dead or a living one. They need never have met him but they must have heard something about him. If their faith is not misplaced, if he really is one who had dwelt in the Overself's sacred light, they will get genuine results. If, however, their faith is misplaced and the name represents nothing divine, no results except hallucinatory ones need be expected from this practice. But where the devotion is given to a great soul, it shall surely be rewarded. For the silent repetition of his name, wherever they may be and whatever they may be doing, will in itself become an easy mystical exercise in concentration. No matter how ignorant the devotee may otherwise be, let him do this and out of the infinite Overmind there will presently sound its Grace as an echo of his inner work. The sacred name will thus have become for him a link with the Divine. The Grace which descends is rich and real.

109

The manifestation of the adept to his disciple in meditation may come in different ways to different disciples at first, or in different ways to the same disciple as he progresses. But in general it is: first one sees his picture or image very vividly appearing before the mind's eye; later there is a sense of his nearness or presence along with the picture; in the image he seems to smile or to talk to the disciple and pronounce words of advice and guidance; in the third stage the picture disappears and only the presence is felt; in the fourth stage the disciple comes into tune with the master's spirit. In the fifth and final stage the student relinquishes the teacher.

110

Abrupt recalls to the inner life, when associated with remembrance of the name, or seeing the image of the guide, are intuitions of real value. The student should at once drop all other activities and concentrate on them, giving himself up utterly to the inward-turning of attention they prompt him to practise.

111

It is a recognized yoga-path in the Orient, especially among the Sufis of Persia, Iraq, and Northern Africa, for the sensitive disciple mentally to merge his own individual being in the being of his master during the period of meditation. The master can be anyone in whom he has most faith, to whom he is most devoted, by whom he is most inspired.

112

The yoga of self-identification with an adept is the most effective method and brings the quickest results because it quickly elicits his grace. After all, it is the result that counts. The fact is that inspiration *does* come with the mere thought of him. This yoga-path involves two techniques; first, formal meditation at fixed periods, focused on the master's mental picture and presence and, second, informal remembrance of the master as frequently as possible at any and all times of the day. In both techniques, you are to offer your body to him just as a spiritist medium offers his own to a disincarnate spirit. You are to invite and let him take possession of your mind and body. First, you feel his presence. Then you feel that he takes possession of your body and mind. Next, you feel that you are he (no duality). Finally, he vanishes from consciousness and another being announces itself as your divine soul. This is the goal. You have found your higher self.

113

The disciple should try to feel the master inside himself, sensing his presence and seeing his image at various times. For the master is really there, but must be sought for and felt after. This self-identification with the master is one of the best of short cuts for those who find it difficult to meditate. Even when working or walking, they should suddenly pull themselves up in thought and imagine the master present in them and working or walking through them. Once such a habit is created and properly established, it will not be long before remarkable results are obtained.

114

If the master practises the technique of silent helping from a distance at the very time when his mind is deeply sunk in the mystic heart, and the mental image of the pupil is introduced there, the latter will suddenly have a beautiful experience. He will feel an inner opening and another consciousness will seem to flow in. Then he will sense the real nearness of the master and savour something of the spiritual quality of his aura.

115

The disciple who practises this kind of yoga imagines himself to be the master, thinks and behaves accordingly. He plays this role as if he were acting in a stage drama. He is to imitate the Master's way of meditating, including even the expression of his face at the time, not only in pictorial vision but also in self-identified feeling. The exercise can be done both during the formal daily sessions of his regular program and even at odd moments or in unexpected leisure at other times of the day. The formula is twofold: remembering the master and identifying oneself with him.

116

Now the ultimate use of a mental image, whether of God or guru, is only to help him do without it altogether in the end. For the ultimate aim of a true seeker must always be to become aware of God for himself, to perceive the Real with his own insight, and to understand the truth with his own intelligence. Therefore when he has reached this stage of meditation, when he is able easily to enter into rapport with the presence of the Guide or guru, it has accomplished its work and he must take the next step, which is to let go this presence, or the image which carries this presence, altogether. If he clings unduly to it, he will defeat the very purpose of his practice. The Overself will, of its own accord, eventually complete the work, if he does not so resist, by banishing the image and the presence and itself stepping into the framework of his consciousness. He will then know it as his own very soul, his true self, his sacred centre. He will then feel God within his own being as the pure essence of that being. Any other feeling of any other individual would be sacrilege.(P)

117

The self-identification with the Master consists of lending his spirit in the disciple's body—not the disciple's spirit in the Master's body.

118

The photograph of the teacher is placed immediately in front of the pupil. The latter fixes his gaze upon it and gives the whole energy of his mind to its contemplation. Thus the photograph becomes "printed" on the mental screen. The practice is continued until it can be "seen" with the eyes closed as clearly as with the eyes open. This after-image must then be meditated upon.

119

Photograph the master's face with your mental camera and then carry the picture with you—not, of course, in the foreground of attention but always in its background. When at odd places and odd times you wish to meditate, preface your exercise by gazing intently at the eyes in your mental picture for a minute or two.

120

When this picture impresses itself so strongly, so vividly, and so frequently on his consciousness that it begins to have a hypnotic effect, the real work of his guide also begins.

121

Merely by concentrating on the mind's image and memory of the guide, the disciple may draw strength, inspiration, and peace from him.

122

The simple practice of holding the master's image in consciousness is enough to provide some protection in the world's temptations or dangers.

123

The personal attraction to, and affection for, the man Jesus can be usefully made into a focus for meditation. To meditate on the character, example, and teaching of one's spiritual Guide has long been a standard path in mysticism. It culminates in a joyous spiritual union, at which time the student becomes aware that the living presence of his chosen Guide is no longer separate from himself—his Real Self. This is what Jesus meant when he said, "I and My Father are One." It is, indeed, one of the shortest paths to the Goal.

124

Meditation on a guru's face, form, or name is only for the preliminary and intermediate stages; it must be followed by dropping *all* thoughts, including the guru-thought, if advancement is to be made.

6

MANTRAMS, AFFIRMATIONS

Mantrams

The practice of mantram yoga is well known throughout India as a method of suppressing the wandering tendencies of the mind. A mantram, usually given by a guru or adapted by oneself from a book, is a word or a phrase or even a whole sentence which the practitioner chants to himself or whispers or even mentally utters again and again. Some Sanskrit mantrams are quite meaningless sounds, whereas others are full of metaphysical or religious meaning. Which one is used does not matter from the point of view of acquiring concentration, but it does matter from the point of view of developing any particular quality of character or devotional homage which the mantram symbolizes. This mental or vocal repetition is to be done periodically and faithfully.(P)

2

The use of mantrams is not peculiar to the Hindu. It is still found in the Roman and Eastern Churches, in the Sufi circles and the Lamaistic prayers.

3

The mantram is a statement in words or a symbol in picture which declares some truth of higher being, law, attribute, and help, or reminds one of a moral quality to be practised, or acts as a useful self-help self-suggestion. The words can be taken from any inspired scripture, writer, or poet or can be quotations from a philosopher of insight and used as an invocation or affirmation. They should be timely, fitted to the immediate spiritual need of the person.

4

The Meditation of Constant Remembrance:

A factor in the integral path, besides moral re-education, to which we have not given enough weight in published writings—indeed have hardly mentioned—is self-recollection, the frequent remembrance of the Overself at all times of the day and amidst all kinds of situations. Such remembrance, during the long intervals between formal meditations, is an integral part of this quest. A brief sacred formula expressed in an invocation or affirmation, called "mantram," is most useful for this purpose and is given the disciple so that his remembrance is automatically aroused when habit causes him to repeat its words constantly and mentally. The mantram is a handy device for attracting him to this remembrance and making its achievement easier and sure. A constant technique throughout the day is usually lacking in the knowledge and practice of Western seekers, so they need to learn its efficiency and use. The long hours between meditation periods are wasted. As a sister exercise to the ordinary meditations, it will be useful to many students—whilst as a means to replace them for those students who find formal meditation too difficult or too inconvenient, it is most valuable. It is equivalent to the "right mindfulness" of the Buddhist eightfold path, to the Sufi "Dikr," and to the "correct polarization" in modern psychology.

In choosing a suitable formula for his own use, the student should bear in mind that it is not only remembrance that is needed, but loving remembrance. The mantram for such repetition must not only remind him of the Overself but attract him to it. Hence, it should be one that inspires devotion and uplifts character. It should embody spiritualizing thought and gather ennobling emotion around it. It may consist of a single-word name or attribute of God or of a chosen spiritual guide, but it is preferable and more powerful to use a phrase of three to ten syllables. This may be an invocation to Divinity, or to the guide, or be a beneficent auto-suggestion. It is better, however, to receive such a word or phrase from a qualified teacher at a personal interview, for he will not only choose one especially suitable to the student's spiritual need at the time and therefore apt and forceful but will also impart his own power into it.

The formula must be repeated many times a day and every day in the year. Yet its words should always carry vivid meaning and never be allowed to become mere parrot utterances. There is no fixed time and no particular posture necessary for the practice. It may be muttered half-aloud in the earlier stages, but should become silent and mental in the later stages.

The purposes, benefits, and results of this practice are several:

1. It has an intellectual effect by acting as a reminder or arouser in a busy material life. Thus, the first effect is to arouse thought, the second is to still it.

2. The constant repetition has a mesmeric effect: it lulls the senses and thoughts into semi-inactivity and sets the attention free to pass inward toward the soul and eventually induces the contemplative mood.

3. It develops an acute, growing self-consciousness of the right sort, a constant obsessive suggestion that there is a higher self.

4. It leads to the necessary concentration, which is a door to inner consciousness.

5. Its rhythmic activity aligns and then integrates the different parts of the personality. It also removes their restlessness.

6. It gradually establishes subconscious orientation towards the higher self, which keeps on breaking into the conscious field to the detriment of the lower self; thus it gives direction to thought and purification to character. It enables the seeker, therefore, to go on with everyday external living, knowing that God is working in him internally.

7. It becomes a focus for continuous concentration during active life, even whilst engaged in work, pleasure, or walking.

Forgetfulness of the quest, or of the Overself, besets most aspirants. Here is a valuable remedy. It brings the chosen goal, or the revered ideal, constantly back to their attention.

5

Practising mantram consists of repeating a selected word over and over, soaking oneself in it. There are three stages: (a) chanting the word out loud; (b) whispering it; (c) repeating it mentally. Then, when repetition ceases, all thoughts cease. Through this constant concentration, the mantram becomes a backdrop to one's daily life. Just as one can hum a tune while attending to other affairs, so the mantram becomes an ever present accompaniment. When one turns full attention onto it and concentrates fully upon it and then stops—all thoughts stop. This is the purpose of the mantram. This result may take weeks or months.(P)

6

There are three types of mantrams:

(a) *the musical (or bhakti) mantram* (for example, "Jai Ram"). The musical intonations in repetition of a word (or two words) create an almost hypnotic effect as in a Gregorian chant or Ravel's *Bolero.*

(b) *the meaningful mantram.* One selects a word representing a quality one desires and chants it slowly to absorb its meaning; one meditates on the word and the meaning of the word. Eventually the meaning floods gradually into one and he identifies with it. Example: "I am Being."

(c) *the meaningless mantram.* A useful technique for intellectuals who wish to surmount the barriers of the intellect is to choose a word without apparent meaning—"Krim" or "Ayin," for example. The word itself becomes a symbol of That which is beyond comprehension. It enables one to go beyond boundaries of the finite intellect to relate to That which is infinite. A good example is "Aum" pronounced "Aah—ooo—mmm." The first letter represents the waking state, the second the dream state, the third deep sleep, with their wide, then narrow, then closed, sounds.

7

Japa is a mantram specifically restricted in meaning to a name of God. Like all mantrams, it is constantly repeated. It is not only one way of prayerful remembrance of God but also a simple easy method of overcoming the mind's tendency to wander about and to bring it into concentration. It can also be assisted by harmonizing its syllables with the incoming and outgoing breaths.

8

The difference between practice of Japa and practice of mantra is that the former uses only sacred words or names but the latter may use nonsacred, secular, or even meaningless words.

9

The repeated invocation of a sacred name, with trust in its saving power, eventually keeps away all other thoughts and thus focuses the mind in a kind of constant meditation. In the earlier stages it is the man himself who labours at this repetition, but in the advanced stages it is the Overself's grace which actuates it—his own part being quite passive and mechanical.

10

A mantra is a short dynamic saying to be repeated to oneself incessantly. The monotony of this procedure does not, as might be expected, produce a boring effect but rather a lulling one which is pleasant.

11

It uses one thought in order to transcend all thoughts, a single vibration of the mind in order to attain a stillness never ordinarily known by the mind.

12

By repeating the same words in the same rhythm frequently during the day, the week, and the year, the mind's resistance to the idea enshrined in those words is slowly worn down. A time comes when not only do the words repeat themselves without conscious effort, but also their meaning impresses itself deeply.

13

This repetition-method may seem somewhat primitive and crude to the sophisticated or educated modern mind, and quite needlessly redundant. But it is based on sound psychological practice. It is an appeal to the subconscious, not to the logical mind. Its kindred is the lullaby which a mother sings and with which she soothes her child to sleep.

14

Indian and Tibetan yogis particularly value and use the *Om* mantram because they are taught, and believe, that its sound was the first one in the world creation and that its repetition will bring the mind back to the stillness which existed before that creation.

15

A fit subject for the mantra yoga meditation exercise is the series of words descriptive of the Overself's attributes. One word could be taken each day.

16

The idea is that this rhythmic incantation will open an avenue of communion with the Overself.

17

A further value of mantram yoga is that it keeps the practiser from thinking about himself. The two things—a specific mantram and a personal matter—cannot coexist in his consciousness.

18

You may devise your own formula, affirmation, or a traditional mantram, if you wish, but the use of one specially prepared by a Master possesses tested merit.

19

The yogic claim is that this *om-om-om-om* sound is cosmic; it is the keynote of the spinning globes in space; it is the humming vibration of all the worlds.

20

Vivekananda: "We can now understand what is meant by repetition. It is the greatest stimulus that can be given to the spiritual *samskaras* [tendencies]. One moment of company with the holy builds a ship to cross this ocean of life—such is the power of association. So this repetition of *Om* and thinking of its meaning are the same as keeping good company in your own mind. Study and then meditate on what you have studied. Thus light will come to you; the Self will become manifest. But one must think of *Om* and its meaning too."

21

The first revelation of the divine world is sound. Before beholding it, one hears it with an inner ear. The name of God has not only the power of easily washing away all sin, but can even untie the knot of the heart and waken love of God. To be severed from God is the only real sin.(P)

22

A mantram becomes most worthwhile when it is heard deep deep down in the practiser's being. It will then produce the effect of profound inner absorption.(P)

23

When one whose Atman is completely wakened sings the name of God, this has the power of waking a sleeping soul. What happens then is called initiation. By listening devotedly, while another sings the name, and by singing it oneself, one's heart is led back to its real nature, which is love.

24
OM means "I am part of (or one with) the World-Soul."

25
Part of his endeavour should be to set up a rhythmic relation between the mantram and his inner being. If he faithfully attends to its practice, the time will come when it will voice itself within him at regular times, such as after waking from sleep and before entering into it.

26
AUM is chanted on a very low note and extended on a single indrawn breath.

27
The mantra "Shantam Param Sukham" means "Serenity is the highest happiness."

28
Do not keep all your attention fixed on the changing scene around you. Hold some of it back for the Word which, in your consciousness, stands for the Supreme Power.

29
To chant mantrams or to affirm declarations, without looking to the kind of life he lives, is not enough.

30
They are known in Tibet as *dharanis*, literally "mystical sentences," and in India as mantrams, literally "sacred syllables" or "sacred chants."

31
Those mantrams like *Hrim, Klim*, and so forth, which have no significance at all may still be meditated on until the meditator realizes through them that the entire world-appearance is itself without significance because of the Voidness which is its reality.

32
The earthly sound of the name of God is only a vessel for the shadow of the Spiritual Sound. Even this shadow helps to lead the heart to God.

33
The continual practice of the mantram leads in time to the awakening of his spiritual forces. They rise up spontaneously from their deeply hidden source within him and begin to saturate his mind and overwhelm his ego.

34
Both poet Tennyson and medico Crichton-Browne passed into the state of illumination by the same method—silently repeating their own name to themselves.

35
All mantrams constituted by meaningless or mystical words are intended to create a mental vacuum.

36

The word *Om* is not the only one whose sound is used by Orientals to quieten the mind in meditation and therefore claimed as a holy word. The Chinese have used *Ch'an*, the Japanese *Zen*, the Hindus *Soami*, the Arabs *Sufi* for the same purpose.

37

The effect of this constant dwelling on the mantram is to come to rest within the mood of mind or the state of heart which it symbolizes.

38

If a sage be one who exists constantly in the awareness of the Overself, then mantram can be a Short-Path technique to emulate his awareness. By putting the cart before the horse and aiming at imitating the sage's awareness, we can come closer to his state of being.

39

The vocal chanting of a mantram belongs to the elementary practice of it. In the more advanced practice, nothing is spoken aloud and the mantram is simply held in the mind—constantly repeating itself as a thought but a thought to which we kind of listen and from which we seem to stand apart so that it has its own inner vitality. This makes a great difference from the spoken practice, because the latter keeps the mantram fixed whereas the former leaves it flexible.

40

In the mantram "Om Mani Padme Hum," inhale after the first word.

41

"Hum" in the famous Tibetan mantram stands for the heart, whereas the first word "OM" stands for the inner reality, the unseen power behind all things.

42

Gandhi often prescribed the continuous recitation of God's name. But he always emphasized that it had to be more than mere lip movement; it had to absorb the practitioner's entire being throughout the period of exercise and even throughout life. While repeating the word "God," he had to concentrate intensely on godliness.

43

When the incantatory words of a mantra by constant practice become fully activated, the mantra becomes fully automatic and circles round and round inside the head or the heart just like a revolving wheel. At this deep stage, he is not concerned with its translated or verbal meaning but only with the kind of consciousness it produces. For now it is not a matter of what he is doing but of what is being done to him. The mantra has brought him into a region of released forces which are very active in him.

44

The mantram must be clearly pronounced. Its meaning must be devotedly, even reverently, felt.

45

In Sanskrit magic and mysticism, not only are complete words and phrases and even sentences used as mantrams, but also certain single letters and syllables are used. Such a mantram is called a seed, and it can be used either in written form on paper or in pronunciation as a sound. The letters also stand as symbols representing certain angelic or other higher beings who are invoked.

46

Mantram = *Al-lah* (*Al* on inbreath, *lah* on outbreath)

47

These mantrams are brought into rhythmic harmony with the breathing of the lungs or the beating of the heart or the chanting of the phrase.

48

Repeatedly sounding the vowel "O" stimulates the bony part of the voice box in the throat and mentally assists attention to concentrate. The mantram *Om*, so well known, is a useful ending to all other mantrams. On the expiring breath, very slowly lengthened out, it leaves an effect which assists the fulfilment of the meditation—that is, a calming one.

49

The master of the mantram becomes a symbol of help, to which the believers can turn in thought at any time or at the special time set aside for it.

50

Mantramic denials and affirmations should be formulated in as impersonal a wording as possible. This keeps the reference to a higher power and away from the ego, with its slender resources.

51

It is good practice to use the mantram on the intake of breath, when doing rhythmic breathing. Deep breathing for use in rhythmic breathing should be with lateral expansion of chest.

52

A story is told of Jowett, a thinker and a man of God, the famous and brilliant Oxford University translator of Plato's Greek, that even during conversations with others he would, while keeping silent and listening to them, move his lips continuously in prayer. He was practising a Christian form of mantram.

53

It has done its duty and served its purpose if the invocation or affirmation ceases of itself and in the ensuing silence a mysterious power rises and takes possession of him.

54

Mantra in Sanskrit means hymn, prayer, invocation, formula for magic, secret, charm, lines of prayer to a divinity. It is something that creates loving devotion to God. The mantra uttered and the divinity called upon are identical. Hence the reverence for it and the importance of its being correctly spoken, and the danger of its being misused for selfish purpose. It should not be spoken, but sung.

55

A mantram depends for its effect not only upon repetition (which brings about concentrated attention) but also on its sound (which brings about a subtler mental contact). The latter may be lower psychic or higher spiritual, according to the word used. *This is important to remember* for though any one of these effects justifies calling the word or phrase a mantram, both in combination provide it with the fullest power and the complete function.

56

A Moroccan mantric dervish dance: A couple of hundred men—young and old—were arranged in a large circle. When the leader, who was squatting in the centre, gave a signal, they all leapt up and yelled, "Allah!" together, swaying from side to side, stamping their feet, and repeating the name of their God dozens of times until they became delirious with joy and absorbed into a half-trancelike state.

57

Nicephoros the Solitary wrote: "We know from experience that if you keep on praying in this manner, that if you practise the 'Prayer of Jesus' with attention, the whole host of virtues will come to you: love, joy, and peace."

58

Because the muttering of these ejaculations and the chanting of these incantations have been perverted into use as part of the techniques of professional witch-doctors and primitive medicine-men, is no reason why their proper use for higher purposes may not be achieved.

59

The Arabic word for God—*Allah*—or the Aramaic (Jesus' spoken language) word—*Alaha*—form excellent mantric material.

60

The endless repetition of the same word is a most important feature of the practice, for when it has passed through the mind a thousand times in less than a day, and this for several days, in the end it becomes fixed as a part of the background of all his consciousness.

61

Muhammed: "There is no act which removes the punishment of Allah farther from you than the invocation of Allah's name."

62

Whether he uses the Hindu one-syllabled *Om* for such repetition or the Muhammedan two-syllabled *Allah* for the same purpose, the results will be the same.

63

The mantram is a means of awakening the power of concentration. But all mantrams differ from one another and thus introduce a secondary effect or influence. The meditation is the primary work, the concentration being intended to develop power for it: the form of the mantram is shaped by its object—communion with God, cultivation of a virtue, and so on.

64

A time comes when there is no need to try to practise the exercise, for the mantram wells up of its own accord. It then repeats itself automatically and silently in his mind alone. Over and over again, like the chorus of a song, it comes to the front or remains at the back of attention.

65

Bhagat Singh Thind: "Negation has to be nullified, you can not take sin into God, but you can take God into sin, and short work He will make of it, if you do. If you are in the habit of doing something that you know is foolish, and you can not shake it off, take a Christ into it, hold *His Name of Truth* in the very heart of it, dare to say the *Word* of Life, even when you are doing the foolish thing. For that is the very time when you most need it, that is the moment when you can test its power. Only stick to it, repeating it with your whole heart and mind, hold fast to the Name of your Divine Self doggedly through anything and everything, letting no old feeling of condemnation sweep it out of your mind, but hang on to it by your eyelids, if you are drowned up to that, and you will find Truth will set you free."

66

To some extent, its use has a purifying effect on the subconscious character.

67

The chosen phrase or selected word should be dwelt upon again and again until it is firmly implanted in the ever-receptive subconscious mind.

68

The Asiatic mystics aptly name them "words of power." They believe that, if intoned correctly, they help to keep away the baser influences and to stimulate the finer ones. The effect is temporary, of course, but by constant repetition it may become permanent.

69

A single word like "God" or a simple phrase like "God in me" must be spoken with the lips without intermission, or repeated in the mind with intensive concentration.

70

Mantram practice was given to Indians to help stop thought from wandering, just as Koan practice was given to Japanese to help stop thought from dominating. The Koan method crippled or even paralysed the intellect; but this was only in its approach to the spiritual goal, not in its worldly business.

71

Those who are unwilling to engage themselves in the metaphysical studies and mystical practices may avail themselves of the devotional attitudes and daily reverential worship of religion, or repeat constantly the affirmations and declarations of mantra yoga.

72

The murmuring of such a phrase over and over again is a useful device to concentrate the mental waves and to turn them into a spiritual direction.

73

Gandhi: "Persevere and ceaselessly repeat *Ramanama* during all your waking hours. Ultimately it will remain with you even during your sleep."

74

It is the common practice in all the Bengali districts of India as well as in parts of the Mahratta districts for large groups of people, as well as solitary individuals, to engage in the protracted chanting of God's name or some phrase incorporating it. The mental level on which it is done is like that of hymn singing in the West.

75

The Master Tao-Ch'o: "Say, without interruption and without any other thought, the Buddha's name, and you will enter the presence of Buddha."

76

A mantra is best and most commonly muttered, but beginners sing it aloud, while the advanced repeat it mentally and automatically.

77

It is like a refrain that keeps on singing in the heart.

78

The repetitious rhythm of a mantram can, with assiduous practice, become almost hallucinating.

79

He may mutter the mantram to himself, moving his lips in an almost unhearable whisper.

80

He must harness himself to the main thought again and again. He must resolutely keep the mantram a chained captive.

81

The mantra is mentally or vocally chanted so many times that the mind is brain-washed: it can resist no longer and from then on the phrase keeps revolving by itself over and over again in consciousness.

82

It is claimed that ordinary methods involve conscious deliberate thinking but the mantra method of meditation does not. It by-passes them all and directly reaches thought-free stillness.

83

Only experience and use can show its worth in rhythmically directing awareness to a certain fixed point, and keeping it there. The word, phrase, name, invocation, sentence, or image provides him with a certain power of concentration.

84

The words of the invocation stabilize attention and steady emotion. They hold the mind in desired states.

85

He uses the mantric repetition to work himself into the state of rapt concentration and then to feel his way into the inner self's presence.

86

It is useful to follow out the mantram system of meditation when the ordinary systems, involving set exercises and formal periods, have been tried and found profitless.

87

Bhagat Singh Thind: "The constant utterance of Holy Name without the agency of lips by Spirit-current develops concentration. The Holy Name that is taught has resemblance to the Sound or current emanating from the nerve centre where the practice is to be performed. This nerve centre is the focus of the Deity. Your constant repetition will one day result in creating harmony with the vibrations inside and bring you into a condition of concord with the Deity therein. You will then be able to participate in the essence of Him, and that will prepare you for further progress."

88

Bhagat Singh Thind, Sikh Teacher: "With the eyes of Mind the disciple sees the image of the guru, with the ears he listens to the Holy Names within, and with the speech of the mind inaudibly he repeats rhythmically the Holy Mantrams given to him by the guru. By this constant daily practice he moves to an ingathering of his whole being towards integration and unity."

89

However, prayer must be mastered first. This, in its purest form, is complete stillness of speech, thought, and body. One thought alone must repeat itself again and again, such as, "God is within me," and it will drive away all other thoughts. Incidentally, *this is Mantrayoga.*

No teacher is needed for Mantrayoga because *you* have to do it yourself. Nor is there any danger. After the 20–45 minutes' distraction, meditation may then come in a moment.

90

The time may come through practice and effort when he will be able to meet a period of trouble or anxiety more calmly by humming slowly and repeatedly the familiar formula.

91

Mantram = Holy Word, the Mystical
Affirmation = Sacred Invocation

92

He who suffers from incessant mental activity could harness it and turn it to profit by Mantrayoga, which solves the problem: "How to transfer attention from foreground to background of mind and yet attend to work?"

93

The venerable heavily bearded Father Joseph, of Mount Athos, a teacher of other monks, claims that the "Prayer of Jesus" becomes with time an unstopping activity, productive of enlightening revelation, and purifying from passions. His own disciples spend several hours every day on the mental repetition of this short prayer.

94

The constant recital of the mantram is a simple effective exercise but it cannot, by itself, win the highest goal.

95

There are many ways of meditation, and the practice of mantram is one of them—indeed, almost the most elementary one of them. Yet it is useful on its level. But one should not remain forever on that elementary level. You may go on repeating the word, the phrase, but a time will come when it will lose its power to help you, when its effects will vanish and its very practice will become boring. Use it as a step not as a stop.

96

Many of the people using this method are as likely to achieve spiritual illumination by their babbling of mantrams as a donkey is by his braying of noises.

Affirmations

97

What Indians call *mantra* is what New Thought calls *affirmations*.

98

When all other methods of meditation prove fruitless or too hard, let him try the simplest of all methods—the Spiritual Declaration—and bring words to his help. They may be reduced to a single one—the name of his spiritual leader, or of a moral quality towards which he aspires, or of an inner state which he seeks to achieve. Of the first kind, a specimen is the name "Jesus"; of the second, "Love"; of the third, "Peace." Or a few words may be combined into the phrasing of any helpful statement, metaphysical/mystical affirmation, or devotional prayer.

99

The Declaration is a word, statement, or verse, affirmation or invocation, which is committed to memory and then often repeated. The purpose is twofold: first, to achieve a state of concentration; second, to direct the concentrative mind upon the idea to be expressed, so constantly or continuously that the idea begins to influence him deeply and almost hypnotically.

100

Affirmations are of two kinds: those for use in meditation and those for constant repetition aloud, whispered, or silently.

101

These divide themselves naturally into two main groups: those belonging to the Long Path and those to the Short Path. Of the first kind, there is Coué's famous suggestion: "Every day, in every way, I am getting better and better." Of the second kind there is Jesus' figurative statement: "I and my Father are one."

102

(a) Both affirmations and denials have their place and usefulness. Philosophy, being integral, rejects neither. The first would seem illusory if they affirm what is true only on a higher level of being while the person himself is unable to rise above the lower one, as in the statement, "I am divine." But still, their concentrative and suggestive power may, given enough time, eventually help him to do so. The second would seem nonsensical at worst in dismissing what stubbornly remains all the time, or narcotic at best in lulling it into brief quietude, yet the Buddha did not hesitate to recommend denials to his disciples: "This is not mine; this am I not," was one formula which he gave them. For even the theoretical separation thus brought about between the man and the weakness or fault denied has some constructive value and is the beginning of a mental-emotional-physical series whose intuition-guided total effort leads to a successful result.

(b) The Declaration habitually repeated and faithfully applied continually renews the Ideal for him.

(c) It is a practice useful for filling unoccupied moments.

103

The affirmation is to be firmly held and unwaveringly trusted. He is not to consider it as a statement of a far-off ideal but of a present actuality. He is to identify himself with it with all his being.

104

The affirmation can even be reduced to a single word. This makes it easier to use, and concentrated in effect. Such simplicity is more akin to the Overself than to the intellect; therefore this type of affirmation should not be dwelt on analytically, not examined and probed with a logical scalpel, but merely held closely, repeated slowly and frequently until the mind is saturated with it. It may be used both inside and outside the special meditation periods. In the latter case, it is defensive against attack from lower thoughts.

105

There is one human activity which is continuous, rhythmic, natural, easy, and pleasant. It is breathing. We may take advantage of its existence by combining it with a simple exercise to bring about a kind of meditation which will possess all these four mentioned attributes. The exercise is merely to repeat one word silently on the inhalation and another word on the exhalation. The two words must be such that they join together to make a suitable spiritual phrase or name. Here is one useful example: "*God Is.*"

106

"I am poised in the Consciousness of Truth." Repeat it audibly, then carry it into the Silence.

107

The Buddha taught his monks to enter daily into the following meditation: "As a mother even at the risk of her own life protects her only son, so let a man cultivate goodwill without measure among all beings. Let him suffuse the whole world with thoughts of love, unmixed with any sense of difference or opposed interests."

108

The thought thus self-given will become transformed into an act.

109

The declaration should be audibly repeated if he is alone, silently if not, or audibly a few times followed by silently for some minutes.

110

At a fixed time each day repeat the declaration for five or ten minutes.

111

The effectiveness of a Declaration depends also upon its being repeated with a whole mind and an undivided heart, with confidence in its power, and sincere desire to rise up.

112

Declarations:

1. "I am becoming as free from undesirable traits in my everyday self as I already am in the Overself."
2. "In my real being I am strong, happy, and serene."
3. "I am the master of thought, feeling, and body."
4. "Infinite Power, sustain me! Infinite Wisdom, enlighten me. Infinite Love, ennoble me."
5. "My Words are truthful and powerful expressions."
6. "I see myself moving toward the mastery of self."
7. "May I co-operate more and more with the Overself. May I do its will intelligently and obediently."
8. "I co-operate joyously with the higher purpose of my life."
9. "O! Infinite strength within me."
10. "O! Indwelling Light, guide me to the wise solution of my problem."
11. "I am Infinite Peace!"
12. "I am one with the undying Overself."
13. "Every part of my body is in perfect health; every organ of it in perfect function."
14. "In my real self life is eternal, wisdom is infinite, beauty is imperishable, and power is inexhaustible. My form alone is human for my essence is divine."
15. "I am a centre of life in the Divine Life, of intelligence in the Divine Intelligence."
16. "In every situation I keep calm and seek out the Intuitive that it may lead me."
17. "I look beyond the troubles of the moment into the eternal repose of the Overself."
18. "My strength is in obedience to the Overself."
19. "O Infinite and impersonal Bliss!"
20. "I am happy in the Overself's blissful calm."
21. "God is ever smiling on Me."
22. "God is smiling on me."
23. "The Peace of God."
24. "I dwell in the Overself's calm."

25. "I smile with the Overself's bliss."
26. "I dwell in Infinite peace."
27. "I am a radiant and revivified being. I express in the world what I feel in my being."(P)

113

What is newer than a new dawning day? What a chance it offers for the renewing of life too! And how better to do this than to take a positive affirmative Declaration like, "I Am Infinite Peace!" as the first morning thought, and to hold it, and hold on to it, for those first few minutes which set the day's keynote? Then, whatever matters there will be to attend, or pressing weighty duties to be fulfilled, we shall carry our peace into the midst of them.(P)

114

A friend told me some years ago of an interesting and useful method of using these Declarations which had been taught her by a celebrated holy man and mystic in her country, when he gave her the "Prayer of Jesus." This is a Declaration which was widely used several hundred years ago in the old Byzantine monasteries and even now is used to a lesser extent in Balkan and Slavonic monastic circles in exactly the same way as in India. The method is to reduce the number of words used until it is brought down to a single one. This reduction is achieved, of course, quite slowly and during a period covering several months. In this particular instance, there are seven words in the Prayer: "Lord Jesus Christ, have mercy on me." They are all used for the first few weeks, then the word "Christ" is omitted for the next few weeks. The phrase is again shortened by detaching from it, after a further period has elapsed, the word "Lord." Then "have" is taken out and so on until only one word is left. The Declaration as finally and permanently used is "Jesus–Jesus–Jesus–Jesus." This method can be applied to almost any Declaration. The selected last word should be a name, if addressed to God or to a Spiritual Leader, or, if that is not part of it, a desired quality.(P)

115

The use of short statements, often strangely worded, made by a master to a disciple as a means of getting the flash of enlightenment flourished in China during the Tang dynasty. It was taken up later by the Japanese, among whom the method's original name "kong-an" changed slightly to "ko-an." Despite extravagant claims made for it, the successful practiser got a glimpse only, not a permanent and full result. It is not the same as, and not to be confused with, the method of meditating upon affirmations, pithy condensed truth-statements (called *Mahavakyas* in India) since these openly possess a meaning whereas koans are often illogical and always puzzling.(P)

116

Philosophy uses these declarations guardedly and does not approve of such potentially dangerous ones as "I am God!" or "I am one with God." Instead, it uses the more guarded ones like "I am in God" or "God is in me," and these only after a preparation has elapsed with self-humbling phrases like "I am nothing" and "Take my ego, swallow it up, O Thou Divinity." Otherwise the truth is half-understood and misused, while the relation between the Overself and its shadow-self becomes a source of mischievous illusion and intellectual confusion.

117

It is better to choose a declaration which pertains to his immediate need than one which does not.

118

Any declaration brings before the mind some specific truth which it wants to realize, but the greatest one, and the most powerful and creative one, is that which affirms the divinity of its innermost nature, the presence of God inside its own being.

119

An affirmation which proclaims a spiritual reality, may seem to be contradicted by outer facts.

120

Deep within him there is an opening out to the infinite being. How this opening is actually effected, no one really knows. One moment he is here, the next moment he is there. It is then that these spiritual declarations become perfectly true, completely in accord with fact.

121

He must deliberately eject each negative thought as it arises. The easier way to do this is immediately to replace it by a "Spiritual Declaration" of an affirmative nature. This is quicker than and not so hard as trying to use willpower alone to get rid of the negative thought.

122

The best of all declarations is the one which represents either the Supreme Power or else the human leader who most inspires us to think of that Power. We cannot go higher in thought or come closer in awareness. Whatever name we habitually give to this Unique Power, be it Truth or Reality, Allah or Jehovah, that is the word to use as our Declaration— unless the leader's name helps us more.

123

If he habitually suffers from a certain mood, or if he may be the victim of it at the moment, it will be useful to choose a Declaration which affirms the opposite mood. In despondency, for example, he may find cheering and upholding sentences for repetition in one of the Psalms.

124

The symbol or declaration must be one to which he can completely give himself, if all its effectiveness is to be realized.

125

It is useless to say to yourself what you cannot bring your mind to believe, to affirm in your meditation what your heart cannot possibly accept. Do not try to violate laws that you trust by beliefs that are contrary to them. Instead of profitable results, you will generate inner conflicts. If your affirmation is not in harmony with the order of the universe, with the possibilities and principles of human existence, you will not succeed in its use.

126

If any declaration seems unnatural and artificial and impossible in relation to oneself, it ought to be abandoned until it has been passed through a prolonged thinking-out process.

127

If no attempt is made to gain understanding of, as well as give feeling to, these utterances, repeating a declaration may become artificial and making an affirmation may become mechanical.

128

He should close his eyes, repeat the phrase slowly several times, and try to penetrate ever deeper into its meaning with each repetition.

129

The practice of these Declarations is a device to recall to the memory of the man his perfect and ideal state which he not only has to retain but which in his Overself he already is. This is a means of recalling him from the periphery of life to his centre.

130

Each stirring of the old weaknesses must be treated as a command to new efforts. But these shall be toward recollection of, and identification with, the Overself—not necessarily toward direct struggle with them. In these efforts, let him reiterate a spiritual declaration—holding to the thought behind it with the deepest intensity. The silent word must become this spiritual warrior's sword.

131

He does not need to practise the declarations in a conspicuous manner, or draw the attention of others to what he is doing. Instead, working quietly, he can and should let it remain a secret between the Overself and himself.

132

A single word naming some divine attribute or human ideal is another good focus for a concentration exercise. It should be slowly but silently repeated to oneself at certain intervals whilst its significance should be held all the time in the mind. Every other idea should be kept out. Words which are suitable to perform this office may be safely left to the aspirant's taste and mood of the moment. Here are instances: reality, truth, love, being, illusion, goodness, pity, purity, and peace.

In this exercise, he repeats mentally and slowly over and over again a significant key word like "Reality" or a pithy formula like "In my higher being, I am beyond weakness and sin."

Incessant repetition of a brief mystic formula, a short holy phrase, will keep out all other thoughts and ultimately even lapse itself. The mind will then fall into stillness, the heart be inundated with quiet.

133

Before attending any interview or group meeting, as well as during the attendance itself, if a clash of wills is to be expected or some trouble is to be feared or some favour is to be requested, silently practise mantric affirmations such as: "All Good is with me," or "The Infinite Power is my perfect supply," or "Perfect Harmony is in me."

134

The way to use these affirmations differs from one to the other, according to its nature and purpose. For example, an affirmation of calmness and peace needs a different approach mentally, emotionally, and even physically from one of power and strength.

135

The general rule for using these affirmations is first to sit comfortably and relax the body in every way. Then slowly repeat the selected words for a few minutes. Lay hold intensely on their meaning. The practice may be done again in the evening with another or with the same affirmation.

136

Of all affirmations, the student who has evolved to the higher stages of development will select those that concern the impersonal rather than the personal self. These are the ultimate truths, the conclusive formulae of philosophy such as: "Mind is the Real," or "The ego is illusory," where the mind calmly rests on the final position to be attained.

137

The student who takes one of these sentences from a piece of inspired writing is seeking to reproduce in his own feelings and thoughts the inner condition which gave it birth. As he ponders over the phrase, he should not only seek to distill every bit of meaning from it, but also let his inner being passively receive that meaning by other than logical ways. This wider concentration upon it may gradually open up its content. Nevertheless, if he returns to it a long time later—perhaps after a year or two—he may penetrate abruptly and unexpectedly to a still deeper layer of meaning and with that experience the joy of new revelation.

138
Select any phrase, sentence, or even single word which makes most appeal to you and pertains to the goal, ideal, or quality you wish to develop. It may be taken from a book (if inspired) or you may construct it yourself. Examples are: *I am infinite peace: harmony–harmony–harmony.* This Spiritual "Declaration" is to be repeated as often during the entire day as you remember to do so—silently and mentally when out or with others, whispered to yourself when alone and in your own room. This means that there may be dozens of repetitions in one day. It is particularly to be practised when any provocation or temptation arises. After the first few weeks the habit should become automatic, when you may try to make it a silent one at all times.

You may, if you prefer, use as the theme for concentration the name of your Spiritual Leader: "Jesus–Jesus–Jesus," for example. This exercise must be done very slowly, the phrase must be long drawn out, and, in the early stages, the meaning pondered on.

139
Each affirmation he decides to accept should be used regularly for a period of twenty-one days before changing to another one.

140
Affirm truth, and let others deny falsehood.

141
It will double the efficacy of this exercise if it is practised at the same time as and united with the regular cycles of breathing activity. When the two are as one, much greater power enters into the declaration or invocation.

142
The value of these declarations and affirmations, these ideas held and repeated, is not a total one. The method they use is only a first step and an easy step. It is not a self-sufficient method.

143
I call it paradoxical thinking as opposed to logical thinking. "I am infinite being" is a declaration which does not fit into the logic of conventional experience.

144
To think only and completely of this truth at the very moment when the ego's voice or passion's demand is loudest, is a necessary step forward.

145

In the beginning of each session it will assist the novice to concentrate if he will say the Declaration several times with his lips.

146

When this delicate intuitive feeling is verbalized into an intellectual statement in the form of a Spiritual Declaration, the latter may help to awaken an echoing feeling in the heart of one who uses it.

147

The words should be descriptive of some attribute of the Overself or some quality of its nature. They should also separate the aspirant from his lower tendencies or ego and identify him with the Overself.

148

The practical technical use of Declarations belongs only to the elementary or intermediate stages of the path. When their purpose of reminding man of his true self is fulfilled by every event, every happening, every situation in a man's life, then he is said to have reached the advanced stage of mantra-yoga. At this stage, there is nothing too trivial to act as a reminder of the higher helpfulness to which the Quest leads. Everything can then be accepted as presented symbolically to the traveller.

149

The declaration is also used in India to purify a place, to uplift the mind, to invite Grace, and to abate sickness.

150

He is to remind himself constantly of the greater truths, whether he is at home in his room or abroad in the public places. "Be still and know that I am infinite power" is one such truth. "Be still and know that I am infinite joy" is another.

151

These truths are not mere metaphysical statements that raise the dust of argument, but spiritual signposts which guide man into the true way of life.

152

It is useful to prepare and keep a list of these silent declarations and select a different one for use during a particular period, whether it be a single day or a whole week. It can be chosen to fit the particular needs of that period, and the experiences which are expected or developed then.

153

An affirmation should be some easily seized, easily held phrase. It is to be said over and over again. It is essential that the fullest faith should be given to it by the person using it.

154

Let the mind dwell constantly on these great truths. Let the hand write them down and carry the record for study at odd moments.

155

"I will try to show forth in my personal life, thought, and feeling the perfect harmony which already belongs to the impersonal Overself within me."

156

A Declaration has creative power only if the mind is firmly fixed on its meaning as it is repeated.

157

"The divine Self in me manifests itself in contentment and strength."

158

The declaration is a simple device for achieving three different objectives at one and the same time. It facilitates the continuous remembrance of the Overself. It holds the ideal and parades the objectives of self-improvement ever before us. It inspires us as a form of concentration, first by keeping us in touch with the Overself and then by getting us ultimately absorbed in awareness of it.

159

The practice keeps away other thoughts if they are of a baser kind, yet it does not keep away those which are necessary to carry on the ordinary affairs of everyday living. The declaration stays in the deep places of the mind like a little island of immovable rock, while the agitated waves of personal activities swirl around it.

160

Let the affirmation rise into central consciousness every moment that the mind is free to attend to it.

161

What affirmation shall he use? He should analyse his character impartially and carefully and let his decision rest on the revelation of positive and negative qualities this analysis affords him.

162

They may also be the opposite of affirmations; that is, they may be denials. An example is: "I will no longer express negatives."

163

These declarations can be formulated in the first person—"I am eternal"—or without reference to any person at all—"God is infinite being."

164

Let him create his own declarations or denials, to suit his special needs and individual aspirations.

165

By affirming a particular virtue, he automatically repudiates its opposing evil quality.

166

These affirmations are taut, compact statements of truths.

167
An affirmation takes a general thought, idea, ideal, and turns it into a precise one. This helps those who cannot find their way among abstractions.

168
Here are some of the more metaphysical declarations for meditational use: (a) "You are me and I am you"; (b) "I Who Am"; (c) "What I have been, I shall be"; (d) "He Who Is."

169
The kind of thinking which makes up the content of your mind, influences always, and creates sometimes, the kind of fortune which makes up the course of your life.

170
Some of these declarations are phrased as auto-suggestions, phrased so as to have evocative or creative value.

171
Suggestion from others and expectancy from himself—if strong enough—help to shape inner experiences, but his own work is essential.

172
How many unacknowledged suggestions do they carry about with them, as part of their own nature now although first put into their heads long ago by others?

173
Once he perceives this truth, he goes his own way and does not allow others to make him a victim of suggestion.

174
The reaction of his environment to his dominant thought is as certain as the operation of a law in Nature.

175
To the degree that a man practises constructive thinking and harmonious feeling, to that degree will he help to draw progressive events and helpful chances to himself.

176
Those who are sceptical of the higher origin of this phenomenon, who assert it to be the work of auto-suggestion, that it is of a mind able to impress its own imaginings upon itself to such an extent that it mistakes them for realities, are themselves guilty of auto-suggestion, for they have impressed their sceptical theories to such an extent upon their own minds that there is no reason for anything else than these complexes.

177
If the dominant trends of his thought are bad, evil, or negative, let him counteract them by repeatedly, persistently, and intensely dwelling on their opposites.

178

In the early stage, when concentration is needed, he will succeed best by giving his attention strong, forcible commands, by directing his mind toward the chosen topic with positive phrases.

179

The Chinese name for these muttered or chanted incantations is very apt: "True Words."

180

As soon as the light is put out and you prepare to sleep, give a command to the deeper mind to work on the problem you present it with. You may state the problem aloud. Then, when you wake up in the morning, look for the solution before you do anything else.

181

Put into the affirmation all the intensity and all the fervour at your command.

182

The call to "pray without ceasing" which Paul made, the recommendation to "think of Buddha" which the Lamas give, and the remembrances of the name of Allah which Muhammedan Sufis practise, are declarations.

183

Joyousness is enjoined in Hindu Upanishadic texts. It is to be practised through self-suggestions (*Svabhutivakyas*).

184

The seeker will profit during his hours of distress or difficulty, whether inward or outward, by pronouncing a mantric affirmation and then making his prayer of petition in a general way. A particular thing should not be included in the prayer. For example, in the case of an environmental want, the affirmation could be: "Within me there is all I need." This kind of petition is a far higher form of prayer and a far more successful one than the common begging for a specific relief or object or change.

185

With every interval of time that he is able to get, however short it be— even a few seconds—he repeats a majestic word like "Peace," or an evocative sentence like "Cast thy burden on my back and I shall give you peace."

186

The affirmation is used in three different ways. It is chanted aloud, muttered or whispered, silently and mentally repeated.

187

There is another special value of the declaration, and that is found during the strains and struggles of living. If established previously by habit, it will be present and available, ready to use at any moment of need or crisis.

188

The instant vigorous and continued practice of a declaration may change the state of mind in a few minutes from a negative one that is agitated or depressed to a positive one that is reposed or cheerful.

189

When an affirmation is used only in and for meditation exercises, it should be mentally pronounced as firmly and as positively and as confidently as possible. It should also be repeated several times. Do not ponder over its meaning but rather be content with letting each word sink into the subconscious mind.

190

The power of the declaration rises to its greatest degree when used in magical rites, when it is solemnly chanted by a suitably attired priest or wizard.

191

The whole of his consciousness is to be withdrawn into the declaration and to remain within it, if he is sitting in solitude at formal regular meditation at the special time, but only a part of it if he is otherwise engaged.

192

These short, specific statements, used persistently as auto-suggestions, are useful to all.

193

He is to live with the name and qualities of his ideal ever before him, for the purpose of drawing inspiration from it. He is to repeat, silently or vocally, at every moment when there is a break in whatever he happens to be doing, and even as often as he can during the act itself, a spiritual declaration. Suitable phrases or sentences can be found in hymns, bibles, proverbs, and poems, and in the great inspired writings of ancient and modern times.

194

The declaration may be intoned loud enough to be heard clearly by himself but by others only as a murmur. This is intended to induce a concentrated state.

195

The yogi who spends years mechanically mumbling the affirmation imparted to him by his teacher will not get so far as the Western aspirant who selects his own declaration and conscientiously, intelligently, works with it.

196

The Spiritual Declaration is to become his magic talisman, to be used in provocative situations, irritating environments, or unpleasant contacts with unliked persons.

197
There is one condition: the declaration must not be longer than a single sentence, and even that ought to be confined to less than ten words.

198
He should make these affirmations firmly, intensely, and confidently.

199
These precious words ought to be printed in capital letters and doubly underlined. For, in a world of polite lies and prejudiced stupidities, they are the TRUTH.

200
The more he can put his loving attention into the declaration or behind the auto-suggestion, the more are his chances of being helped by the Overself's Grace.

201
A Spanish friend, who put into his mysticism all the ardours of his people, called this practice "inner work." The monks of Mount Athos, who use hundreds of times a day the same declaration which the Rumanian mystics used, call it "work."

202
In this loving remembrance, this turning of the mind through devotion to its parental source, the Quest finds one of its most effective techniques.

203
Sufi Declaration: "I am the Truth!"

204
Equipped with this knowledge and these exercises, the aspirant will be able to use well those idle minutes which would otherwise be wasted.

205
Simone Weil tells how the highly concentrated recitation, with all needed tender feeling, of a devotional-metaphysical poem by the seventeenth-century Englishman, George Herbert, turned her from an agnostic into a mystic as the Christ-consciousness took possession of her. This result was as unsought as it was unexpected.

206
The sacred declarations are to be hummed in some cases, chanted in others, or spoken in still others.

207
These inspired sentences or phrases can also be used as amulets against his own dark moods as stronger hands to hold on to during depressed moments or weak phases.

208
The practice seems to have a hypnotic effect on the mind and to draw him with a magnetic spell to the idea behind the declaration, as the latter is frequently and solemnly repeated.

209

It is from these declarations that the idea was derived of magical incantations which were supposed to bring about extraordinary results, for some men were able by their aid to induce a trancelike state which, like the hypnotic state, temporarily released paranormal powers of mind.

210

Stand in front of a mirror and pronounce the constructive auto-suggestive affirmations with dramatic, intense feeling.

211

The secret is simplicity itself. It was written down by the Sufi poet Shams Tabriz in eight little words: "Keep God in remembrance till self is forgotten." If he keeps the declaration half-whispered on the tip of his tongue and joyously fondled in his mind, it will serve him well.

212

An affirmation fixes attention and elevates emotion: this is its primary purpose, but it may also offer wise counsel.

213

In the finer homes of Japan, the reception room will contain a silk or paper scroll hanging, upon which some master has drawn, in calligraphic characters, a pithy and wise affirmation.

214

These exercises can usually be practised wherever a man happens to be and, often, whatever he happens to be doing.

215

The declaration comes up from the subconscious and gets itself uttered and repeated. The process of articulation is a pleasant one, sometimes even an ecstatic one.

216

By learning to live with the declaration, even if it seemed remote, fantastic, and impossible at first, it will come to evoke a veritable ecstasy of acceptance.

217

The declarations need to be pondered with faith and held in the mind with persistence if their effectiveness is to be demonstrated.

218

The exercise is a powerful counterweight to the restless nature of our thoughts. It forces them to take anchorage in the declaration.

219

As he perseveres with this practice, the intervals when he forgets to repeat the Declaration get fewer and fewer in number, shorter and shorter in time. Its constant utterance or remembrance then becomes more and more a realizable aspiration.

220

The practice also has a purifying effect so far as it prevents the rising of wrong thoughts and helps the eradication of those which do appear.

221

The formula can be selected from an upholding Psalm, like the ninety-first, or from the Book of Prayer.

222

One of the great *Mahavakyas* is *"Ayam Atma Brahma"*—"This Atman is Brahman."

223

When these declarations are chanted, Orientals find them to help breath control, which in turn helps meditation.

224

A book which is truly inspired will contain many a sentence that can be used suggestively in meditation. Linger over some of them as long as you can. It is not movement which matters here but depth.

225

The effect of using affirmations and recollections is to tint his nature with diviner qualities. These work upon and gradually transmute his lower ones.

226

When he is practised enough, he will find that meditation charges him with an inward glow.

227

What he meets with outwardly as well as inwardly on this quest should be tested against these affirmations and scrutinized in the light of these truths.

228

This exercise can be used with success only if there is the utmost attraction to the idea phrased or the fullest love for the Divine Name or spiritual leader mentioned in it. If the feeling is weak, the remembrance will be fitful and unsteady, the practice will only be occasional and hence insufficient. If the feeling is strong, the mind will be able to hold the idea or the name more easily and unbrokenly, for then it is like the feeling which exists between a pair of separated young lovers. They are able to remember each other's name constantly, to hold each other's mental picture quite spontaneously. They do not need to make any deliberate effort at all.

229

This practice makes it possible for the otherwise restless mind to think of one thought and live in one purpose constantly. In this way it steadies the mind and keeps its attention concentrated.

230

The moment any activity is at an end, his attention will instantly return to the declaration and continue the inner work with it.

231

When his last thought at night and first thought in the morning refers to the Overself, he may appraise his progress as excellent.(P)

MINDFULNESS, MENTAL QUIET

Mindfulness

Although everyone must begin by making meditation something to be practised at particular times only, he must end by making it an essential background to his whole life. Even under the pressure of inescapable outward occupation, it ought to be still continuing as the screen upon which these occupational activities appear.

2

Keep on remembering to observe yourself, to watch yourself, to become aware of what you are thinking, feeling, saying, or doing. This is one of the most valuable exercises of the Quest.

3

Whatever one is doing, to stop suddenly at an unarranged moment and in an unforeseen position becomes a useful exercise when repeated several times every day. It is necessary to hold the whole body rigidly fixed in exactly the posture which had been reached at the very moment of command. Even the expression on the face and the thought in the mind must be included. This is one of the "Awareness" exercises; they are performed when sitting, walking, working, eating, or moving.

4

This exercise of self-vigilance is a daily and hourly one, for the intrusions of negative moods and destructive thoughts are daily and hourly, too.

5

Walking meditation: The practice of meditation can be continued even while walking. This is done in a slow dignified way, starting with the right foot and the heel touching the ground first, on the *expiring breath*. Then continue rhythmically, slowly, a measured pace—without haste and without turning the head right and left. The monk I saw was walking with head down, and looking at the ground. He was in Thailand.

6

In the end, he will make no separation between everyday ordinary routine and the period of meditation—for the whole of his life will become one continuous meditation. His actions will then take place within its atmosphere. But in the beginning he must make this separation.

7

As you go about your daily work in your ordinary life and in relations with other people, in hours of toil or pleasure, or indeed at any period of your life, remember the Overself.

8

The Way of Mindfulness in Buddhism, of deliberately being conscious of each physical action quite apart from the action itself, produces a different state from that of the ordinary person who may outwardly perform the same action. It develops concentration and an awareness which ultimately leads to the awareness of the being himself who practises the exercise. The ordinary person is lost in the action itself, in the thought itself, in the speech itself, and has no separate awareness of them. Practice of mindfulness gives a conscious responsibility for what is being done, what is being thought, and what is being said quite apart from what is observed and heard. It lights him up from within with intense concentration. This is a mental discipline practised daily by the Buddhist monks and useful to other seekers.

9

By means of this exercise in mindfulness, whatever he is doing and whatever he is working at is no longer the mere work or action itself. It is also a part of his spiritual training, his self-discipline, his concentration practice, and ultimately his separate awareness and responsibility for himself.

10

A housewife wrote to me that she found herself too busy with her duties to sit down and meditate; but by thinking about spiritual subjects as she went about her work, she found with time that this not only lightened the drudgery but also developed into a kind of meditation itself.

11

A valuable exercise is one which practises transferring awareness to the body as and when it is being used. This is done by moving across a room, a courtyard, an open space, with slow-walking feet, as slow as he can make them. The physical movement must be accompanied by a deliberate effort to *know* what one is doing, fully mindful and concentrated on each step forward.

12

This practice of persistent recall does more good to help a man not only in an inward uplifting sense but also in a practical manner by its prevention of falling into bad courses.

13

Responsibility, according to its measure, cannot be shrugged off. "Our thoughts are ours," as Shakespeare says.

14

He will give, and he ought increasingly to give, more attention to scrutiny of the kind of thoughts which occupy his mind. And he will take the opportunity following every such scrutiny to cleanse, correct, improve, or uplift these thoughts and thus bring them under some control.

15

He can use books as a preliminary guide to working on himself. The study and observation of his conduct, the analysis of his past and present experiences in the light of his highest aspirations, the attempt to be impartially aware of himself in various situations, will open the way to more direct guidance through intuitions from his higher self.

16

It is true that the space of time during which he tries to gain control of his thoughts every day is a short one, whereas his habitual carelessness in the matter continues for the rest of the day. Some critics have asked what is the use of this control if it ends with the meditation period?

17

Even while he is acting in a situation, he trains himself to observe it.

18

The practice should also be continued at mealtimes. When eating anything, keep in mind the idea, "The body (not *my* body) is eating this food." When taking particularly appetizing food, hold the thought, "The body is enjoying this food." All the time, watch the bodily reactions as an impersonal but interested spectator.

19

Bangkok monastery meditation exercise: The monks paced around very, very slowly, slowly lifting a foot and consciously deliberately putting it down again for the next step. All the while they tried to keep the mind empty. The eyes were cast downward.

20

The intenser the longing for enlightenment, the easier it is to practise recollection.

Mental quiet

21

Emotional ecstasies are not or should not be the final goal of meditation practice. They may be welcomed, but the quest ought not be pursued so far and allowed to end with them. Better the Great Peace, the Self melted in Divine Being, the mind enlightened by Divine Truth, the result a return to the world with the heart suffused by a Great Goodwill. Such is the philosopher's goal. It does not depend on meditation alone. To those struggling in and with the world as it is today, it may seem inaccessible, utterly beyond one's ambitions.

22

The higher purpose of meditation is missed if it does not end in the peace, the stillness, that emanates from the real self. However slightly it may be felt, this is the essential work which meditation must do for us.

23

The cultivation of a tranquil temperament promotes the practice of mental quiet. The cultivation of mental quiet promotes the attainment of the Overself's peace.

24

The bored or gloomy silence of some old persons is not at all to be mistaken for the sacred silence of a true mystic.

25

If he practises mental stillness until he masters it, he will benefit proportionately. For in its deepest quietude he can find the highest inspiration.

26

It is partly because the Overself waits for us in silence that we have to approach it in silence too.

27

The belief that meditation is only an exercise in quiet reflection is a half-true, half-false one. It may begin like that, but it must not end like that. For when it is sufficiently advanced, thoughts should be dropped and the mind emptied. This will not be possible in a few days or months, but if one sits for it daily, regularly, this utterly relaxed state will suddenly be realized.

28

It is also an affair of waiting, waiting for the repose to settle on his being. The doing is simply to brush off intruding thoughts, to hold attention in a concentrated manner.

29

In those moments when a mysterious stillness holds the heart of man, he has the chance to know that he is not limited to his little egoistic self.

30

If the mind could but listen to itself, and not to its thoughts, it might get closer to truth.

31

To renounce the self in meditation is to sit still and let the ego listen to the Voice of the Overself.

32

It is the calm which comes from profound reflection, the repose which repays adequate comprehension.

33

If we can train the mind to be still, it will clear itself of muddy thoughts and let the Soul's light shine through.

34

What ordinary thought cannot reach, pacified thought can. This happens when mental quiet is fully and successfully entered, even if briefly.

35

There is the silence of the mentally dull and spiritually inactive. There is also the silence of the wise and illumined.

36

God will not enter into your heart until it is empty and still.

37

But why must the mind be stilled, it will be asked, to know God? Because God moves in and through the universe itself so silently and in such stillness that atheists doubt whether this divine power is really there. In the state of rapt mental quiet, the human mind approaches the divine mind and, as the quietness deepens, is able to make its first conscious contact with it.

38

It is not easy for a man to believe that a greater wisdom may be received by his mind if he keeps it still than if he stirs it into activity.

39

What they do not know, and have to learn, is that there is a false silence within the mind as well as a true one. The one may resemble the other in certain points, and does—but it is a psychic state, not a spiritual one. It can deceive and lead astray, or reflect earthly things correctly, but cannot let them hear the voice of the Overself.

40

When the brain is too active, its energies obstruct the gentle influx of intuitive feeling. When they are extroverted, they obstruct that listening attitude which is needed to hear the Overself's gentle voice speak to the inner silence. Mental quiet must be the goal. We must develop a new kind of hearing.

41

If he is really deep in meditation, not a single muscle of his body will move.

42

With most people a completely thought-free mind may be impossible to attain in their present situation, but a tranquillized mind is possible.

43

Meditation may begin as a dialogue between the meditator and his imagined higher self; it may pass beyond that into a real dialogue with his Overself. But if he is to go farther all dialogue must cease, all attempt to communicate must end in the Stillness.

44

As mental agitations and emotional dominations fall away through this patient waiting, a hush falls upon the inner being. This is a delicate, gentle, and important state, for it is approaching the threshold where a new and rare kind of experience may be near.

45

Mental quiet, if fully attained, frees the time-bound consciousness, which then floats all-too-briefly into Timelessness.

46

He is to keep absolutely still during this period, letting no movement of the body distract the mind; because of the interaction of these two entities, the one influencing the other, the mind will become increasingly still too.

47

The layman of the West is just beginning to learn the art of mental quiet, but he has not yet penetrated deeply enough; he has far to go.

48

The "natural" (returning to one's true nature) condition of consciousness has not only to be attained but, by unremitting practice, also retained.

49

The bustle of the world's activity and of personal preoccupations must be inwardly silenced before the knowledge of what underlies both the World-Idea and the ego-thought can reveal itself.

50

It is good practice to put one's questions or state one's problems before beginning a meditation and then to forget them. Unless the meditation succeeds in reaching the stillness, the full response cannot be made.

51

Mental silence is what is ordinarily called yoga in India. From the philosophical standpoint, it is valuable, but still not enough where it is mere mental inactivity. The ego, or the thought of the ego, has also to be overcome so as to allow the higher power, the higher self, to take possession of the mind thereafter.

52

Because thinking is an activity within time, it cannot lead to the Timeless. For this attainment, mental quiet is necessary.

53

The clearness of mind which pervades this state is extraordinarily intense. It lights up every person and every incident coming into the area of thought, but even more—himself.

54

To sit with another person for several minutes in complete silence yet in complete ease is beyond the capacity of most Occidental city people. The Orientals still have it but, as the West's way of life makes its inroads, are beginning to lose it.

55

It is only when this emotional calm has been attained that correct thinking can ever begin.

56

Chou Tun-Yi (eleventh-century Chinese philosopher): "The Sage makes stillness the ruling consideration."

57

There is an air of venerable dignity about a figure sunk in meditative quiet and withdrawn from earthly concerns.

58

As the mind's movement ebbs away and its turnings slow down, the ego's desires for, and attempt to hold on to, its world drop away. What ensues is a real mental quiet. The man discovers himself, his Overself.

59

He sees into himself as he has never known himself before.

60

How far is all this utter emotional stillness and grave mental silence from all the noise of religious disputations, from all the tension of sectarian criticism, from all the puerilities of textual hair-splitting!

61

It is when the mind is still that high spiritual forces, be they from God or guru, can reach a man.

62

The body becomes strangely still, the sinews quite relaxed, the breathing greatly subdued; sometimes even the head droops.

63

Only the regular deep breathing shows that the spirit has not withdrawn from the body.

64

The quietness uncovers the essential being.

65

A mind filled with thoughts about things, persons, and events, with desires, passions, and moods, with worries, fears, and disturbances, is in no fit condition to make contact with that which transcends them all. It must first be quietened and emptied.

66

Thoughts flicker across the screen of consciousness like a cinema picture. Who pauses to see what this consciousness itself is like and what it has to say for itself? Has not the time come for Western man to learn the art of mental quiet?

67

The effort to hold thoughts back, to touch their calm source deep deep below them, must be made.

68

The way his body moves, works, walks, behaves, reveals something of the inner man, the ego. But non-movement, sitting quite still, can reveal even more—the being behind the ego. However, this remains a mere unrealized possibility if the man is without knowledge or instruction.

69

"To be in Mental Quiet is to observe the mind's own nature," wrote Lao Tzu.

Index for Part 1

Entries are listed by chapter number followed by "para" number. For example, 1.199 means chapter 1, para 199, and 6.112, 138, 143, etc., means chapter 6, paras 112, 138, 143, etc. Chapter listings are separated by a semicolon. Please note also that, for the reader's convenience, the first number in the right-hand running heads throughout the text indicates chapter number.

T

tantra yoga 3.260; *see also* Tibetan
tantra
Tao-Ch'o 6.75
teacher 2.121, 149–50, 153; 5.106–
24
telepathic interaction 2.149, 151
themes for meditation, *see* 4.1–103
thinking 1.140; 4.4, 6–7, 9–12, 14,
17–18, 25, 29–32, 36–38, 47, 53–
60, 61, 63–64, 68, 71–73, 80–82,
92–93, 96, 102–3
Tibetan Buddhist initiations 3.228
Tibetan tantra 3.254–255
Tibetan meditation 2.25, 327
times for meditation, *see* 2.4–62
evening 2.31, 33, 36–38, 49, 51, 56,
61–62
morning 2.4–28, 31, 33, 46, 51,
347
night 2.33, 44, 49, 53, 57
trance 1.238, 448–50
tratak 3.253; 5.7

V

vichara 4.9
visions 1.417–18, 503
visual phenomena 1.503
visualization 1.131; 3.141; 4.202, 205
Visuddhi Magga Sutra 1.489; 2.257
Vivekananda 6.20
Void 1.145, 216

W

Wai-Tao 2.152
walking meditation 7.5, 19
Weil, Simone 6.205
Westerners, and meditation 1.4, 52–
55, 64, 67, 107, 109, 118–19, 121,
200; 2.327
What am I? exercise 4.36–37, 44

Whirling Dervishes 3.244
Who Am I? exercise 4.61
Wood, Sir Henry 3.142
Wu Wei 3.241

Y

yantra 5.64, 91
yoga
definition of 1.116, 165, 168
different schools of 1.113–15
intellectual over-analysis of 1.134
and metaphysics 1.18
as both method and result 1.123–
126
misrepresentation of 1.114, 117
and monasticism 1.49, 63, 100,
102–4, 109–10, 121
P.B.'s views on 1.120
and philosophy 1.118
of self-identification 5.111–13,
5.115–117
and Westerners 1.106, 118, 121
yoga sleep 1.290, 465; *see also* sleep,
and meditation

Z

Zen meditation 1.465; 3.255

The 28 Categories from the Notebooks

This outline of categories in *The Notebooks* is the most recent one Paul Brunton developed for sorting, ordering, and filing his written work. The listings he put after each title were not meant to be all-inclusive. They merely suggest something of the range of topics included in each category.

1 THE QUEST
> *Its choice —Independent path —Organized groups —*
> *Self-development —Student/teacher*

2 PRACTICES FOR THE QUEST
> *Ant's long path —Work on oneself*

3 RELAX AND RETREAT
> *Intermittent pauses —Tension and pressures —Relax body,*
> *breath, and mind —Retreat centres —Solitude —*
> *Nature appreciation —Sunset contemplation*

4 ELEMENTARY MEDITATION
> *Place and conditions —Wandering thoughts —Practise*
> *concentrated attention —Meditative thinking —*
> *Visualized images —Mantrams —Symbols*
> *—Affirmations and suggestions*

5 THE BODY
> *Hygiene and cleansings —Food —Exercises and postures*
> *—Breathings —Sex: importance, influence, effects*

6 EMOTIONS AND ETHICS
> *Uplift character —Re-educate feelings —Discipline emotions —*
> *Purify passions —Refinement and courtesy —Avoid fanaticism*

7 THE INTELLECT
> *Nature —Services —Development —Semantic training —*
> *Science —Metaphysics —Abstract thinking*

8 THE EGO
> *What am I? —The I-thought —The psyche*